HAND-LOOM WEAVING

Domestic Loom   From a Lyonnese Woodcut, 1510

"*A winter garment now demands your care,
   To guard your body from th' inclement air ;
   Soft be the inward vest, the outward strong,
   And large to wrap you warm, down reaching
      long :
   Thin lay your warp, when you the loom prepare,
   And close to weave the woof no labour spare.
   The rigour of the day a man defies
   Thus clothed, nor sees his hairs like bristles rise.*"

"*The matron cheerful plies the loom at home.*"
                              Hesiod "*Works and Days*"

HAND-LOOM WEAVING PLAIN & ORNAMENTAL

BY LUTHER HOOPER : WITH LINE
DRAWINGS BY THE AUTHOR &
NOEL ROOKE: ALSO SEVERAL
ILLUSTRATIONS FROM ANCIENT
AND MODERN TEXTILES

PITMAN · LONDON
TAPLINGER · NEW YORK

A PENTALIC BOOK

PITMAN PUBLISHING LIMITED
39 Parker Street, London WC2B 5PB

Associated Companies
Copp Clark/Pitman, Toronto
Pitman Publishing New Zealand Ltd, Wellington
Pitman Publishing Pty Ltd, Melbourne

Published simultaneously in the USA by Taplinger
Publishing Company Inc, 200 Park Avenue South,
New York, N.Y. 10003

First published in Great Britain, 1910
Revised reprint 1960, reprinted 1926, 1930, 1934, 1937,
1940, 1947, 1949, 1953
First published in paperback 1979

UK ISBN 0 273 01267 3
US ISBN 0-8008-3805-X

Reproduced and printed by photolithography in
Great Britain at The Pitman Press, Bath

EDITOR'S PREFACE

IN issuing this volume of a series of Handbooks on the Artistic Crafts, it will be well to state what are our general aims.

In the first place, we wish to provide trustworthy text-books of workshop practice, from the points of view of experts who have critically examined the methods current in the shops, and putting aside vain survivals, are prepared to say what is good workmanship, and to set up a standard of quality in the crafts which are more especially associated with design. Secondly, in doing this, we hope to treat design itself as an essential part of good work-manship. During the last century most of the arts, save painting and sculpture of an academic kind, were little considered, and there was a tendency to look on " design " as a mere matter of *appearance.* Such "ornamentation" as there was was usually obtained by following in a mechanical way a drawing provided by an artist who often knew little of the technical processes involved in production. With the critical attention given to the crafts by Ruskin

v

and Morris, it came to be seen that it was impossible to detach design from craft in this way, and that, in the widest sense, true design is an inseparable element of good quality, involving as it does the selection of good and suitable material, contrivance for special purpose, expert workmanship, proper finish and so on, far more than mere ornament, and indeed, that ornamentation itself was rather an exuberance of fine workmanship than a matter of merely abstract lines. Workmanship when separated by too wide a gulf from fresh thought—that is, from design—inevitably decays, and, on the other hand, ornamentation, divorced from workmanship, is necessarily unreal, and quickly falls into affectation. Proper ornamentation may be defined as a language addressed to the eye ; it is pleasant thought expressed in the speech of the tool.

In the third place, we would have this series put artistic craftsmanship before people as furnishing reasonable occupations for those who would gain a livelihood. Although within the bounds of academic art, the competition, of its kind, is so acute that only a very few per cent. can fairly hope to succeed as painters and sculptors ; yet, as artistic craftsmen, there is every probability that nearly every one who would pass through a sufficient period of apprenticeship to workmanship and design would reach a measure of success.

vi

In the blending of handwork and thought in such arts as we propose to deal with, happy careers may be found as far removed from the dreary routine of hack labour, as from the terrible uncertainty of academic art. It is desirable in every way that men of good education should be brought back into the productive crafts : there are more than enough of us "in the City," and it is probable that more consideration will be given in this century than in the last to Design and Workmanship.

●　　●　　●　　●　　●

This volume on Weaving, the seventh of our series, is an interesting account of a very ancient and a very remarkable art. With weaving from early days has been associated the making of patterns which repeat a given unit, and the commerce in such fabrics has been the chief means of disseminating patterns over the world. Considering the utility, the universality, and the wonderful nature of the art at its simplest and the splendid triumphs of its maturity, weaving must have a strong claim for being the most extraordinary of man's inventions.

W. R. LETHABY.

PREFATORY NOTE TO THE 1920 REPRINT

It was unfortunate that the first edition of "Hand-loom Weaving" became exhausted at a time when the difficulty of producing such books was almost insurmountable, especially as its success and the increasing demand for it called for an immediate reprint. Happily the lengthy period of delay has come to an end, and the present volume, which is an exact replica of the first edition, except for a page or two of necessary addenda, is now ready for the use of students and others interested in the fascinating textile arts.

The favourable opinions of "Hand-loom Weaving" so generally communicated to the author have been highly gratifying, and have more than compensated for the care and labour bestowed on the preparation of the work. These communications are hereby gratefully acknowledged.

LUTHER HOOPER.

AUTHOR'S PREFACE

NOTWITHSTANDING the competition of its formidable rival the power-loom, the hand-loom still survives, and seems likely to continue in use for the weaving of the best webs, in several branches of textile manufacture.

In various districts of Great Britain, as well as in France, Germany, Italy, and other European countries, hand-loom weaving continues to be, though much decayed, an important industry. In the East—in India, China, and Japan—the hand-loom weavers outnumber by several millions the workers employed in attending to the textile machinery of Europe and America.

The fact that hand-loom weaving has so long survived gives hope, that, now that there is a growing demand for the best in all departments of workmanship, the future may see an extensive revival of this beautiful and ingenious art.

There is more hope for such a revival since numerous handicraft societies and guilds, as well as many independent art workers, have been led to

study and practise weaving, and have met with
much encouragement, both as regards the quality
of the work they have been able to produce, and
its appreciation by the public.

It is a pity that the introduction of machine
spinning and weaving should have had the effect
of almost entirely superseding the domestic loom
and its auxiliary the spinning-wheel. Spinning and
weaving are ideal domestic occupations, especially
in the country home. Since they ceased to be
universally practised, no home industry at all
approaching them in usefulness or interest has
taken their place. It is true that some branches
of the art, such as the weaving of fine silk into
elaborate damasks or brocades, require special
training and constant application in the worker.
This has always been so ; but the weaving of linen,
cotton, woollen, and the coarser silk threads, into
materials of strength and beauty for domestic use,
can quite well be carried on intermittently together
with other household occupations.

There can be no doubt of the superiority of well-
made hand-woven webs, whether they be of the
finest silk or of the coarsest wool. This is plainly
shown if the best hand-made and the best machine-
made productions be compared.

Hand-loom weaving, too, is superior to machine-
weaving if judged by the effect it is likely to have

on the worker. The hand-weaver is employed in
a pleasant, ingenious occupation which exercises all
his faculties, while the attendant on a power-loom
is engaged in a monotonous toil, in which no
quality but intense watchfulness is required.

The object of the present volume is to inform
the student of hand-loom weaving of the best
methods of preparing warps, fitting up looms,
and making or selecting the various appliances
necessary for the work, as well as inventing,
planning, and weaving plain and ornamental webs.
The assistance of the domestic and the artistic
weaver has been particularly borne in mind in the
preparation of the book.

I hope that this volume will also prove of use
to all who are interested in textiles artistically,
commercially, or in any other way. The principles
of weaving, traced out from their origins, to their
greatest perfection in the eighteenth century, are
identical with those of the most highly developed
modern inventions—inventions which have succeeded in accelerating the speed of weaving at more
or less cost to its artistic perfection.

For assistance in the preparation of the book my
thanks are due to the authorities of the Victoria
and Albert Museum, the National Art Library,
and to the authorities of the British Museum, for
facilities of research, and for permission to photograph

Author's
Preface

examples of choice textiles, &c., in their various collections ; to Miss Charlotte Brock and Mr. Noel Rooke for valuable assistance in preparing the illustrations, and to Mr. W. H. Abbott, M.A., and other friends for much helpful advice and many practical suggestions.

LUTHER HOOPER.

ARMS OF THE WEAVERS' COMPANY
LONDON 1700

CONTENTS

PART I

PLAIN WEAVING

CHAPTER I

THE RUDIMENTS OF SPINNING AND WEAVING

CHAPTER II

THE INDISPENSABLE APPLIANCES FOR SIMPLE WEAVING

CHAPTER VI

THE BEAMING DRUM

CHAPTER VII

THE HAND-LOOM FOR AUTOMATIC WEAVING

CHAPTER VIII

THE ACCESSORY APPLIANCES OF THE LOOM

PART II

SIMPLE PATTERN-WEAVING

CHAPTER IX

TAPESTRY-WEAVING

CHAPTER X

THE SIMPLEST WARP AND WEFT EFFECTS OF PATTERN

CHAPTER XI

SINGLE-HARNESS PATTERNS

CHAPTER XII

THE SATINS AND DOUBLE CLOTH

CHAPTER XIII

SHEDDING MOTIONS

CHAPTER XIV

DOUBLE-HARNESS PATTERN-WEAVING

CHAPTER XV

AUTOMATIC MACHINES FOR SHEDDING MOTIONS

PART III

COMPLEX PATTERN-WEAVING

CHAPTER XVI

THE DRAW-LOOM AND THREAD MONTURE

CHAPTER XVII

THE SHAFT MONTURE

xix

Contents

CHAPTER XVIII

BROCATELLE AND TISSUE WEAVING

CHAPTER XIX

THE COMPOUND MONTURE

CHAPTER XX

FIGURED-VELVET WEAVING

LIST OF PLATES

xxi

PART I
PLAIN WEAVING

PART I

PLAIN WEAVING

CHAPTER I

THE RUDIMENTS OF SPINNING AND WEAVING

The Comparative Importance of the Weaver's Art—
Scope of Hand-loom Weaving—Weaving Universal
—The Construction of Plain Cloth—The Warp—
The Weft—Relative Size of Warp and Weft—Pre-
paration of Threads for Weaving—Flax and its Use
Prehistoric—Retting and Skutching of Flax—Pre-
paration of Cotton, Wool, and Silk—Carding, its
Purpose and Method—Fine Spinning by Machinery
—Ancient Spinning with Distaff and Spindle—The
Distaff—The Spindle.

IT may be confidently affirmed that the art of weaving occupies a place of importance and usefulness to mankind second only to that of agriculture. We shall reach this conclusion whether we take into consideration the number of persons engaged in the various branches of the art, the universal practice of weaving in ancient and modern times, or the necessity and value of the productions of the weaver's craft and industry to society in general.

The Scope
and Value of
the Weaver's
Art
If necessary it could be proved by statistics that at least one-fifth of the working world is occupied either with weaving and its allied trades, or in the distribution of its finished materials. It would be found also that a similar proportion of the general expenditure is for woven goods of one kind or another.

It is not only, however, from an economic point of view that the art of weaving is of such interest and importance, but also on account of the vast amount of invention and ingenuity, both of a mechanical and an artistic kind, that it has been the means of calling forth. These qualities have been shown during the course of its development from the elementary and laborious attempts of primitive tribes to the elaborately finished and swiftly wrought, though complicated webs woven on the modern power-loom. It is this aspect of the subject—viz., the development of textile art from its earliest beginnings—that the present volume is intended to set forth. A clear account of the principles and practice of the art of weaving, and the possibilities and limitations of the loom and its accessories, cannot fail to be of interest and value to the antiquary and to the collector of ancient textiles, as well as to the designer, the weaver, the distributor, and the purchaser of the various kinds of modern woven fabrics.

It will not be necessary, nor, indeed, would it be possible within the compass of this handbook, to follow the subject of weaving beyond the point when it ceased to be a handicraft, owing to the introduction of the Jacquard machine and the application of steam-power to the loom, which events took place at the end of the eighteenth century. These changes in the construction and mechanism of the loom did not alter the principles of weaving in the least, nor add any new effects of combinations of threads to those previously in use. The inventions only affected the exactness and speed of the weaving, the motive power by means of which the loom was driven, and rendered easy a frequent change of pattern. No real advance in weaving technique has taken place for a hundred years, as nothing more perfect is possible in the weaver's art than the sumptuous webs of silk, of exquisite texture, which were deliberately woven by hand on the perfected draw-looms of Europe during the seventeenth and eighteenth centuries.

The first principles and practice of the art of weaving, wherever they are found, are universally similar. Primitive peoples of to-day follow the same methods and use the same appliances as those of ancient times. And as it is on these that all later textile developments are based, it will be necessary in the first place to define them clearly. A visit to the ethnographical department of any of our museums, and an examination of their contents, will prove that there is scarcely a savage tribe, however primitive, which has not some more or less proficient acquaintance with the art of making thread and of utilising it in the weaving of cloth (see plate I). Also, the specimens of ancient handicraft, such as those shown in plate II, which remain to us, as well as other less direct evidence, will show decidedly that the people of antiquity were familiar with the arts of spinning

3

and weaving, which they practised with a great deal of skill and carried to a high pitch of perfection. Indeed, so universal and so ancient are the occupations of making thread and weaving webs that they appear to be instincts as natural to the human species as to the caterpillar and the spider.

If we look carefully at a piece of plain cloth we find it to consist of a number of longitudinal threads placed side by side, and intersected, or interlaced, by a continuous single thread. This thread passes alternately before and behind the longitudinal ones, and has been introduced between them from edge to edge, by some means and in such a manner as to bind them together and hold them in position. When thus united the threads are woven into a flat, orderly, and uniform-surfaced material, of more or less durability, according to the strength of the threads of which it is composed and the closeness and evenness with which the crossing thread has been pressed down and beaten together. By means of plate III the arrangement of the longitudinal threads and the continuous thread crossing and intersecting them should be made quite clear. The longitudinal threads of a woven material are always

called the *warp*, because, in order to allow of their being intersected conveniently by the continuous crossing thread, they have to be *warped*—that is, tightly strained in their position on some kind of frame prepared for the purpose. The longitudinal threads are known as the *warp* and by no other name, but the continuous crossing thread has several technical names, the most usual being

weft, *woof*, or *shoot*—sometimes spelt *shute*.

4

In the magnified piece of plain cloth (plate III) the warp threads are seen at once to be much finer than the weft thread. This is always the case, except in the most elementary attempts at weaving. And the threads differ not only in size, but in the manner in which they are prepared for use. The warp threads need to be hard, having thin strands strongly twisted together. The weft thread is only slightly twisted; this makes it soft and yielding, and enables the weaver to press it well down and to beat both warp and weft together into firm, good material. The selection of properly proportioned threads is of the highest importance in weaving, for the good appearance of the finished work depends almost entirely upon it, as also does its durability.

The simple methods and appliances for making thread and weaving adopted by different ancient peoples and by primitive tribes of to-day are remarkably similar in kind. But the raw materials used and the manner of preparing them differ considerably, and depend, of course, on the natural products with which the particular people happen to be familiar, and the inventive skill which they possess. The most obvious and simple of all raw materials for weaving were the long grasses and rushes, or other plants, with which the weaver was acquainted, which could be readily split into filaments or used entire. But the rudest people readily become aware that many animal and vegetable substances are capable of being drawn out and twisted together into a continuous thread, of more or less firmness and strength, and they accordingly soon invent for themselves some simple appliances for performing this operation.

5

Previous to the introduction of cotton from India and the marvellous development of the cotton industry in this country during the last century, the most important of all the various kinds of thread for weaving purposes was obtained from the stems of the family of plants known as the *Linum* family, of which the flax has always been the chief member. Animal wool and silk—the only natural continuous thread—have been chiefly used for ornamental fabrics, but flaxen or linen thread has always been the most used and the most useful for ordinary purposes. The earliest specimens of knitted and woven thread at present known are fragments that were found amongst the remains of the lake-dwellings in Switzerland, and which are attributed ; by the most reliable authorities, to the age of stone. These venerable relics are therefore prehistoric. They consist of small bundles of flax fibre, both raw and twisted into threads of various thickness. Some are made into ropes and nets and others knitted or woven into pieces of cloth (see plate IV). In Egypt, in Greece and Rome, and, with one or two exceptions, in all the more or less civilised countries of the ancient world, flax was used and preferred above all other fibres for weaving purposes. It is remarkable that the cultivation and preparation of flax, even at the present day, is almost identical with that in use in ancient Egypt four or five thousand years ago. Probably the reason why cotton has, within the last century, almost superseded the use of linen, is because it is better adapted for preparation and weaving by machinery and takes more kindly to all sorts of abominable adulteration, so that it can be more cheaply put upon the market.

6

The valuable portions of the flax plant are the dark brown seeds, usually called *linseed*, and the inner fibres of the stems, which by a severe course of treatment become linen thread. After the flax has been pulled up by the roots the seeds are first shaken out. The plants are then made up into small bundles and immersed in water until they begin to ferment. As soon as the fermentation has begun they are taken out of the water and allowed to dry in the open air. This process is called *retting*, and when it is complete the leaves and outside membrane of the stem are easily removed. The roots and small stems are next cut away, and the main stems are then ready for the next operation, called *skutching*. The purpose of the skutching process is to thoroughly clear away all remains of the outer membrane and the short, useless veins of the leaves, and to straighten out the inner fibres and lay them all in

𝔉𝔩𝔞𝔠𝔥𝔰.

FIG. 1
Flax Plant

one direction ready for twisting into thread. Sharp
toothed combs of various sizes are used for this

F<small>IG</small>. 2.—Stripping Hemp in Burgundy.

skutching, coarse ones at first and finer ones afterwards. The fibres are finally made up into convenient bundles. By this process the filaments of
8

the flax are thoroughly cleaned and separated, and converted into a fine, silky kind of tow. This, in brief, is the manner in which the best flax is prepared for the linen thread of to-day, and there is evidence to show that it was in just such a manner that the flax was prepared for the thread of the state robe of "fine linen" given by Pharaoh to Joseph in ancient Egypt as a mark of his royal favour.

The down of the cotton plant and the fleece of the sheep need much less preparation than the fibre of the flax. The former only have to be cleaned and the fibre cleared by the process of *carding*, which will presently be explained, and the cotton or wool is ready to be operated upon by the *spinster* who makes it into thread.

Silk is produced ready spun by the silkworm in a continuous double thread, and only requires to be unwound from the cocoon, as the case is called which the caterpillar twists and winds curiously around itself when ready to change into the chrysalis form. When unwound the cocoon is found to consist of a continuous double thread of silk about one thousand yards in length, but of such exceeding fineness that it takes from ten to twelve hundred cocoons to weigh one pound. So fine, indeed, is the natural filament that twelve strands have to be twisted together in order to make the finest thread of silk that it is practically possible to use for weaving. The twisting and cleaning of these threads of silk is technically called *silk-throwing*, and is a most delicate and elaborate process.

The operation of carding by hand requires the use of a pair of implements called *cards* (fig. 3A).

9

FIG. 3.

FIG. 3A.—Pair of Cards.

They are made of hard wood, and each has one of its flat surfaces covered with tough leather, into which a large number of points of thin steel wire have been very strongly and evenly fixed. A small quantity of clean cotton down or fleecy wool is spread as evenly as possible on the steel points of one card. This card is then held by the handle, with the points upward, in the left hand of the operator, who sits to the work and rests the implement flat upon her knee. The other card is then taken in the right hand, and its points pressed firmly down upon the fibre to be carded. The right-hand card is then drawn smartly over the left-hand one in the direction shown in fig. 3, which movement tears the fibres apart and straightens them out. When this action has been repeated a few times the straightened fibres will be found lightly attached to one edge of the lower card. They can then be transferred to the smooth back of the other card, and with a few deft taps of the back edge of the one from which they were taken, may be made to assume the curled shape shown at the foot of fig. 3A. When it has been worked into this neatly curled form the carding is ready to be drawn out and twisted into thread.

Spinning, as its name denotes, is the process by which the short filaments that have been separated and combed into order by the carder or skutcher, are drawn out and joined by being twisted or spun together into a continuous thread, or *yarn*. This yarn can be spun to an astonishing degree of fineness. The finest ever known to be made was spun by machinery and shown at the great Exhibition of 1851. It was a cotton yarn, and a single pound of it, it was said, would measure one thousand and twenty-six miles in length. This yarn was only made for exhibition, and was of no practical use. The finest cotton yarn used in weaving is spun by machinery, and *runs*, as it is called, three hundred miles to the pound weight. Needless to say, the ancient method of spinning by hand could never produce a thousand miles of thread from a single pound of cotton, but the hand-spinners of India spin, for use in the Dacca muslin industry, one pound of cotton fibre into a length of thread which measures two hundred miles. The Eastern spinners can also spin wool or flax into yarn of a hundred miles to the pound weight. These figures have been approached if not quite reached by good spinsters of Europe.

The figure of a spinster (plate v) is copied from a painting on a Greek vase preserved in the British Museum. It gives a fairly good general idea of the method of spinning by the primitive means, viz., by the use of the *distaff and spindle*. It is not wise, however, to put much faith in the details of ancient pictures of this kind, as we shall have occasion to notice particularly when we come to consider the representations of ancient looms. Artists and poets, in ancient times, seem to have been content if they succeeded in conveying a general impression of a figure or scene they intended to repre- sent, without much regard to accuracy of detail. In this case the graceful figure is holding up a stick, the distaff, on which a tightly wound ball of thread is fixed ; and at the end of the thread, which passes through the right hand of the figure, a spindle is turning. All that we can learn from this figure is that the distaff and spindle were used in ancient Greece for the purpose of making thread, but neither the details of the process of spinning are explained nor is the position or action of the figure suitable for the work. When only the distaff and spindle are used for spinning, the distaff is usually fixed under the spinster's left arm, so that the prepared flax, loosely wound upon its end, may project in front of her. By this method of fixing the distaff the hands of the spinster are both left free, the one to twist the thread and the other to keep the spindle duly rotating.

The *distaff* (fig. 4) is simply a round stick of wood about fifteen or eighteen inches in length, at one end of which the flax, or other raw material prepared for spinning, is loosely wound in such a way that

The Distaff

Fig. 4
The Distaff

13

FIG. 5.—Spinning with Distaff and Spindle.

the fibres can be readily drawn out and twisted together by the spinster. The distaff is sometimes, although not generally, used for cotton and wool—these are for the most part spun from the cardings, which are joined on as required ; but the distaff is always used for the spinning of flax. When the distaff is fitted up, or the cardings ready to the spinster's hand, she deftly draws out a few filaments, sufficient, in her judgment, for the thickness of the thread required, and gradually twists them into an even thread without detaching them from the distaff or carding. When a sufficient length of thread is thus twisted it is attached to the spindle, which is then made to revolve, and as it spins it assists in evenly twisting the gradually drawn out thread. As the length of thread increases, the twisted yarn is wound upon the spindle from time to time, until it is conveniently full ; then the thread is cut, and a fresh spindle attached in place of the full one (fig. 5).

The spindle (fig. 6) is simply a slender metal or hardwood rod, from six to ten inches in length, having at one end, or in the centre, a round weight, and at the other end a hook, or notch, for the purpose of holding it in a vertical position

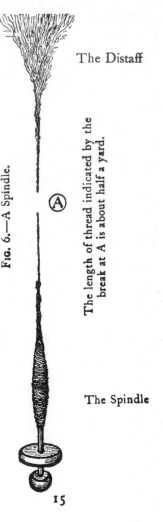

The Distaff

Fig. 6.—A Spindle.

The length of thread indicated by the break at A is about half a yard.

The Spindle

15

FIG. 7.—Spinning with Wheel.

when the thread is attached to it. Spindles are of The Spindle
various weights and dimensions, according to the
size of the yarn for the spinning of which they are
used. Plate VI shows ancient spindles preserved in
the British Museum.

This method of spinning with these simple
appliances, the distaff and spindle, seems to have
been universal. It is still used by primitive peoples,
and the best, strongest, and most durable thread is
even now produced by its means. The method
also illustrates perfectly the essential principles of
the making of all thread. The use of machinery
for spinning, whether it be only the simple, pic-
turesque, mediæval spinning wheel (see fig. 7), or
the elaborate machinery of the cotton-spinning industry of the nineteenth century, did not alter the
principles of the process in the least. These only
enabled the work to be carried out with increased
speed and with greater exactness of result.

CHAPTER II

THE INDISPENSABLE APPLIANCES FOR SIMPLE WEAVING

The Origin of the Loom—Looms in Ancient Art and Literature—Egyptian and Greek Looms—The Essential Part of the Loom—The Cross in the Warp—The Simplest Practical Loom—Demonstration of the Cross—Special Need for the Cross in Long Warps of many Threads—Preparation of the Warp—Ancient Warping—A Simple Method of Warping for Domestic Looms.

Origin of the Loom

THE weaving of mats and baskets from natural grasses and rushes can, of course, be manipulated without the use of any special appliance for holding or stretching the materials whilst in working. But as soon as pliant thread has to be woven, and any considerable length of web is required, it becomes necessary to devise some kind of frame to hold and stretch the warp threads upon, so that the weft may be readily interlaced with them. The more or less elaborate frame constructed for this purpose, with the properly arranged warp mounted on it, together with the various contrivances added from time to time by the weaver's ingenuity, has by universal consent been called a *loom*.

The representations of looms in ancient sculp-

18

tures, paintings and drawings, are exceedingly scarce, and what few there are, are for the most part so incomplete, not to say incorrect, in detail, that it is difficult for the most expert weaver to see how they could have been used effectively. Textile art seems to have been a more attractive and interesting subject to the ancient poets than to the artists, as their allusions to the loom, the needle and the various operations of weaving and needlework are frequent and interesting, and prove beyond doubt that the weaver's and embroiderer's occupations were held in very high estimation and were very extensively practised in the ancient world. These literary allusions to the loom and to textile art will be considered in a subsequent chapter, but a reference to the available pictorial representations is necessary at this point.

The most ancient illustrations of looms and weaving are to be found amongst the wall-paintings in a tomb at Beni Hasan, in Egypt. Fig. 8 represents a warp apparently stretched on the ground, and a figure in an impossible attitude weaving what may be supposed to be a mat. Fig. 9 shows an upright frame having a few threads fixed to it, at which two women are working. One of the women may be presumed to be introducing the weft between the warp threads, and the other beating it together. A later Egyptian painting represents a loom of more elaborate construction (fig. 10). This painting is at Thebes, and shows a weaver very actively at work at an upright frame, on which he is evidently weaving cloth by means of a stick having a hook at its end. No threads, however, in this instance are shown, either of warp or weft. These are all the instances

19

at present discovered of representations of Egyptian looms, except that there is a kind of hieroglyphic on a sarcophagus of an early period which is supposed to stand as a sign for a loom, or weaving. The scarcity of these pictorial records is remarkable when we consider that Egypt was the seat of a great

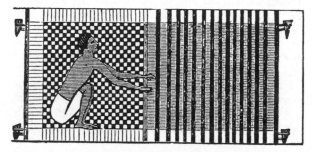

FIG. 8.—Egyptian Loom.

linen-weaving industry, which not only supplied the large domestic market with woven materials, but was famous throughout the ancient world for the manufacture of "fine linen," and exported great quantities of it to contemporary nations with whom the Egyptians traded.

Although in ancient Greece and Rome weaving was a common domestic occupation universally practised, as we gather from many classic literary allusions, drawings or other representations of looms seem to be even more rare than are those of Egypt.
It appears that only in two Greek vase-paintings is there anything of the kind to be found. One of these (fig. 11) represents the loom of Penelope, and the other that of Circe (fig. 12). They are

20

both upright looms, and differ from those of Egypt in that the warp strings are stretched by means of a weight being hung on each separate string, instead of the threads being tightly stretched all together on the frame, as were those of Egypt.

FIG. 9.—Egyptian Loom.

There are a few other ancient drawings extant, purporting to be of Roman looms, but these are absolutely unreliable, as they are from Byzantine and Eastern manuscripts of later periods, and only show the kind of weaving appliances in use at the time when, and in the places where the drawings were made. In all these ancient pictures of looms the artists have shown the stretched threads of the warp, and suggest the insertion of the weft thread. We can also gather that, owing to the

21

different methods of stretching the warp peculiar to
Egypt and Greece, the Egyptians beat the weft
together down from *above*, whilst the Greeks beat

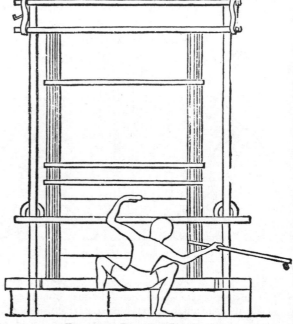

FIG. 10.—Egyptian Loom.

theirs up from *below*. This is an important difference, and was noticed by the Greek historian
Herodotus when he visited Egypt. Beyond these
meagre details we can learn nothing definitely from
the ancient pictures. We may conjecture and

22

argue, as learned authors and antiquarians are constantly doing, as to the methods by which the ancient weavers obtained the fine results which they certainly did, but the pictures are no help in the matter to anything beyond conjecture. It is

FIG. 11.—Greek Loom.

remarkable that all the artists have neglected to observe and show one simple but universal and indispensable contrivance used in weaving, the ONE thing we know must have been there, and without which no loom, however simple or complicated, could be set to work or kept in order by the weaver.

By means of fig. 13 the nature and value of this simple but essential part of the loom can be readily explained. The figure represents a board, which may

23

be of any convenient size; for the present purpose we will say it is four inches wide by sixteen inches long. The construction is shown at no. 1. At the ends A, a and b, B a piece of beading, having a rounded edge, is fixed. The beadings are four and a half inches long, so that when fixed on the ends of the board they project slightly beyond its edges. No. 2, is a section of the board, showing the position of the rounded edges of the beadings. This

FIG. 12.—Greek Loom.

board, when fitted up with a warp, is perhaps the simplest possible form of loom. But notwithstanding its simplicity many beautiful and ingenious narrow webs suitable for braiding and other trimmings may be made on it, as will be shown in a subsequent chapter. At no. 3, the board has a string wound upon it lengthwise. In this case it is wound so as to make a warp of nine strings, but these may be of any number possible to the width of the board. Before the string is wound on to the board a loop is made at its end, which is caught on to the projecting end of the beading at A, no. 2. The string being looped on to the beading, the winding proceeds, and when the desired number of strings is complete the string is carried down the back and tied to the other

24

projecting end of the beading B. At no. 4, the strings on the board are shown intersected by the two rods C, in such a way that alternate strings go over and under each rod. In the space between the rods, the alternate strings cross each other in regular succession. This cross is clearly shown in the diagram between

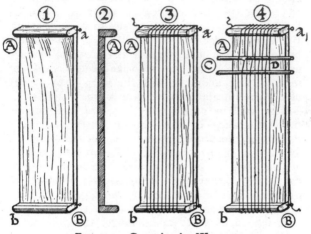

FIG. 13.—Cross in the Warp.

the points marked C, D. It will now be understood that whilst the rods C, are kept in their position in the warp, it is impossible for the threads to get out of place or to get hopelessly entangled, as they otherwise would certainly do. This cross in the warp, sometimes called the *lease*, is really the one indispensable part of the loom. It is no doubt prehistoric, and is universally used in weaving. All other parts and appliances of the loom may vary,

25

and be of either the most complicated and elaborate
or of the rudest possible description, but this simple
yet perfect contrivance for keeping the warped
threads in order cannot be dispensed with, and is
never likely to be superseded.

The difficulty of keeping the warp from getting
entangled when only a few threads are used in it,
and when the finished work is not required to be
longer than the loom itself, is not so very apparent.
But when in place of the fixed bars, or other limits
between which the warp is stretched, rollers are
used, and it is desired to make several yards of
material, and, added to this, the warp is to consist
of a great number of fine threads, the difficulty, it
is clear, will be considerably increased, and, but for
the contrivance of the crossing of the alternate
threads of the warp, as described above, would be
found to be insurmountable. This would especially
be the case with warps many yards in length,
consisting as they often do of several hundreds of
threads of fine linen, cotton, or wool, or, it may be,
of several thousands of threads of fine silk.

A length of warp much longer than the loom
itself cannot, of course, be prepared upon it, as a
short one may readily be. This being the case,
some contrivance has to be resorted to in order to
build up a series of threads of exactly the required
number, and of the length determined upon ; and
not only this, but to keep the threads as nearly as
possible at the same tension, so that when transferred to the loom and stretched between its front
and back rollers they shall give the weaver as little
trouble as possible with loose and uneven threads.
This process of preparing the threads for the loom

is, obviously, called *warping*, and is a very important one, requiring great exactness and care in the doing—as, indeed, may be said of all the operations connected with weaving, from beginning to end.

Preparation of the Warp

The ancient method of warping, a method that is still practised in India, where weaving as a simple domestic art still survives, is as follows. A row of sticks in pairs, fixed upright in the ground, is set out, of the required length. The warper, holding two reels of thread, in such a way that they will readily unwind, ties the thread to the first pair of sticks, and then passes along the line from end to end, backwards and forwards, crossing the threads at each pair of sticks, in order to keep the tension even. When he has the required number of threads piled upon the sticks, he inserts a cord in the place of the last pair but one, at both ends of the row, tying it up securely so that it cannot slip out of the cross. Finally he binds the warp firmly together at both ends, looses it from the sticks, and winds it upon a hand-stick, or rolls it into a ball convenient for carrying it to the loom and turning it on to the rollers.

Ancient Warping

A more compact and convenient, though similar, method of warping to the ancient one, is by means of a board fitted up with a number of pegs, in place of the row of sticks planted in the ground. As this is a very easy and effective way of warping a moderate number of threads, such as would be required for a domestic loom, and at the same time perfectly illustrates the principles of warping, which it is necessary for the student of weaving to understand clearly and definitely once for all, it will be well in the next chapter to carefully describe it and demonstrate its use.

A Simple Method of Warping

27

CHAPTER III

THE WARPING BOARD

The Warping Board—The Necessity for Strength in all Weaving Appliances—The Warping Board in Use—Securing the Crosses in the Warp—Warping Several Threads at Once—The Reel- or Bobbin-carrier, and its Use in connection with the Warping Board—The Portee Cross—Taking off the Warp—The Hand-stick.

The
Warping
Board

THE board with its arrangement of pegs for warping is shown in fig. 14, nos. 1, 2, and 3. It may be of any convenient size, according to the place where it is fitted up, but it should not be less than six feet long by one foot broad, and it must hang firmly on a wall at such a height from the ground that the operator can reach to any part of it without difficulty. On a board of the size indicated a warp of ten yards in length, and of any reasonable number of threads, can quite easily be warped. A longer length may be warped either by increasing the length of the board or by increasing its width and adding to the number of pegs with which it is furnished. One peg added below each of the pegs 2, 3, and 4, will add four yards to the length possible to be warped on the board. The pegs, indicated by the letters and

28

numerals, must not be less than six inches long, and not more than nine inches in projection from the surface of the board. The pegs must be made of

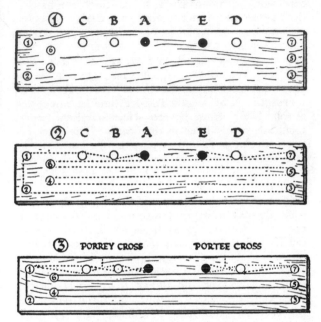

FIG. 14.—Warping Board.

hard wood, not less than one inch in diameter, as they have to bear a great strain when some hundreds of threads are stretched upon them, and they must be well made, be perfectly smooth and have nicely rounded ends. The board itself must also

The
Warping
Board

Necessity
for Strength
in all
Weaving
Appliances

The Board
in Use

be strong and smoothly finished, and must not be less than one inch in thickness if six feet in length, and an inch and a half, if longer. It may be remarked here—and it cannot be with too much emphasis—that, EVERY APPLIANCE CONNECTED WITH THE LOOM REQUIRES TO BE MUCH STRONGER THAN WOULD AT FIRST APPEAR NECESSARY. THE WEIGHT OF THE REPEATED BEATING OF THE WEFT TOGETHER, AND THE MULTIPLIED STRAIN OF THE MANY THREADS OF WARP, ARE MUCH GREATER THAN WOULD BE SUPPOSED. The pegs marked A and E, and filled in solid black, must be movable, but all the others should be firmly fixed in the board. The space between the pegs A and B must not be less than one foot, and the space between B and C six inches. The space between pegs D and E should also be one foot.

The board being ready and fixed in its place on a wall, we may now proceed to use it. We will suppose that we require quite a small warp, of say twenty threads, ten yards long. We take a reel of thread and, placing it on a short rod of thick wire, in order that it may turn freely, we begin operations by tying one end of the thread to the movable peg A (no. 2, fig. 14). Now, holding the wire with the reel on it in our left hand, with our right hand we guide the thread *under* peg B and *over* peg C. Then, following the dotted line shown, we carefully guide the thread outside pegs 1, 2, and 3 back to peg 4, then to pegs 5, 6, and 7 in succession until it reaches peg D, which it goes *under*. The thread must now be carried *over* and *under* peg E, and thus begin its return. Before returning, however, it will be well to compare the

thread on the board with the dotted line of the
drawing, in order to make sure that we have
exactly followed in its course. Having ascertained
that all is well, we may now carry the thread *over*
D on to peg 7, and so back in the same course
till we again reach peg 1. Having carried the thread
over peg 1, it must be taken *below* C over B and
arrive *below* A ; this will complete one course.
We have now warped two threads, and the warping board should be as represented at no. 3, with
the threads crossed between pegs B and C, and D
and E. Taking into consideration the size of the
board, it is clear that we have warped two threads
of a length of ten yards between the two crosses.
The second thread being carried round and over
peg A, goes *under* B, following exactly the course
of the first thread, and duly arrives at E ; then,
following the second thread back, it reaches A,
goes under and over the peg, and four threads, out
of the twenty required, are warped. By the time
ten forward and ten backward journeys are made
our sample warp of twenty threads will be finished,
and may be removed from the board as soon as
the crosses we have taken so much trouble to make
are secured. This important matter of securing
the crosses is easily done, but if forgotten, and
the warp be removed from the board, it will be irre-
trievably spoiled, especially if it consists of a great
number of fine threads. Not only the labour,
but the thread itself will be wasted. Fig. 15 will
make clear the method of operation. The letters
A, B, C, D, and E, are the pegs of the warping board. The thick lines are the threads of ?
warp, which may be of any number, large or small.

31

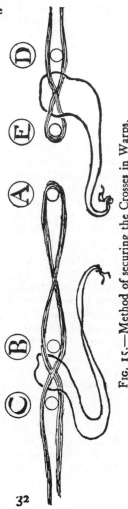

FIG. 15.—Method of securing the Crosses in Warps.

32

Between C and B, and D and
E, are the two important
crossing places of the alternate threads. The thin lines
represent two pieces of strong,
pliable cord, each about two
yards long, which have been
inserted from the front in the
openings of the warp made
by the pegs C and E. These
cords have then been passed
between the first thread
and the board, and brought
through from the back in the
openings made by the pegs B
and D. The ends of the
cords have been firmly tied
together, and by their means
the cross is perfectly secured,
whatever may happen to the
warp. It will be noticed
that there is another cross in
the warp between pegs B and
A, but this is not so important. It is useful, however,
to pass a short cord through
the loop at peg A and tie the
threads all together. If our
small warp of twenty threads
were now taken off the
board and the cords which
secure the crosses stretched
out, the two ends of the
warp would be represented
by fig. 16.

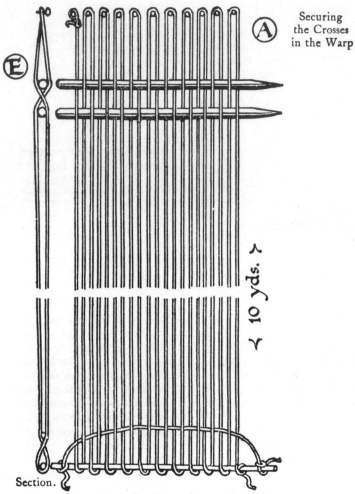

Ⓔ   Ⓐ

← 10 yds. →

Section.

FIG. 16.—The Warp displayed.

It would be a very tedious proceeding to warp a great number of threads, one at a time, and it was only suggested as advisable to do so in order that the principle of warping might be made clear. Eight threads can quite easily be warped together, so that when the warper has carried them once from the peg A to peg E and back again, sixteen

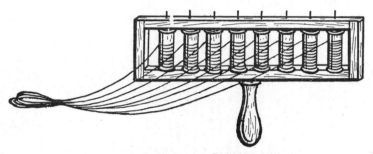

Fig. 17.—Bobbin-carrier.

threads will be placed in order. To effect this saving of time and labour we must use a *reel- or bobbin-carrier* (fig. 17). The bobbin-carrier is an oblong

The
Bobbin-
carrier.

frame, in which there is room for eight bobbins to stand and turn, when they are fitted up with wires for the purpose. A convenient handle for holding the frame is firmly fixed to it at the bottom. The top of the frame is pierced with eight holes, and in the bottom, corresponding holes are drilled about half through the thickness of the wood, so as to fix the eight wires and not allow them to fall through. The wires are passed through the top

34

edge of the frame, through the bobbins, and are then
caught and fixed by the holes in the bottom edge.
As the frame is held upright, the weight of the bobbins
standing in the frame will be found to give the
tension to the thread which is required for warping.
When placing the reels in the carrier care must be
taken so to fix them that the threads all unwind on

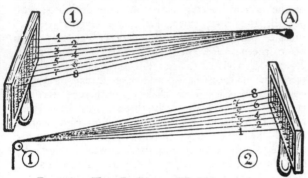

FIG. 18.—Two Positions of Bobbin-carrier.

the same side, and cause all the reels to revolve in
the same direction.

Having got the bobbins properly set up, the
ends of the threads must be gathered together and
tied in a convenient way for fixing on to peg
A of the warping board (fig. 14). The threads
being fixed to the peg A, no. 1, fig. 18, and the
carrier held in the left hand of the warper, in an
upright position, it must be taken past the pegs B
and C and held there a little above their level,
so that the threads are well separated and taut.
Then with the first finger and thumb of the right

35

hand the warper must pick out and draw downwards the second, fourth, sixth, and eighth threads,
as numbered in no. 1, fig. 18, and place them
below peg B in the same position as the first thread
in the warp of ten was placed. This will leave
threads 1, 3, 5 and 7, above the peg. Again
tightening the threads by a slight further movement
of the carrier, taking care that they do not slip off
peg B, the first, third, fifth, and seventh threads
must be picked out and pulled downwards so as to
place them *below* peg C, leaving threads 2, 4,
6, and 8 above it. It will now be found that
we have a crossing of alternate threads between
pegs B and C. After making quite sure that the
crossing is correct, the eight threads must be grasped
by the right hand of the warper and carried steadily
round the seven pegs in exactly the same course
as the single thread was carried when guided by
the dotted line, no. 2, fig. 14. After having
traversed the seven pegs the carrier arrives at the
peg D. It is not necessary to take a cross of single
threads here, as at B, C, but altogether, the eight
threads must be taken *below* peg D, *over* and *under*
peg E, then *over* peg D, and so back again the
whole round to peg 1. When arriving at peg 1 the
carrier must be transferred to the right hand, without twisting the threads, so as to leave the left
hand free to manipulate the return cross between
pegs C and B. The position of the carrier and
threads is now represented at no. 2, fig. 18,
and the threads marked 1, 3, 5, and 7 must be
pulled down and placed *below* peg C, leaving
threads 2, 4, 6, and 8 above it. Again with a slight
movement, the threads must be tightened, and

36

threads 2, 4, 6, and 8 placed below peg B, leaving threads 1, 3, 5, and 7 above it. The crosses are now complete, and it only remains to take the group of eight threads *below* and *over* peg A in order to finish the first PORTEE, as such a collection of threads warped in one round is called. The use of the portee cross (no. 3, fig. 14) will be explained later on. Before beginning the second round it will be well to examine the threads between pegs C and B in order to make sure that the sixteen threads are all "in the cross" in proper succession, as they will certainly be found to be if the above directions have been accurately followed. After a little careful practice it will be found that, the portee of eight threads can be warped in the same time as that taken for warping one thread. As soon as a few portees have been warped it will be found difficult to remember how many threads are gathered together on the pegs, so it becomes necessary to use some contrivance for readily counting them, in order that we may know exactly when the warp is finished. This account can be quite easily kept if half a yard of narrow tape or coloured cord be attached to the top edge of the warping board above the portee cross (no. 3, fig. 14). The tape has to be turned back until five portees have been made; then it must be allowed to hang over the front until five more have been built up, and so on, forward or backward, after every fifth portee. By this means the number of portees can at any time be counted. Thus, five portees of sixteen threads contain eighty threads, and these multiplied by the number of fives warped will give the total number of threads reached. The warp, of any required number of portees, being

37

finished and the crosses secured, as directed at
p. 32, it may be taken off the board and wound
on to a stick, for convenience in transferring it
to the loom. For reasons which will afterwards
be explained, it is necessary in winding on to a
handstick, to begin at the beginning of the warp,
peg A, fig. 14; this will leave the portee cross

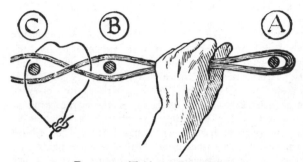

FIG. 19.—Taking off the Warp.

outside when the warp is all wound on to the
stick. The handstick should be a short round
stick, smoothly finished and with rounded ends, in
size about an inch and a half in diameter by eighteen
inches long. This being ready, the warp must be
firmly held by the left hand of the warper at the
point shown in fig. 19. The peg A is then to be
removed and the loop of warp taken in the right
hand, the fingers being thrust through it. The
loop being securely held, the left hand is free to
remove the warp from pegs C and B and from
peg 1. The cross having been previously secured,
the loop between A and B may be made of a

38

convenient length for the next operation, which a
careful study of figs. 21 and 21A will make quite
clear, so that it needs no verbal description. It
may be remarked that the loop shown in this
figure is a most useful one, and is much used in
the fitting up of looms; it should therefore be well
mastered once for all. The loop having been
formed, the handstick must be inserted and the loop
tightened as indicated in the bottom compartment

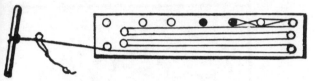

FIG. 20.—Handstick and Warp off Pegs **A, B, C,**
and 1, 2 of Warping Board.

of fig. 21A. The warp looped on to the handstick
ready for winding off the pegs is shown at fig. 20.
It may be found advisable to enlist the help of
an assistant in taking off the warp, especially to
hold it at the pegs and prevent its coming off too
freely. The warp may now be gradually and
firmly wound upon the stick, care being taken to
start the winding in the direction of the arrow,
bottom compartment, fig. 21A. If wound in this
direction the warp will not slip round the stick or
come loose. When the portee cross is reached
the warp may be taken off the pegs D and E,
carried away and kept quite safely till the loom is
ready to receive it.

39

Forming the
Loop

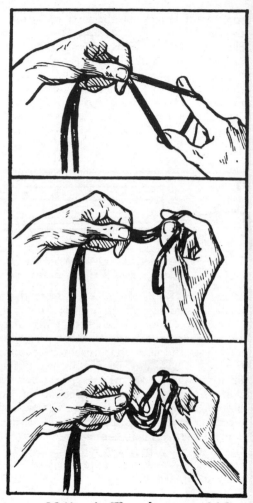

FIG. 21.—Making the Weaver's most useful Loop.

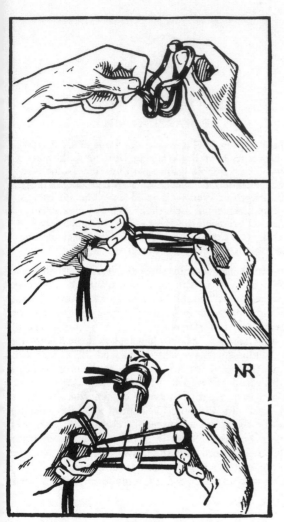

Forming the
Loop

FIG. 21A.

CHAPTER IV

THE WARPING MILL

The Warping Mill necessary for Long, Full Warps
—Description of the Warping Mill for Silk-weav-
ing—The Bobbin Frame—The Heck-block—
Demonstration of spreading a Warp—Regulating
the Length of Warps—The Heck—The Gatherer
—The Count and Length of Warps; how calcu-
lated—Threading the Heck—Beginning a Warp—
Taking the Cross—The Rachet and Wheel of the
Heck-block—Mending Threads.

The Warp-
ing Mill
necessary for
Long Full
Warps

ALTHOUGH the warping board described in the last
chapter is very useful for small warps of moderate
length, such as would be used in a domestic loom,
it would not be convenient for very long warps, or
accurate enough for warping several thousands of
fine silk threads. For such warps as these a warping
mill is necessary, on which, if need be, as many as
twenty thousand threads can be made into a warp
of a hundred yards in length.

Description
of the Warp-
ing Mill for
Silk-weaving

The warping mill now to be described is of the
kind used in conjunction with the silk-weaving
draw-looms of the seventeenth, eighteenth, and part
of the nineteenth centuries. It is perfectly adapted
to its purpose, and, like the draw-loom itself, was the
result of centuries of gradual development.

The warping mill, fig. 22, is made entirely of hard,

42

tough wood, perfectly smooth and strongly fitted
together. Its chief feature is a large skeleton reel,
A A A A, generally five yards in circumference, though
sometimes seven and a half yards, and about two
yards long. The reel has an axle, B, which has a
long iron pin at each end, shown plainly at no. 2. A
strong frame, consisting of two uprights, C, C, and
two cross-pieces, D, D, is very firmly fixed up, and in
the centre of the bottom cross-piece there is a socket
to receive the iron pin, E, of the axle when the reel is
set on end in its place, as in the diagram. The
reel is kept in an upright position by the pin F,
which passes through the upper cross-piece and terminates about ten inches above it. This arrangement allows the skeleton reel to turn freely on its axle.
A grooved wheel, G, is strongly screwed to the end
of the axle where the pin E enters it, and another
wheel, H, also grooved, is attached to a handle which
can be turned by the warper, who sits on the seat I.
The seat I is movable, and may be placed in any
convenient position, being kept there by heavy
weights, J. The grooved wheels G and H are
connected by a continuous cord, as indicated in
the ground-plan, no. 3. It is now obvious that
the warping reel may be turned at any required
speed, and in either direction, by means of the
handle K.

The front upright of the frame, C, is divided into
two for the greater part of its length, and a solid
block of wood, L, is fitted to it, so that it can slide
up and down the frame opposite to any part of
the reel. Fig. 23, which is an enlargement of
the sliding block, will explain this mechanism.
Between the uprights a pulley, M, is attached

43

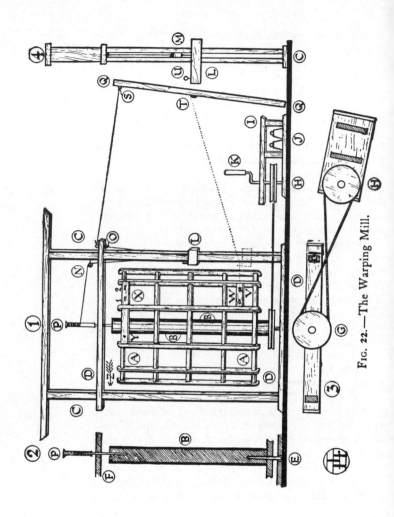

Fig. 22. — The Warping Mill.

to the top of the block. At the top of the frame (fig. 22, no. 1) is another pulley, N, and a strong

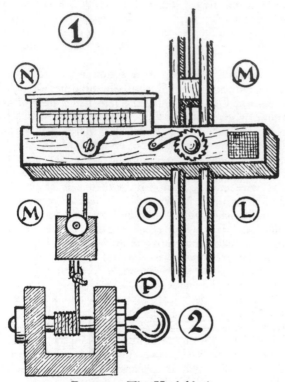

FIG. 23.—The Heck-block.

staple, O. The axle-pin F, no. 2, terminates in a small cylinder, P, which fits over it and is fixed so that it will revolve with the reel. A hole is made in the cylinder near one end, a strong, smooth cord being passed through it, and a knot tied to prevent its slipping out. This cord is next passed over the pulley N, down to the pulley M in the block, then up again to the staple O, and tied there.

The side elevation of a frame made to hold a large number of bobbins of silk or other thread, is shown at QQ, no. 1, fig. 22. A front view of the frame is given in fig. 24. The wires on which the reels are placed are fitted into holes drilled half through the sides of the uprights of the frame. On one side a groove of the same depth as the hole is cut, of the shape indicated at RR, so that the wire can be removed by lifting it at one end and drawing it backwards. This is necessary for changing the bobbins as they become empty. The position of the frame, in regard to the warping mill, is clearly shown in the drawing. S, fig. 22, is a strong staple screwed to the mill frame, from which a cord passes to a similar staple fixed in the centre of the bobbin frame, fig. 24, S. This cord keeps the frame from falling backwards, and at the same time allows it to be readily adjusted. The frame stands freely on the ground, inclining backwards, and the weight of the bobbins of silk, added to that of the frame itself, gives just sufficient tension to the threads when in process of warping. Before going into further details, the action of the warping mill, in so far as it has been described, must now be noticed.

In the block L, figs. 22 and 23, centres the whole mechanism of the warping mill. On it the

appliance for *taking the cross* is fastened. It is   The
also the means of spreading the warp truly and   Heck-block

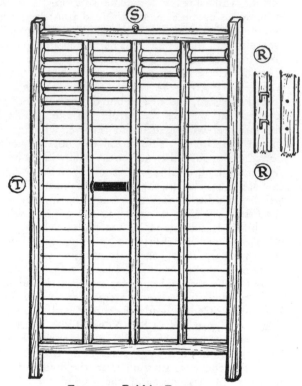

FIG. 24.—Bobbin Frame.

evenly upon the large reel of the mill.   The
apparatus for taking the cross will require careful

47

explanation of further details, but everything for
spreading and regulating the warp has been described and is ready for demonstration. For this
purpose a single reel of stout thread must be placed
on the reel frame, fig. 24, at about the centre, T
(see also no. 1, fig. 22). The dotted line passing
from the reel at T, fig. 22, indicates the course of the
thread. At the point in the block marked U (no. 4)
a temporary screw-eye is fixed. Through this the
thread is passed, and tied to one of the staves of the
mill reel at V. By the turning of the handle K
the mill reel will be made to revolve, winding the
thread upon itself. The thread will not be wound
horizontally, but rather diagonally, and will gradually
rise on the reel, until it will be found, on the completion of one revolution, that the second round of thread
will begin a little space above the starting point of
the first, V. This is owing to the cord on which
the block is suspended by the pulley M (fig. 22,
no. 4) having been shortened by being wound upon
the cylinder, P, at the top of the axle. The
shortening of the cord has gradually raised the block
L, and if the cord and cylinder are properly adjusted
the block will have risen an equal distance at each
revolution. Consequently the thread will be exactly
distributed over the mill. Now, if the thread be
fixed at the top of the reel and the handle turned
backwards, the reel will revolve in the opposite
direction, the cord unwind from the cylinder, the
heavy block descend, and the second thread will
follow exactly the same course as the first until it
reaches the bottom. In the same manner, if a
hundred bobbins were placed in the frame and all
the threads drawn through the eye in the block and

tied together to the mill reel they would be laid and spread as easily and evenly as the single thread.

Again, any length of warp desired, from two yards to a hundred, can be measured and determined at the beginning, by the revolutions of the mill reel. For instance, we will suppose the block, carrying the warp, is wound to the top of the mill. This is always its position on starting. Let the warp be tied to one of the pegs on the top of the reel at X, no. 1, and the handle K turned so that the block descends. The mill being five yards round, at the end of one revolution there must be five yards of warp on it. It follows that we have only to count the convolutions on the vertical line from the starting point and multiply them by five to ascertain the length wound upon the mill reel. For instance, if twenty-five yards of warp are required, five revolutions of the reel must be completed in each direction. In order to make different lengths of warp at will, there must be provided some means of holding the threads at the beginning and end of the length required. The first and last of the pegs, five in number, shown in fig. 22, no. 1, at Y, W, and X, answer this purpose. The three pegs at the top of the mill, Y and X, are fixed in that position, as the warp always begins at the same place. The board in which pegs W are inserted, is movable, and is so made that it can be fixed by a wedge at any height on the reel between any two of the staves. The threads are first looped on to peg Y, and the mill caused to revolve in the direction of the arrow Z. When a place on the mill is reached where it is wished to terminate the warp, the peg board W is moved to the spot, the

49

threads are looped round the right-hand peg, and the motion of the reel reversed. As the block continues to fall and rise between the top of the mill and peg W, the threads of the warp will all be laid of an equal length.

The spaces between the rounds of thread formed by each revolution can be regulated by altering the size of the cylinder P, no. 1, fig. 22. An increase in the size of the cylinder causes the block to rise quicker. This lays the thread in a steeper diagonal and increases the space between each round. A smaller cylinder, of course, has the reverse effect. The pegs X, no. 1, fig. 22, correspond with the pegs B and C in the diagram or the warping board, fig. 14, and the pegs W with the pegs D and E of that appliance. The former are for use in building the cross of alternate threads at the beginning of a warp, and the latter for making and preserving the portee cross at its end.

Use of the
Fixed and
Movable
Pegs

The Heck

The next detail of the warping mill to be described is the important fitting which gives the name to the block L, fig. 23, by means of which the cross in the warp is made quite easily, however many threads are used. Fig. 25 is a representation of the HECK, which is the name given to this useful appliance. There are variously constructed hecks in use, but they are all made on the same principle. The drawing shows one of the simplest both to make and keep in repair. It consists of a strong, hardwood frame of an oblong shape, having an attachment, at the bottom, pierced with a hole, by means of which it is firmly fastened with a thumb-screw to the heck-block, as at N, fig. 23. On

the inside, at both ends, the heck frame is grooved
(B, fig. 25), and two smaller frames are fitted
into the grooves loosely enough to be easily moved
up and down in them separately or together.   Tied

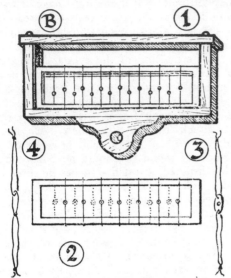

FIG. 25.—The Heck.

at regular intervals on the two small frames, are a
number of loops of fine, strong thread, as in no. 2,
which shows one frame detached. The loops are for
the purpose of holding a row of eyes in the centre of
the frame.   These may be either smaller loops of
string, as in no. 4, or smooth glass beads, or *mails*, as
they are called in weaving (no. 3).   These can be
obtained perforated with three holes, one large for

51

the thread to pass through and two smaller ones for attaching them to the loops (no. 3). For the sake of clearness, only seven loops are shown on the frame in the illustration. Any number, however, may be used, but each frame must have at least half as many loops as there are reels of thread on the bobbin-carrier. Thus, if eighty bobbins are to be used in making a warp there must be forty eyes on each frame. The position of the eyes and loops on the second frame is shown by the dotted lines in no. 2.

The next appendage to the heck-block to be described is placed at the back of it, opposite the centre of the heck frame. It is shown screwed to the block in fig. 26, no. 1, A. No. 2 is an enlargement of it. It will be seen to consist of a block of wood (it should be boxwood), very smoothly finished, about five inches by three inches, and an inch and a half thick. Projecting from the top edge are two strong steel points, about three inches long, and two inches apart. Upon these points two round, hollow, boxwood pegs are made to fit. In the drawing one of these, B, is represented in its place on the point, but the other is shown separately at C. The pegs are not fixed on the points, but are fitted so that they will easily revolve on them. The reason for these pegs being loose, is to prevent friction when a large number of threads gathered together is passing quickly between them, from the reel frame, through the heck, to be spread upon the revolving mill.

In the centre of the heck-block shown in fig. 23 at O a ratchet and wheel will be observed. This is to enable the warper to regulate to a greater nicety the spreading of the warp on the mill reel.

52

The section, no. 2, will explain its construction. The pulley M is attached to the axle of the ratchet wheel by a piece of strong catgut, which on the

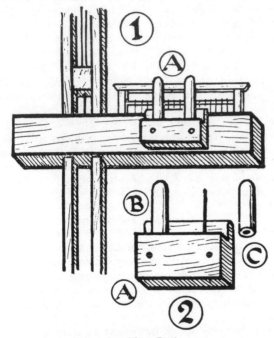

FIG. 26.—The Gatherer.

wheel being turned ever so slightly winds the cord on to the axle and brings the pulley nearer to the block. This has the effect of raising the block a little, and prevents the accumulating threads of the

53

warp from piling up in one place on the mill, as they would otherwise do.

The description of the warping mill is now complete, and it only remains to demonstrate its use in the preparation of a large warp of fine silk, say of twenty thousand threads fifty yards long. In warping, the first thing to determine is the number of bobbins of silk to be used, and to arrange them on the bobbin frame, fig. 24. The frame must be fixed in the position shown at QQ, fig. 22, no. 1, and all the other fittings of the mill must be in working order. Fifty bobbins will be a convenient number, as twenty thousand divides equally by fifty. This number of bobbins will make each portee consist of one hundred threads (see pp. 34–37).

It must next be calculated how many portees of one hundred threads each, will make up the number required for the whole warp.

$$20,000 \div 100 = 200.$$

Two hundred portees, then, will be needed. In order to build this number up on the warping mill the heck-block must be caused to travel down and up the mill frame two hundred times, a cross being taken at the beginning and the end of each journey.

The bobbins of silk must next be arranged on the frame, which is shown to be capable of holding a hundred, so that the fifty we propose to use will just fill the upper half of it. It must also be noted that the reels are counted in rows, beginning at the top of the left-hand row. This order must be maintained in threading them through the heck. When placing the bobbins on the wires care must also be taken that they will all unwind in the same direction (see p. 35).

see p. 35

The bobbins being ready on the frame the warper must stand between it and the mill with the right hand to the bobbin frame. The end of silk hanging from the first reel must be taken and threaded through the first eye of the heck, which will be seen by reference to fig. 25, no. 1, to be on the front frame of that appliance. The thread must be drawn well through the eye, taken between the revolving boxwood pegs, and left hanging there. In like manner the second thread must be passed through the second eye of the heck, which will be found on the back frame. The silk from the third bobbin must then go through the third eye, which is on the front frame, and this order of alternate threading must continue until all the threads pass in regular order from the frame through the heck, and hang all together between the boxwood pegs.

The heck-block, which has been standing at any convenient height for threading the silk, must now be worked gently up to the level of the pegs at the top edge of the mill, and all the loose ends of silk, hanging from the heck, being tied together, must be looped on to the peg Y, fig. 22, no. 1. On the mill being now moved a few inches in the direction of the arrow Z all the threads will be tightened, and the heck must be examined in order to see that they all pass in regular alternation through the eyes of its front and back frames. Any error in the threading will be at once detected if the frames are lifted in succession so as to raise

Order of
Bobbins on
the Frame

Position of
Warper
when
threading
the Heck

Position of
the Heck-
block at
Beginning
of a Warp

first one half and then the other of the fifty
threads. This being found correct, the collection
of threads which passes between the frame and the
heck must also be examined. They should come
off the bobbins in five distinct vertical rows, so that
the warper may be able to see at any moment that
the reels are all revolving properly, and detect at once
threads that require mending or any other attention.

It will next be necessary to remove the silk
from between the revolving pegs of the heck-block,
gently turn the mill by hand until the peg Y stands
about two feet to the left of the heck, and then all
will be ready for the important operation of *taking
the cross* which is done in the following manner.
Care being taken to keep the threads all taut, the
front frame of the heck must be first raised. This will
lift half of the threads and make an opening through
which a short glass rod or the finger and thumb
of the warper's left hand must be passed. The
opening thus made can then easily be moved along
the threads and transferred to the first peg X, which
is nearest to Y. By another slight movement of
the mill the silk must again be tightened, the *back*
frame of the heck raised, and the rod inserted in the
opening, which is then to be transferred in like
manner to the second peg X. The cross should
now be complete and perfect, and as soon as it is
seen to be so the silk must be replaced between the
revolving pegs of the heck, and the warping may
proceed. The length of warp is next to be arranged
for and spread as described at p. 48. The fifty yards
will need ten revolutions of the mill to spread, and
these are to be made by turning the handle K,
no. 1, fig. 22. Great care must be exercised

in order to turn the mill steadily and firmly and
keep an unrelaxed tension on the threads of silk.
When the ten revolutions are complete the movable
board holding the pegs W must be wedged
between the staves of the mill just below the
termination of the tenth round of the warp. Here,
as previously explained (p. 37), only the portee
cross is required. Accordingly the fifty threads,
taken all together, will pass above the first peg W,
below the last one, then round it, and under the
first, which completes the portee cross. The revolution of the mill must now be reversed, the silk
being wound upwards in the same course until the
heck-block again reaches the pegs at the top, and
the mill is stopped gently for taking the return
cross. This time, as the first opening has to be
transferred to the second peg, the *back* heck frame
must be the first raised for the insertion of the glass
rod. When this has been done the front frame
will be lifted, the opening transferred to the first
peg X, and when the warp has been looped round
peg Y the first portee will be finished, and a
hundred and ninety-nine others will have to be
done in exactly the same manner. An excellent
way of keeping account of the portees as they are
warped is shown at fig. 27. A stroke is made for
every portee completed until nine are reached, and
at the tenth one the nine are crossed out.

On arriving at peg Y, fig. 22, after the last
portee has been warped the half-portee must be
divided and the threads cut from the heck and tied
in such a manner as to loop over the peg.

As the warping proceeds it will be found
necessary to make use of the ratchet and wheel

57

marked O in fig. 23. Without the help of this
extra means of regulating the length of the cord by
which the block is suspended the threads would be
piled up in one place in an unmanageable heap, and
when stretched out in the loom would be of various
lengths and cause great inconvenience to the weaver.
After a few portees have been laid on the mill,
therefore, the cogged wheel has to be turned so that
the ratchet may catch the next tooth. This will

FIG. 27.—Method of Counting Portees.

obviously raise the block a little and cause the next
round of warp to be laid a trifle higher on the mill.
As this movement of the ratchet wheel is repeated
from time to time the warp will gradually fill in the
space between the rounds and lie flat in a spiral
band on the mill. This filling of the space needs
to be done judiciously, and must never be carried
so far as to merge one round into the next. Warps
of a high count naturally require greater space
between the rounds. This is regulated, as has been
described (see p. 50), by the size of the cylinder P,
fig. 22, no. 1.

However great the care taken by the warper may
be, it is impossible to prevent threads occasionally
breaking. These must be most carefully watched, and
if possible detected before the broken thread has passed
away through the heck. To find and mend threads

58

between the bobbin frame and the heck is an easy
matter if done in the right way. The warper must
reach down from the top between the vertical row
of threads in which the broken one should be and
the row nearer to him, bring both ends up, seeing
that they come direct from the bobbin on the frame
and from the heck, and tie them together. If this
has been rightly done the thread will find its proper
place as soon as the mill begins to revolve again.
Should the thread have passed the heck it is more
difficult to find and mend. In this case the end
must be brought from the bobbin and threaded through
the vacant eye in the heck. If the end to be joined
has disappeared, as will be most likely the case, the
half-portee must be unwound with the greatest care
and searched for the missing end. As the silk is
unwound from the mill the warper temporarily
winds it upon his hand until the missing thread is
discovered. When found, it is tied to the loose end
from the reel, and the half-portee replaced gently
and accurately in its proper position as the mill is
turned by hand, until the heck is again reached, and
the warping proceeds. This is rather a difficult and
tiresome process, and needs to be avoided as much
as possible by watchful care. Immediately on the
warp being finished the crosses must be secured in
the manner described at p. 32, the greatest care
being taken that the cords pass clearly through the
openings kept by the pegs.

There are, of course, numberless points with
regard to warping which only experience will
teach, but enough has been advanced to explain the
method itself and to indicate the uses of the various
parts of the warping mill.

CHAPTER V

TURNING ON, OR BEAMING

Turning on, or Beaming—The Raddle, or Vateau
—Selection of a Raddle for a particular Warp—
The Cane Roller and Cane Sticks—The Raddle
Stand for Small Warps—To separate the Portees—
Distributing the Portees in the Raddle—Turning on
in the Loom—Position of the Cane Roller in the
Loom—Means of turning the Roller—Assistance
required in turning on—Method of keeping the
Warp hard on the Roller.

Turning
on, or
Beaming

IN order that the warp may be stretched in the
loom ready for the weaver to make into cloth, it has
to be attached to a roller and spread out and wound
evenly and tightly upon it. This roller fits into the
back or top of the loom frame, and when spread out
upon it the warp has to be a little wider than the
web is intended to measure when finished. This
process is called *turning on* or *beaming*—beaming
because beam is the old name for the roller of a
loom. When we read in history or poetry of a
"weaver's beam" we may know that the roller is
the part of the loom referred to.

In Chapter III. the use of the warping board
was demonstrated, and a finished warp, with the
crosses properly secured, was described as left wound

60

upon a hand-stick, with the portee cross exposed, and ready for beaming (p. 39).

For the demonstration of turning on we will suppose that the width of material to be woven is twenty-two inches, that the warp contains nine hundred and sixty threads, and that this number is made up of sixty portees having sixteen threads in each.

We have first to spread the warp out evenly to a width of a little more than twenty-two inches. This must be done by means of an appliance called a *raddle*, or *vateau* (fig. 28, nos. 1 and 2). The raddle is simply a comb with a movable cap to cover the ends of the teeth (no. 1). The frame is made of wood, but the teeth are of hard brass wire. The cap has holes in it, near the ends, through which the sides of the frame pass in order to fix it on, as shown at no. 2. Metal pins or small wedges passing through the projecting ends secure the cap in its place. The cap also is deeply grooved above the range of teeth, and when fixed on the comb effectually separates all the divisions of the raddle. The teeth of the raddle are accurately spaced and marked, so many to the inch. A warper has to be provided with a set of raddles, so as to be able to deal conveniently with warps made up of different numbers of portees and various thicknesses of yarn.

In order to determine the proper raddle required for a warp, the number of portees it contains must be divided by the number of inches it is to occupy on the roller. Thus, the warp with which we are dealing contains sixty portees, and as it is to make cloth twenty-two inches wide, it should be

61

Selection of
the Raddle
for a Warp

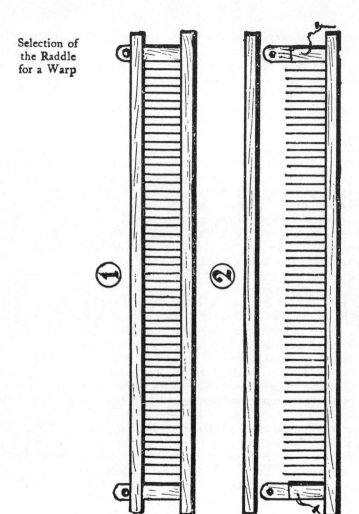

Fig. 28.—The Raddle.

spread out to at least twenty-four inches in the
raddle.

$$60 \div 24 = 2\tfrac{1}{2}.$$

We find then that every inch of the raddle must have two portees and a half distributed on it. A raddle having five spaces to an inch will accordingly suit our purpose, and in every space we

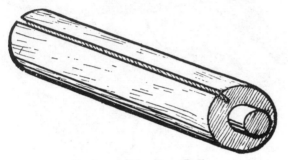

F<small>IG</small>. 29.—The Cane Roller.

must place half a portee. This can be quite readily done, as each portee is divided into two at the cross.

Fig. 29 represents the back or top roller of a loom such as the warp is to be spread and wound upon. It is called the *cane* roller, to distinguish it from the *breast* roller, in front of the loom, on which the woven cloth is wound. It has a groove ploughed in it from end to end deep enough for two smooth, wood or metal sticks to be placed easily one above the other in it. One of these rods we shall require to use at once in spreading the warp.

The warp is shown on the hand-stick in fig. 30. Into the opening at A the cane stick must be inserted, and through the opening B, another cord, a little longer than the cane stick, has

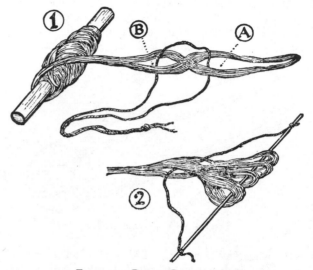

Fig. 30.—Portee Cross in Use.

to be passed and tied securely to the ends of the stick. As soon as this is done the first cord may be cut away. The portee cross will now be safely kept by means
of the cane stick and the cord as at no. 2. Two little supports for the raddle will now be required in order to fix it in an upright position on a table, as shown in fig. 31. Fig. 32 shows the warp in the proper position for distribution in the raddle. A

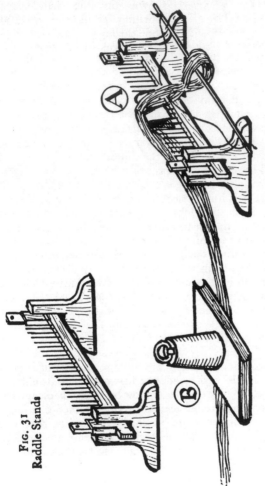

FIG. 31
Raddle Stands

FIG. 32.—Warp ready for distributing in Raddle.

heavy weight of some kind, B, is placed on the warp three or four feet from the raddle, and the portee cross, secured by the cane stick and cord, is on the opposite side. A piece of card folded as at A and placed on top of the teeth of the raddle, makes a handy rest for the warp while the portees are being picked out and placed in order. It will now be found that on taking the cane stick in hand and gently pulling the warp tight the portees can readily be separated and entered in regular succession along it. By this means the warper is enabled to distribute the portees at will in the raddle spaces.

The raddle will probably be more than twenty-four inches long, but that is quite immaterial. We must first find the central space and count off twelve inches to the right of it, marking it as the starting place of the distribution. The folded card may be moved to within a few inches of the mark, with the warp resting upon it. The first portee must now be separated from the bulk of the warp and divided, the first half of it, which will come out of the cross naturally, being placed in the first space, and the second half in the second space. The second portee, in like manner, will fill the third and fourth spaces, and so each portee will follow in succession, until all are distributed. It will be found necessary, during the distribution, to keep the cane stick as much below the level of the raddle as possible. If this be not done, the distributed portees are apt to escape from their appointed spaces, and the work of distribution has all to be done again. As soon as the whole warp is in the raddle the cap must be fixed securely in its place, and then all will be safe and ready for the actual turning on.

66

Such a warp as the one we are dealing with, made on the warping board, is just suitable for a domestic loom, so we will suppose it has to be turned on, in the loom, with the roller, on which the warp has been wound, fixed in its place. This can readily be done, but an important silk warp, such as the one described as made on the warping mill, requires the use of a special turning-on machine, with facilities for very heavy weighting and a means of keeping a steady and even tension on the multitude of fine silk threads.

Turning on in the Loom

This is not the place to explain the method of fixing the roller to the loom, that will be done when the whole construction of the loom itself is treated of. We must therefore, for our present purpose, imagine it bracketed to the loom-posts as shown in fig. 33, in which A, A are the back posts of the loom, B the cane roller, and C the groove in the roller into which the cane sticks fit. Two assistants will now be required, one to turn the roller and the other to hold on to the hand-stick, on which the warp is at present wound. Before we can actually begin the turning on, however, some means of turning the roller must be devised.

The Position of the Cane Roller in the Loom

Into the roller at the place marked D, fig. 33, a very strong, short screw or nail must be driven, deep enough to take firm hold but at the same time to leave the head about an inch out of the wood. About six feet of strong cord will also be wanted ; this must be tied together at the ends so as to form a long loop. One end of the loop must be caught on to the screw-head, and the double cord wound round the roller two or three times, crossing itself

Means of turning the Roller

67

Means of turning the Roller

as it winds. It must be wound in the direction shown at fig. 33A, leaving the loop E for the insertion

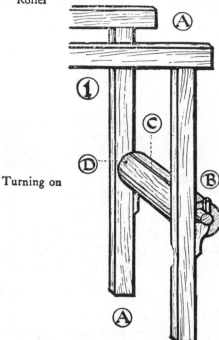

FIG. 33.—Loom Posts with Roller.

of the stick as at F, fig. 33B. By means of this stick and cord, the assistant will be enabled to turn the roller, hand over hand, and wind the warp upon it quite easily, although a good deal of strength be exerted at the other end in order to pull the warp tight on the roller.

The actual process of turning on will be readily explained with the assistance of figs. 34 and 35. At fig. 34, no. 1, the warp is shown with the raddle, GG, and the cane stick, HH, in their proper places in the warp. One assistant, we will suppose, is holding the hand-stick, with the bulk of the warp upon it, at some little distance off

Turning on

in the direction of the arrow. The other assistant is holding the raddle, GG, and the cane stick, HH, in the relative position, with regard to the loom-posts, shown in the drawing. The warper must now

68

stand behind the loom-posts, and, reaching between them, take from the assistant the cane stick, HH, to which the warp is attached by the portee loops. This he must slip into the groove in the cane roll. To fix the cane stick in the groove, another stick must be passed underneath the roller and the warp, into the groove, as shown at no. 2, fig. 34. The

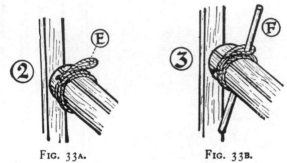

FIG. 33A.   FIG. 33B.

Loop and Stick for turning Roller.

raddle must now be brought close to the roller by being slipped along the warp, and the roller itself must be turned once round. This will fix the warp securely in its place, and at the same time spread it evenly upon the roller. When placing the cane stick in the groove care must be taken to leave equal spaces, or whatever proportion of space may be necessary for the working of the loom, at each end of the roller.

The warper and the assistant holding the raddle will now have to change places, but before doing so the roller must be fixed so that it will not turn

69

back although the tension be kept on it. This may
be done at any time, by placing the turning stick, F,
in the position shown in fig. 35. This drawing
(fig. 35) represents the stage of the operation now
arrived at. The warper must take the raddle in
hand and see that all the portees are in their proper

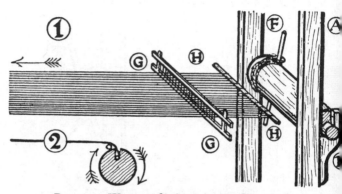

FIG. 34.—Warp ready for fixing in Cane Roller.

places, and that the raddle can be moved easily and
without obstruction along the threads. All being
in order, the turning on may now proceed. The
warper must guide the warp, as it is turned on, by
means of the raddle, gently shifting it about so as to
lay the threads on the roller as evenly as possible round
by round. All the time of turning he must look out for
broken or tangled threads, being careful to place any
that have to be mended in the portee to which they
belong. If all goes well and the warp is turned on
easily, it will prove that the warping has been properly
done. All this time, from the first turning of the roller,

70

the assistant holding the hand-stick with the warp
upon it must have been pulling with all his force
and steadiness against the turning. If, indeed, the
warp is of any considerable size, the services of
two or three people are necessary in order to give
sufficient tension to it. When a few turns have

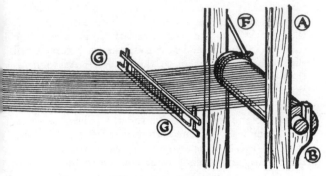

FIG. 35.—Warp ready for turning on.

been given, it may be well to place a sheet of very
thick paper or tough card underneath the warp,
between it and the roller. This being wound on,
will prevent any threads sinking in and giving
future trouble, as they would otherwise be apt to
do. A long warp may require several of these protecting cards to be wound in with it, but the need
for them will depend very much upon the weight
and evenness of the tension kept during the turning
on. If the warp on the roll begins to feel soft and
flabby, it may be known that a card is required.
As soon as the important cross is exposed on the
hand-stick, the warper must call a halt, leave the

71

raddle, and spread the crossing threads out on the securing cords. This will not be found difficult to do if the weight be kept well on. When the cross is spread out clearly, two smoothly polished, round, wooden rods, pointed at one end, about an inch thick and six inches longer than the width of the warp, must be put into it, in the openings made by the securing cords, and left there together with them. When the rods are safely in place, the turning must proceed and continue as before, until the rods are close up to the raddle. As soon as they are in this position the cap must be taken off the raddle and the raddle itself removed, its work being done. One or two more turns will wind the cross and the rods on to the roller. The hand-stick may then be detached from the warp, and the turning on, or beaming, will be completed, the warp being quite ready to be entered in the loom.

CHAPTER VI

THE BEAMING DRUM

The Essential Part of Beaming Machinery—The Drum and its Fittings—Friction Brakes—Ropes of the Drum—Space necessary for Beaming—Importance of Accuracy of Detail in Weaving Operations—Turning-on Posts—Appliance for Beaming in Confined Space—Winding the Warp on the Drum—Beaming with the Drum.

THE beaming of such a warp as that described in Chapter IV. necessitates the use of some mechanical appliance in order to give to the threads a great and unintermittent tension during the whole operation. This want is met by the essential part of any turning machinery, the beaming drum.

This drum is a strongly, solidly made, large reel, with an iron axle, on to which the warp to be beamed has to be wound instead of being turned on directly from the hand-stick, as was done in the case of the small warp described in the last chapter. The drum, furnished with all its fittings and fixed in position, is represented by figs. 36, 36A, and 36B. It should be in size at least two feet in diameter and two feet six inches to three feet in length. It must be perfectly smooth and well joined, so that there may be no danger of the finest silk thread being caught or broken on any part of it. The two stands on which it revolves must be firmly bolted to the floor of the workshop, as the strain they have to bear is very heavy and continuous, and they must be carefully adjusted in order that the

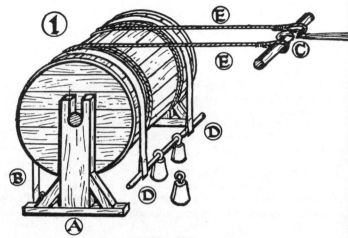

FIG. 36.—The Beaming Drum.

revolutions of the drum may be level and true. The drum itself must be provided with two friction brakes (figs. 36A and 36B, B, B). Each of these brakes consists of a strap of tough leather, about two inches in width, and long enough to reach from the ground at the back of the drum—where they are fixed by strong staples (C, C, fig. 36A)—to the bar DD at the front (fig. 36B). It is by means of these straps that the tension is given to the warp as it is being turned on.

74

Weights are hung on the bar, and the tension given to the warp can be regulated to a nicety by their means.

The drum must also be furnished with two well-made ropes capable of bearing a heavy strain, and long enough to reach from the drum, after going once round it, to the frame on which the roller

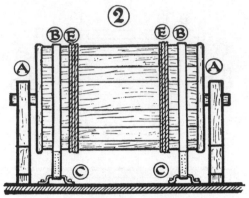

FIG. 36A.—The Drum : Back View.

for turning on is fixed. These ropes must be permanently fastened, at one end, to the drum, as near as possible to the straps of the friction brakes, but not so near as to interfere with them when working. The ropes are wound on to the drum, care being taken to avoid crossing them, as shown at E, E, figs. 36A and 36B. The free ends of the ropes must be looped in order that a thick, round stick, almost as long as the width of space between the straps, may rest in them (F, fig. 36B). To

75

Ropes of the
Drum
Length of
Space
necessary for
Beaming

this stick one end of the warp to be turned on is
attached as shown at fig. 36.

The next necessity for good beaming is a long
workshop, in which a clear space of thirty or forty
feet is available. Where such a space can be had,
the drum, fitted up in the manner described, is the

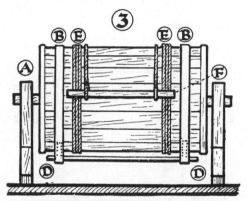

FIG. 36B.—The Drum : Front View.

only apparatus that is required, with the exception
of two posts, answering to the back posts of the
loom, on which the cane roller is placed for beaming the warp, as described on p. 68 and shown in
fig. 33. The posts specially made for turning
on must be fitted up exactly opposite to the
drum, and as far from it as convenient. They
must be adjustable—that is to say, whatever width
apart they may have to be in order to accommodate
different lengths of rollers, the centre of the space
between them must be exactly opposite to the
76

centre of the drum. ALL THESE MATTERS OF DETAIL
ARE OF THE UTMOST IMPORTANCE IN WEAVING. IN
THIS CASE, FOR INSTANCE, A LITTLE INACCURACY IN
ADJUSTING THE POSTS WILL CAUSE THE DISTANCE OF
THE DRUM FROM THE ROLLER TO BE GREATER ON
ONE EDGE OF THE WARP THAN THE OTHER. THIS

DIFFERENCE WOULD BE
MULTIPLIED SEVERAL
TIMES IF THE WARP
WERE A VERY LONG ONE.
IN CONSEQUENCE OF THIS,
WHEN IT WAS IN THE
LOOM THE WEAVER
WOULD DISCOVER THAT
ONE SIDE OF HIS WARP
WAS LOOSER THAN THE
OTHER, AND HE WOULD
HAVE TO WASTE A GOOD
DEAL OF TIME IN
CONTRIVANCES FOR RE-
MEDYING THE DEFECT.
The posts may be made
adjustable in the manner

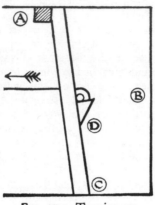

FIG. 37.—Turning-on
Post fitted

indicated by fig. 37. A strong cross-beam about eight
feet long, a section of which is shown at A, must be
fixed to the roof of the workshop, as far from the drum
as possible and exactly parallel with it. As stated
above, the space between the beam and the drum
should be at least thirty feet. At the same time
the beam must not be less than four feet from
the wall indicated in the diagram by the line B,
for in this space the assistant stands to turn the
roller. A permanent mark should be made on the
beam A exactly opposite the centre of the drum,

and a line may be painted on the floor also marking the centre of the space from the drum to the beam. This line and mark will make the nice adjustment of the posts, when they are fixed up, quite easy. The two posts need to be very strong, and should be about six inches wide by three inches thick. Their length will, of course, depend on the height of the workshop, as they must reach from the roof to the floor. It will be seen from the diagram that the posts do not stand quite upright, but lean against the beam in the direction of the drum, so that although when not in use they can easily be removed, when the tension is on the warp they are firmly fixed in their places. In order to make the posts stand firm when the weight is not on, their ends are accurately cut to the angles of the beam and roof and of the floor, so that when in position a tap with a mallet at the place marked C, fig. 37, will at once fix them. It will also be seen that the roller simply rests upon brackets fitted to the posts at a convenient height for the turner-on to work at.

If a space of thirty feet is not available for the beaming it is possible to do it in a much smaller one by means of rollers fitted in a frame. The frame with rollers is fixed to the wall, or placed opposite the turning-on posts, as far away from them as possible. The drum, with its front facing the rollers, stands between them and the posts, as near the latter as convenience will allow. This arrangement of the beaming machinery is shown at fig. 38. The warp in this case unwinds from the drum A, passes under the roller B, over C, and then, turning back, escapes the top of the drum and is turned on at the opposite posts. The simpler arrangement without rollers

78

is better for several reasons, the principal one being that when the silk goes direct from the drum to the cane roller there is much less friction and strain on it.

The process of beaming when the drum is used is exactly the same as that described in the last chapter, except for the management of the drum itself, which takes the place of the assistant who holds the hand-stick and pulls, in order to give the

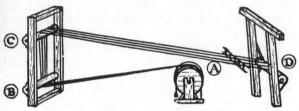

Fig. 38.—Beaming in a Smaller Space.

necessary tension to the threads. It will only be needful, therefore, to give instructions for the management of the drum and refer to the previous explanation for the rest.

In taking the warp off the warping mill on to the hand-stick, when a beaming drum is to be used, the *portee cross* end of the warp must be looped first to the hand-stick, so that when it is all wound on the *porrey cross* (see fig. 14) will be left outside. This is the reverse of the former direction (p. 38), and is necessary because the warp has to be rewound on to the drum. When this has been done the warp will be found in the same position on the drum as regards the crosses, as it was in the former case upon the hand-stick. In order to wind the warp on to the

79

drum, the stick C, fig. 36, must be detached from
the ropes E, E and placed in the opening made
by peg Y, fig. 22, no. 1. The stick must then
be reattached to the ropes, and the drum turned so
as to wind the warp tightly and evenly upon it.
Of course while this is being done the weight must
be taken off the bar of the friction brakes ; the straps
themselves may even have to be removed. As soon as
the warp is all wound on the drum, the friction brake
must be replaced and a light weight put on the bar.
The warper must then take in hand the portee end
of the warp and carry it over to the cane roller posts,
where the raddle is for the present fixed, in a convenient manner, in the place that the cane roll will
eventually occupy. He will then proceed to insert
the cane stick in the warp, distribute the portees in the
raddle, and fix the cap on. Then the roller will take
the place of the raddle and the cane stick be dropped
into its groove. One turn given to the roller will
fix the cane stick, and the necessary weight being
put on the drum, the beaming may proceed.

When the warp is all off the drum, and the stick,
to which it is looped, is in the position shown at
fig. 36, the weight must again be taken off the brakes,
in order to allow of the spreading and straightening
out of the cross and the cords securing it. When
this is done and the two rods inserted as directed at
p. 72, the weight must be again put on and the
beaming can be completed, the tension being kept
even by means of the unwinding ropes.

The directions for finishing off the beaming, which
are the same in large or small warps, are also given
at p. 72.

CHAPTER VII

THE HAND-LOOM FOR AUTOMATIC WEAVING

Opening or shedding the Warp for Wefting—
Shedding the Warp without Appliances—Simplicity
of Egyptian and Greek Weaving—The Headle-rod—
Ancient Horizontal Looms and Automatic Sheds—
Indian and Chinese Looms—The Old English Hand-
loom—The Loom Frame—The Rollers—The
Ratchet and Wheel—Friction Brake for Cane
Roller—Comparison of Indian and English Looms
—Automatic Method of opening the Shed—The
Long Comb or Reed—The Batten—Position of
the Harness and Batten—Preparations for entering
the Warp in Harness and Reed—Gating the Loom.

THE warp, its special characteristics and the
manner of preparing it, have been carefully and
minutely explained ; this will therefore need no
further consideration. The method of opening the
warp for the intersection of the weft thread next
claims attention, for in this consists the whole art
and mystery of weaving. Thus briefly stated,
weaving may appear to be a very simple matter, but
it will be found, as the subject is developed, that the
warp may be intersected by the weft in an infinite
variety of ways, and that the contrivances for doing
this are numerous, and many of them most elaborate.

Opening or
shedding
the Warp

So much is this the case that, instead of being altogether a simple art, weaving, in its highest perfection, is perhaps the most complicated of all the arts of life.

In order to explain the method of opening the warp for inserting the weft, it will be necessary to turn back to fig. 13, no. 1. In this drawing, as was intimated at p. 24, is represented the simplest possible form of loom. The method of weaving plain cloth is all that must concern us at present, the weaving of patterns being left for later consideration. The tools required are as simple as the loom itself, being only the spindle, with the weft wound upon it as it was spun (see pp. 14 and 15), and a flat stick to be used for keeping the openings wide and clear for the passing of the weft, and for beating the weft itself together.

The loom for the demonstration of weaving being prepared as directed at p. 25, the cross-rods must first be secured in their place at the top of the loom. This may be done by attaching loops of string to the projecting ends of the beading, and twisting it round the two rods as shown in the end view of the rods, fig. 39. The flat rod E must next be placed in the opening made by the lower cross-rod, brought a little way down and turned edgeways, as shown in the section of the loom, fig. 39A. This flat rod is usually called the *shed-stick* because it is used for widening the shed, shed being the technical name for any opening made for the

passing of the weft. Through the opening F, fig. 39A, the spindle, G, with the weft upon it, must now be passed, after sufficient thread has been unwound to reach across the warp, and leave the end of it projecting at H. All the warp threads at the

back of the shed will now be covered by the weft,
whilst those in front are still exposed. The latter
must now be covered by the return of the spindle
and weft. For this pur-
pose a different opening
or shed must be made as
shown at I, fig. 39B.
This is effected by
pressing back the front
threads with the top joint
of the forefinger of the
left hand, and hooking
each back string on to it
in succession. To do
this quickly requires a
good deal of practice; it is
well, therefore, to begin
by raising and passing
the weft through only a
very few threads at a
time. For example, let
the warp consist of
seventeen threads, nine
being in front. Be-
ginning at the first
thread on the left-hand
side, and pressing it
back, the back thread

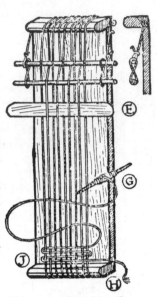

Fig. 39.—Primitive Loom
and Shed-sticks.

can easily be caught on to the finger, which
must next press in the same manner the second
front thread and catch up the second back one.
Next the third front and the third back, and lastly
the fourth front and the fourth back threads must
be taken up. It will now be found that four

83

of the back threads nearest the left-hand side of the loom are on the finger, and if the shed-stick be placed flat in its original position, E, fig. 39, they can easily be raised sufficiently high for the weft spindle to be passed through the opening. When this is done and the shed-stick again placed edge-ways, the remaining four back threads have to be raised in the same manner, and the weft passed through. After the weft has been drawn straight, the shed-stick being again in a flat position, its edge may be brought down smartly upon the whole weft in order to beat it together. The two shoots of weft will now appear as drawn between H and J, fig. 39, and the shed-stick being returned to its position at F, fig. 39A, the opening for the third shoot will be ready. The fourth opening is made by picking up, in the same way as the second, and so shoot by shoot the weaving may be regularly continued. After a little practice the picking up of the back threads for every second shoot will become quite easy, and may be very quickly done. It will also be found that if the cross-rods are of a good size the shed-stick may be dispensed with. The weft, too, may be wound in convenient balls or skeins, small enough to pass

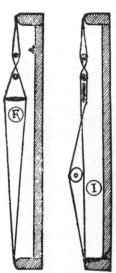

FIG. 39A.   FIG. 39B.

84

through the opening, so that the only tool actually requisite for this simple weaving is a heavy fork or comb to press the weft and beat it together from time to time (see plate II).

The above may be taken as typical of all primitive weaving, both ancient and modern. There is no evidence to show that the "fine linen" of Egypt or the famous textiles of Greece and Rome were woven in a less simple manner. Frames of various sizes for stretching the warp upon were certainly used, and the warps often consisted of a great number of fine threads. Rollers also were added to the loom, enabling the weaver to make long lengths of cloth, but the actual methods of weaving appear to have been as stated.

There is, in use amongst some primitive tribes of to-day, a contrivance for bringing forward the back threads of the warp all together or in sections, instead of picking them up separately on the fingers as above described. This is sometimes called a headle-rod. It is a rather obvious improvement, and, where the threads are very fine and numerous, would save a great deal of time. It may have been used in ancient Egypt and Greece, but there is no evidence to prove it. This appliance is a strong rod, a little longer than the warp is wide. It is suspended in front of the loom a little below the cross-rods. Each back thread of the warp is enclosed by a loop which passes between the front threads and is fastened to the rod (fig. 40). When this appliance is fitted to a loom the first opening is made by means of the shed-stick as already described. The second opening is made by the weaver giving the headle-rod a vigorous pull forward, and into the

85

The Headle-
rod

Horizontal
Looms and
Automatic
Sheds

opening thus made the flat shed-stick is carefully
thrust. When quite through the warp it is turned
edgeways, and effectually clears the opening for the
passing of the weft.

It is impossible to say how early in the history of weaving two most important steps in its

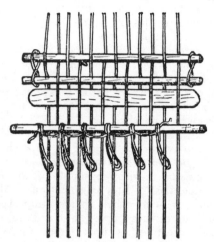

FIG. 40.—Headle Rod.

development were made. These steps were
(1) placing the warp horizontally ; (2) arranging an
automatic motion by which both the necessary
openings or sheds can be made with equal speed
and certainty. There is little doubt that it was
in China that these improvements were first made.
From that country they spread to India and the East
generally. There are in existence very ancient

86

representations of Chinese and Indian horizontal looms with such automatic arrangements. Moreover, the fine silk webs of China and India, so much valued in ancient Greece and Rome, could hardly have been made in the simple manner described above.

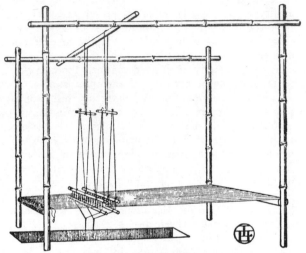

Fig. 41.—Indian Loom.

Fig. 41 is a drawing of an Indian loom made for the weaving of fine muslin. Such looms as this have without doubt been commonly used in India from a time long anterior to the Christian era. The framework is of bamboo, and the warp is stretched between bamboo rollers. There are many details lacking, as we have seen is usual in these ancient drawings, but the automatic motion for opening the

87

shed, just referred to, is quite clearly shown.
Altogether in its general arrangement the Indian
loom bears a close resemblance to the hand-loom
of old English pattern (fig. 42) and the domestic
loom in the old French woodcut of the frontispiece.
The stuffs carefully made by hand on such looms
as fig. 42 cannot be equalled either in appearance
or durability by the productions of the power-
loom, notwithstanding all its claims to perfection
of mechanism.

A careful study of this old English loom in all its
parts will now be both useful and interesting.

The hand-loom, like the warping mill, was the
result of the experience of many generations of
craftsmen. Simple as it may appear, it is perfectly
adapted for use either in the weaving of the finest silk,
or of the coarsest linen, woollen, or cotton materials.
The parts already described will be at once recognised—viz., the back or cane roller, the warp with
its cross or lease, and the cross-sticks protecting it ;
but the new features, the loom frame and its other
fittings, now claim attention.

Strength and rigidity are the chief qualities
requisite in the loom frame, in order to enable it
to withstand the continual heavy beating down of the
weft, on which the making of good cloth so largely
depends. The four posts must be made of sound
wood, and be about six inches wide by three inches
thick and not less than six feet in height. The posts
must be joined together in pairs by being mortised
into the long side-pieces of wood D, D, which
should measure in length not less than eight feet.
The cross-pieces, E, E, need not be mortised, but
may be simply fixed in their places by screws, in

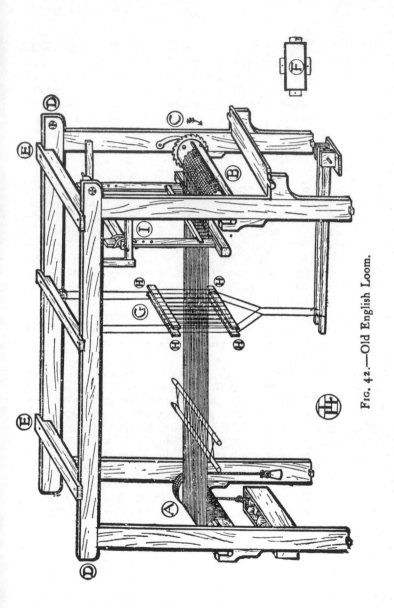

Fig. 42.—Old English Loom.

the way shown in the drawing. The length of the cross-pieces will depend on that of the rollers, and the length of these depends on the width of the web to be made. For a twenty-three-inch warp the rollers should be thirty-six inches long. There is no necessity for cross-pieces to join the posts together at the bottom. These would, in fact, be rather in the way of the weaver, who should be able to get conveniently to any part of the warp. In order to fix the frame solidly in its place and prevent the posts from shifting, four little blocks can be nailed to the floor at the foot of each post, as shown in the plan F, fig. 42. In erecting the loom frame care must be taken to fix it exactly square (see Note 1 at end of chapter), so that the front and back rollers are perfectly parallel to one another. Stays also should be fixed between the top-pieces, from the ends marked with a cross, and the nearest solid beam or wall above or behind the weaver, who sits to work facing the front roller. Constructed in this manner, of well-seasoned wood, the loom frame will be found to resist any amount of strain it may have to bear.

The back, or cane roller, A, has already been described (p. 63), and the front or breast roller, B, is exactly like it, having a groove in which two cane-sticks are put, in order to fix the warp.

The breast roller has in addition a ratchet and wheel attachment (C, fig. 42), which allows it to be turned only in the direction indicated by the arrow. The back roller is not so rigidly fixed, but is weighted by a friction brake at each end, the arrangement of which fig. 43, nos. 1 and 2, will readily explain. A is the roller, with the rope

90

wound three times round it at each end. B is a box suspended between the two ropes, into which any amount of weight, that may be required, can be put. C is a small weight just heavy enough to prevent the rope slipping too freely when the box is heavily weighted and set in the position shown. The warp being placed in the loom, is first sufficiently unwound for its end to reach to the front roller, where it is fixed, in the same manner as in the cane roller, by two rods. It will now be obvious that the warp will be stretched in proportion to the amount of weight put into the box suspended from the back roller.

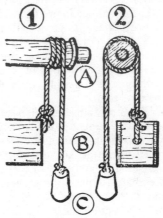

Fig. 43.—Cane Roller and Weighting.

Tapestry looms and some other simple looms for coarse weaving are made with a ratchet and wheel on the back roller, instead of the friction weight. This arrangement would not do for the weaving of fine threads, especially if they be silk, as the tension obtained by two ratchet wheels is rigid, instead of being elastic. When the friction brake is used, no matter how heavy the box may be made, the weight will give slightly at every blow of the beating down. This kindly giving prevents the breaking of the slender threads. The friction brake

91

Advantages
of the
Friction
Brake on the
Cane Roller

Comparison
of the
Indian and
English
Looms

also admits of a nice adjustment of the tension to
the requirements of the weaving, and has also many
minor advantages unnecessary to mention here.

If the Indian loom, fig. 41, be compared with the
English one, fig. 42, it will be at once noticed that
they are both alike in two most important
particulars. Both have the warp arranged in a
horizontal position, and the contrivance used for
making the opening or shed in the warp is the
same in each.

The horizontal position of the warp in the loom
was no doubt originally adopted because, in the
first place, it enables the weaver to throw the weft
swiftly through the opening by means of a shuttle,
instead of slowly passing the ball or spindle across
the warp ; and, in the second place, because it is
easier to arrange for the automatic opening of
the alternate sheds. In fact, if the interlacements
of the warp and weft required are at all complicated, it would be practically impossible to
arrange mechanically for the necessary succession
of openings on an upright loom.

In fig. 41 and at letter G, fig. 42, the simplest
possible automatic arrangement for opening the sheds
is represented. It consists of four laths of wood, H, H,
H, H, fig. 42, joined together in pairs by threads
passing from those above the warp to those below it.
Each pair of laths thus joined together is called a
headle, or *heddle*. The threads joining the laths
together are not simply single ones, but are made up
in the same manner, although on a larger scale, as the
loops of the part of the warping mill called the heck,
shown at fig. 25, nos. 3 and 4. These compound
loops are known as *leashes*, and any number of

92

them mounted on the two laths is called a *headle*.*
The front headle of the English loom will be seen
to have ten leashes, and the back one nine, thus
allowing all the threads of the warp to pass
through the eye of a leash. The first, third,
fifth and all the odd-numbered warp threads pass
through the eyes of the front headle, and the second,
fourth, sixth, eighth and all the even-numbered
threads occupy the eyes of the back headle. Only
nineteen threads are represented in the drawing of
the warp, for the sake of clearness, but it might, of
course, consist of any number in reason, and the
effect would be the same. It will now be seen that
if the headles are raised successively, by some means,
the alternate threads of the warp will be raised with
them, and the necessary sheds opened for weaving.

There are various devices in use for the purpose
of governing the headles in order to make the shed.
These will be described later on, but the opening
made by means of the arrangement of cords, pulleys,
and treadles shown in figs. 41 and 42, as well as in
the French loom of the frontispiece, is most simple
and effective. By its use the pulling down of
one headle causes the other to rise, so that while
one half of the warp is rising the other is falling,
and the clear opening required is consequently
made in half the time it would otherwise take.
Fig. 44, in which a longitudinal section of the
loom is given, will explain the action of this contrivance. A and B are the rollers of the loom, C, C
are the cross-sticks, and D is one of the two pulleys
suspended from the centre cross-piece at the top of

* Sometimes the loop itself is called a *heudle* or *hook*,
and the collection of them a *leaf* or *lam*.

93

the loom frame, just above the ends of the two headles. A cord passes from the front headle over the pulley, and is tied to the top lath of the back headle. The cord is made just long enough to allow the whole warp, when the headles are at rest,

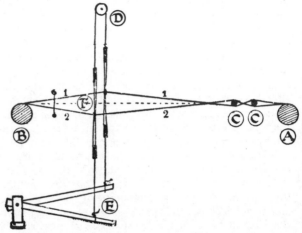

Fig. 44.—Section of Opened Warp.

to lie flat, as shown in fig. 42 and represented by the dotted line in fig. 44. At E are the treadles of the loom, tied separately to each of the lower laths of the headles.

The opening F shown in fig. 44 is obtained by pressing down the right-hand treadle and allowing the left-hand one to rise. The falling treadle draws down the front headle with all the threads of warp carried by it, and at the same time, by means of the pulley D, draws up the back headle

94

with all its threads, the result being a clear open shed as depicted. In like manner the second shed is made by releasing the right-hand treadle and pressing down the left.

It is impossible to say at what period the important improvement in the apparatus of the loom was made, which consists in lengthening the short, heavy, independent comb, by which the weft had hitherto been beaten together, and attaching it to the loom itself, enclosed in a heavy swinging frame. It may be that at first the long comb was only fixed in the loom, near the front roller, in order to keep the warp threads from gathering together in places, as they are so apt to do. It is still used, for this purpose only, in looms built for the making of tapestry. When the long comb is fixed in this manner the short comb has to be used as well for beating down the weft. It led, however, to a great advance in the weaving process, when the idea occurred of hanging the long comb loose in the loom, in order that it might be used, not only for keeping the warp threads evenly distributed, but also for beating the weft together.

By the adoption of the long swinging comb, needless to say, much time is saved. But more important than this, the blow of the comb is by this means evenly distributed across the whole width of the warp, and is so equalised that even the most delicate threads of silk or cotton, composing the warp, are not unduly strained, although a surprising amount of force may be used, after each shoot of weft, to beat the cloth together.

The name given to the long comb by weavers is the *reed*, because the divisions were originally made

95

Signification of fine strips of cane or reed, most carefully pre-
of the Name pared and fixed between four half-round laths, in the
Reed

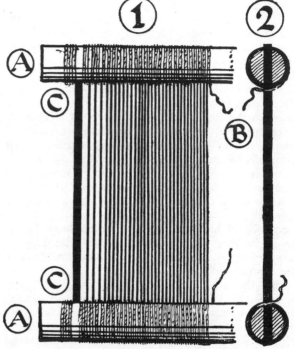

Fig. 45.—Method of Reed-making.

manner shown at fig. 45. A, A, no. 1, are the ends
of four half-round laths, shown also in the section
no. 2, bound together in pairs by a fine waxed cord,
one end of which appears loose at B.

96

In order to make the reed, the laths had to be
fixed in pairs about four inches apart, and, starting
at one end, a rather thick strip of cane—shown
at C, no. 1, and B, no. 2, fig. 45—was placed
between the laths and bound in with the cord as
there represented. This thick strip of cane was for
the protection of the finer strips which followed after
about a quarter of an inch of the binding cord had
been wound about the laths. The fine strips were
put in, one to each round of cord, the spaces between them being regulated by the thickness of the
cord itself. The whole length of reed being thus
built up, the end was finished off in the same way as
the beginning. The bound laths were finally steeped
in melted resin in order to fix everything securely.

The spaces in the completed reed between the
strips of cane were called *dents*, and for fine silk-
weaving there were often as many as a hundred
and twenty to the inch. Often several threads of
fine silk were passed, or *entered*, as it is called, in each
dent of the reed. These combs still retain the name
of *reeds*, although, since the middle of the eighteenth
century, metal has taken the place of cane for the
strips. The best metal reeds are still made by hand
in the same way as the old cane ones, but they are
now for the most part made by machinery.

The heavy swinging frame in which the reed is
fixed is called the *batten*, and the method of
hanging it is clearly shown in the drawing of the
old English loom (fig. 42). Fig. 46 represents a
batten for use with a hand-shuttle. It is constructed as follows. A is a heavy block of hard
wood called the *race-block*, having a groove cut in
the top, at the back edge, the same length as the

97

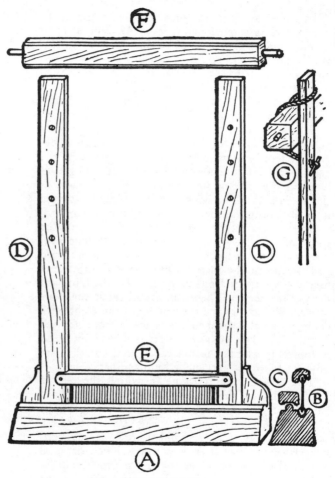

Fig. 46.—Hand-batten.

reed, and of the shape shown in the section at B.
It also has a piece of polished beading along the top
front edge. This is for the shuttle to run on (letter
C in section) as it is thrown through the shed of
warp, which is so regulated that the threads held
down by the treadle press upon the beading and allow
the shuttle to pass over them. D, D are called the
swords of the batten, and are mortised into the race-
block. E is a grooved cap, also shown in the section ;
it is movable, and its use is to fix the reed in its place.*
F is the rocker by means of which the batten is hung
in the loom as shown in fig. 42. When the batten
is attached to the rocker by a double cord, as indicated
in the side view G, its height can be nicely regulated
by means of the peg at the back, which shortens, or
lengthens the cord, by twisting, or untwisting it.

In order to complete the description of the old
English loom, it only remains to point out that the
cross-piece, from which the headles are suspended, is
movable, and may be fixed at any distance from the
front of the loom necessary for the regulation of the
shed. The nearer to the reed the headles are hung,
the clearer and wider the opening in the warp will be.

The position of the batten can be regulated by
moving the rocker backward or forward in the
brackets on which it rests (fig. 42, I). When the right
place for it has been determined it is fixed there by
means of small screws being partially driven into the
bracket at the front and back of the rocker pins.

All the essential parts of the loom for plain
weaving are now described, and it is next necessary
to explain the method of entering the threads of the
warp in the *harness*, as a collection of two or more
headles is called, and the reed. Entering has to be

* See Addenda, page 340.   99

To enter the
Warp in the
Harness and
Reed

done with great care and accuracy, as one mistake will throw out the whole succession of remaining threads. It is also very difficult to rectify mistakes when the entering is finished. In some cases the whole of the warp, beyond the faulty place, has to be drawn out and re-entered.

Fig. 47 shows a warp in the loom prepared for entering. At p. 72 the turner-on is described as finishing his work by winding the cross-rods with the warp on to the cane roller. If not turned on in the loom itself, the roller, with the warp on it, was brought to the loom and placed on the brackets of the back loom-posts. Two strong, side cords, A, C, C, C, were then firmly attached to the front posts of the loom, and, being carried over the ends of the back roller, were rather heavily weighted. The warp was then gently unwound, and the ends of the cross-rods were allowed to rest on the side cords at A. The unwinding was continued until the rods rested at B. The side cords were then twisted once round the ends of the rods, as shown in the drawing, and by this means they were securely fixed at that point, but at the same time could be readily moved backward or forward on the side cord weights being lifted. The warp can now be regulated so that the loops hanging below B will reach to the front of the loom.

The headles had next to be specially fixed for entering, and for this the short pieces of wood D were provided. These were tied, as indicated in the drawing, to the top of the loom frame and to temporary staples driven into the floor. The ends of the top shafts of the harness rest upon the upper pieces of wood, and the bottom shafts are tightly held down

100

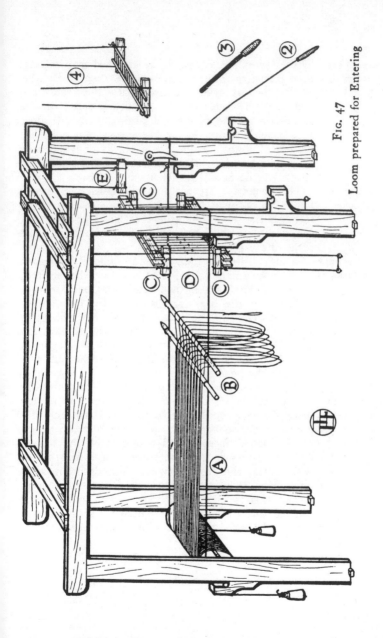

FIG. 47
Loom prepared for Entering

by the lower pieces, which are attached by slip-loops
to the staples in order to regulate them. By this
means the leashes of the headles are rendered quite
taut and the eyes can be readily selected in due
succession by the enterer. To make them still more
secure, which is necessary in the case of a rich, full
harness of many headles, little blocks of wood may
be placed between the ends of the shafts and the
latter may be bound together with cords.

Nos. 2 and 3 are the hooks necessary for entering. No. 2 must be slender enough to pass easily
through the eyes of the leashes, and the flat hook
No. 3 must be thin enough to go through the fine
dents of the reed.

It may be noted here that entering only needs to
be done when the loom, or at any rate the harness,
is new. After a length of cloth has been woven,
sufficient of the old warp is left in the loom, with
the cross-rods in it, to allow of a new one being tied
on to it thread by thread. When the threads are
all joined the old piece of warp is drawn forward,
and of course the new threads follow the old ones
through the headle-eyes.

These preparations all being made, the entering
can proceed. The enterer's assistant sits in the
space D, between the warp and the harness. Beginning at one edge, he takes up a small bunch
of the looped threads, and first cuts off the looped
end; he gives it two or three sharp, firm pulls,
which clear the cross between the rods and make it
quite easy to select and separate the first thread.
When this is done the thread is held ready to be
hitched on to the enterer's hook as soon as it is
pushed through the first eye in the harness.

The enterer himself sits in the loom in front of the
harness, with the slender hook, no. 2, ready for use.
He selects the first eye in the front or back headle
and pushes the hook through it.* The assistant places
the first thread on the hook, which, as it is drawn
back, takes the thread with it. The enterer holds
the thread in his left hand and repeats the operation
with the hook, only selecting the first eye on the
next headle, and draws through the second thread,
which his assistant has picked out at the cross and
placed on the hook. However many headles there
may be in the harness, the first hook in each is filled
before the first headle is returned to for the beginning of the second course. The keeping of this
regular course all through the harness is of the
utmost importance. As the entering proceeds, the
entered threads are loosely tied together in small
bunches, in order to prevent their slipping back
again through the eyes.

Another pair of slings, marked E in the drawing,
is placed in front of the harness. To these the reed
is tied as shown at No. 4. The assistant now
sits in front of the harness, and the enterer stands
over him. The enterer thrusts the reed-hook No. 3
down through the first dent of the reed. The assistant holds the first bunch of threads in one hand,
after having untied the knot. He traces out the
thread coming through the first eye in the harness
and places it upon the hook, which is then drawn
up and treated in the same manner as when drawn
through the harness. The first thread in each
headle is taken in succession, and then the second,

* In England usually the back headle is first ; on the
Continent it is the front.

and so on to the end. When the reed is all entered
and the bunches of threads safely knotted, the loom
will be all ready for the weaver to *gate*, as the
adjustment of the parts of the loom for actual
weaving is called.

The gating of the loom is always done by the
person who is to weave the material upon it, as
every weaver has his, or her own ideas as to the best
way of adjusting the various parts for the work. It
will therefore only be possible on this point to state
the principal matters that have to be attended to.
In the first place, cords must be attached to the top
laths of the headles, preferably the back one, and
passed over the pulleys of the centre cross-piece, in
order to meet and be joined to short strings coming
from the other headle. It is necessary that these,
and, in fact, all the cords of a loom, should be
so tied as to be easily adjusted to a nicety as regards
length ; the manner of doing this is, once for all,
explained in Note 2 at the end of this chapter.
When the headles have been securely connected by
the cord, the slings at D, fig. 47, must be removed
as well as those on which the reed is resting. The
reed itself may, for the moment, be allowed to hang
loosely from the harness, suspended by the knotted
warp. The space in front of the headles being
thus cleared, the batten must next be hung on its
rocker in the position and manner shown at
fig. 42. The cap of the batten, E, fig. 46, being
removed, the reed can be fitted into the groove at the
back of the race-block. This groove must be deep
enough for the round edge of the reed to be completely buried, so that the silk or other threads of the
warp may press on the smooth shuttle-race, and not

104

fray against the lower edge of the reed as the batten is
moved backward and forward. The top edge of the
reed is next to be caught in the groove of the reed-
cap and the latter screwed by wing-nuts to the
swords of the batten. The harness must then be
brought to its proper place, by moving forward
the cross-piece from which it hangs. The nearer
it can be allowed to be to the reed the better,
so long as it does not interfere with the swing of
the batten. The greater the space between the
batten and the harness, the larger the opening has to
be made in order to be effective in front of the reed
where the weft has to be shot. A large opening
has the disadvantage of increasing the strain on the
warp threads. The harness and the treadles will
now be ready to be connected. A long cord must
be tied, at both ends, to the bottom laths of each
headle, as in fig. 42, and from the separate treadles,
exactly underneath these cords, a double cord must
be brought up, and joined to them by the adjustable
slip-knot described in Note 2. It now only remains
to arrange the friction brake on the cane roller as
in figs. 42 and 43, to remove the side-cords and
weights, A, C, C, C, fig. 47, to gently clear and
separate the warp threads and move the rods as far
back as possible, in order to finish the preparation,
or *gating*, of the loom for actual weaving. (See end.)

Note 1, p. 90.—It is very important that the loom-posts
should be set up exactly square, in order that the two
rollers may be parallel to one another. Before they are
permanently fixed they may be tested by a diagonal
measurement being taken from the back left-hand post
to the front right-hand one. If the distance between
the back right-hand post and the front left-hand one

proves to be the same as that between the two others, the loom will be found perfectly square. The posts should be tested with a plumb-line for uprightness, and the rollers and all horizontal parts with a spirit-level.

NOTE 2.—In order to nicely adjust the length of the various cords for tying up the loom, a very simple slip-knot is used. A reference to figs. 21 and 21A, pp. 40 and 41, will be of use in describing it, as the first loop of the slip-knot is there illustrated. It is usual to *tie up* with double cords, as these always terminate either in a loop or two ends, both of which are necessary for the adjustable slip-knot. The cords to be thus joined are shown at A, fig. 48. The loop for the slip-knot is made at the end of the looped cord in the manner shown at figs. 21 and 21A. Through the loop thus made the two ends of the cord are passed as at B, fig. 48, and tied together in a single knot, after the loop has been drawn close round them, as at C. By pulling the two ends of the single knot the latter is drawn close to the loop, and it will be found, that, whatever weight is hung on the cords at D, the knot will not give way in the least. If, however, the ends of the cord are pulled up, it can be shortened at will, and if the knot is loosened the cord may be adjusted with great accuracy.

NOTE 3.—A large number of cords of exactly the same length are often required in tying up a loom. A simple way of measuring the lengths off, is to drive two nails into a board, or wall at the necessary distance apart, and to wind the cord on to them. If double cords are wanted the skein so made can be cut through at one end only, but if single cords are required both ends will have to be cut.

NOTE 4.—The weaver must know how to make the leashes for the headles of the harness, as well as the smaller ones for the heck of the warping mill (fig. 25, No. 4), as they often break and have to be renewed. For use with coarse warps of linen, woollen, or cotton threads

the leashes act quite as well if made separately and
simply slipped, or tied on to the headles. When such

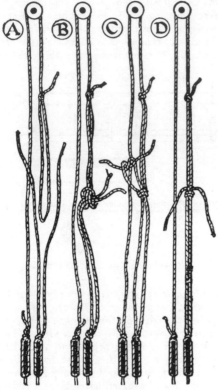

FIG. 48.—Knots.

a warp is entered the action of the loom in working is
sufficient to keep the leashes in their proper places on

the headles. When the leashes are thus separate and movable the harness can be adapted for different counts and widths of warp, so that, when practicable, it is as well to have them so. But in the case of fine silk or cotton warps, of a great number of threads, the leashes must be fixed, and carefully spaced and knitted together on the headles. The appliance for making the separate

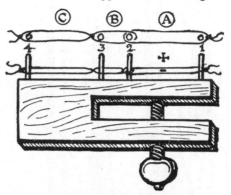

Fig. 49.—Headle or Leash Gauge.

leashes is shown at fig. 49. It is simply a board about fourteen inches long, one inch thick, and six inches deep. On the top edge are four smooth metal, or strong wooden pegs, arranged as in the drawing. The short loop A is made first, on the pegs 2 and 1. The thread is passed through it, and the centre loop, B, is tied round pegs 2 and 3, being double-knotted to prevent its slipping. The leash is finished off by the ends of the thread being tied together round peg 4. The size of the small loop or eye B, is regulated by the position of the pegs 2 and 3. When a large number of leashes are wanted, time may be saved by tying several A loops

108

before turning the board to tie the double loops B, C.
The board may either be held between the knees of
the worker or be fixed on a table in such a way as to be
easily turned.

NOTE 5.—The knitted and spaced leashes for fine
weaving have to be made on a frame prepared for the
purpose (fig. 50). It is constructed as follows: Two

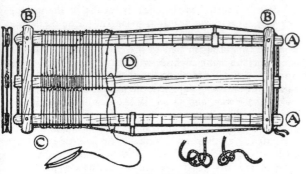

FIG. 50.— Headle Frame.

strong laths, A, A, four inches wide by half an inch
thick, and at least three feet long, are neatly mortised
into two thick end-pieces, B, B, so as to form an oblong
frame not less than fourteen inches wide. The corners
are not permanently fixed, but are held together by
movable pegs. A wooden lath or brass rod crosses the
frame, from end to end, passing through the end-pieces
rather nearer to one lath than the other. The diameter
of the rod or lath is determined by the size of the eyes the
leashes are required to have. Both laths, A, A, are marked
out in inches from one end to the other. This is for
the spacing of the leashes, so many to the inch. The
harness thread, which is made specially strong for the

109

purpose, is wound upon a small *mesh*, such as is used for the making of string nets.

The leashes are knotted to a strong, thin cord, which is tied and wound several times round one end of each lath and tightly stretched along the outer edge of the frame to the other end, where it is also wound and tied. As in the case of the separate leashes, the small loops of the continuous leashes are made first. The thread must be double-knotted to the cord by means of the mesh at the place where the headle is to begin. The mesh must then be passed round the brass rod, underneath the lath, and the thread again tied to the cord. Another loop is made in the same manner without severing the thread, and so on until the right number are made to the first inch. These being adjusted, the second inch can be made in the same way, and so on till the complete number required has been reached. In the drawing the loops are shown loose in order that their interlacement may be indicated, but they must actually be just tight enough to lie straight on the frame without bending the rod. The thread for the double loops must be tied at the beginning to the opposite lath in the same way as for the single ones. The mesh must then be passed under the frame and brought up through the opposite loop, over the rod, and, usually, double-knotted close by it; then, being brought over the lath, it must be knotted at the place it started from. The first leash will now be complete, and all the others must be finished in the same way. The eyes of the leashes for silk-weaving are not always double-knotted; many weavers prefer single knots as being less bulky. Single knots are, however, especially when the harness is new, very apt to slip out of place and give trouble. When finished the centre rod is drawn out of the frame, the pegs removed from the corners, and the collection of leashes thus freed is tied, by the cord to which they are knotted, to the laths of the headle.

CHAPTER VIII

THE ACCESSORY APPLIANCES OF
THE LOOM

The Hand-shuttle—Superiority of Hand-shuttle
Weaving—The Fly-shuttle—The Batten for the
Fly-shuttle—The Raceboard—The Shuttle-boxes
—The Pickers—The Picking Stick—The Action
of the Fly-shuttle—Advantages of the Fly-shuttle
—The Temple—The Skein Reels—The Doubler
—The Quill-winder—Other Tools—Method of
Weaving with Hand-battens—Method of Weaving
with Box-battens.

THERE can be no doubt that as long as the upright   The Hand-
loom only was used, the weft was passed through the   shuttle
opening in the warp in little skeins wound on the
hand, or on the long spindles on which it had been
spun.   But as soon as the horizontal position of the
warp was adopted, especially for plain weaving, it is
certain that some kind of shuttle for carrying the
weft came into use.   The advantage given by the
invention of the shuttle, was, that it could be
thrown swiftly by the weaver through the opening,
from edge to edge of the cloth.   The ease and
speed of the work would thus be considerably
increased.

The hand-shuttle now used for silk-weaving is a

The Hand-
shuttle

Qualities
required in
the Hand-
shuttle

Description
of the Hand-
shuttle

very different tool from the shuttle of the ancients, if we may judge from the few specimens preserved in the British and other museums. The general shape of it is, however, very similar. The chief qualities required in the shuttle are slenderness combined with a capacity for carrying a great length of thread, weight, in order to steady it in its rapid movement, and perfect smoothness of finish, so that it may run from side to side over the most delicate threads without catching up or fraying them.

The best hand-shuttles are made of good, hard, boxwood. They are about eight inches long and one inch wide by three-quarters of an inch deep. The general shape and section are shown in fig. 51. The front edge, lower line, no. 1, is straight, and the back edge, which, when the shuttle is thrown, is towards the reed, is curved near the ends. At the ends, which are sharp and smooth, slips of metal are inserted in order to protect the points from damage should the shuttle fly out and fall. The curved shape of the ends is beautifully adapted for delicate throwing and catching. The top of the shuttle is flat, with rounded edges, but the bottom has the edges not only rounded, but slightly raised, in order to present less surface for friction with the threads over which it slides. The shape of the bottom is shown by the section at no. 2. In the centre of the top of the shuttle an oblong hollow is carved, as deep as it is wide. This is for the reception of the *quill*, as it is called, on which the weft thread is wound. At each end of the hollow a small, flat hole is made, and into one of these a minute, spiral spring is fixed. By means of this spring a piece of thin, hard steel wire, bent

112

in the form shown at no. 3, is kept in position, after
it has been inserted by pressing one end against the
spring and allowing the other end to be pushed by
it into the opposite hole. The bent wire is for the
purpose of holding the quill in the hollow of the
shuttle, and it is bent to the shape shown in the
drawing in order that it may act as a gentle brake
to prevent the quill being unwound too freely. By

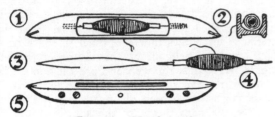

FIG. 51.—Hand-shuttle.

means of closing up or extending the ends of the
bent wire the tension of the thread on the quill can
be regulated to a nicety. At no. 4, the quill,
with weft wound on it, is shown on the wire ; it
may also be seen in its place in the hollow of the
shuttle in no. 1. The quills are now mostly made
of paper, but occasionally a weaver will prefer a quill
made of a small piece of hollow reed. Originally,
no doubt, feather quills were used, as the name
denotes. As the shuttle is thrown from side to side,
the weft is unwound through the small hole shown
in the centre of no. 5, into which a porcelain
or glass eye is fixed. The quill must be short
enough to move longitudinally as the weft is unwound, or the latter will be apt to break, how-

113

ever skilfully it may have been put on to the
quill.

Fig. 52 represents the hand-shuttle in use. It is
lightly held in the right hand of the weaver, partly
within the open shed, and resting on the race-board,
ready to be thrown by a slight, quick wrist movement. The throw causes it to glide along the
beading, over the lower warp threads, to the opposite
edge, where it is caught by the fingers of the left
hand and guided into the palm. As soon as it is
out of the shed the hand is withdrawn from the
batten. This allows the reed, fixed in the batten,
which has been held off by the thumb of the left
hand, to fall against the weft and press it home. In
the meantime the right-hand thumb is prepared, as
soon as the blow has been given, to push the batten
away for the next throw of the shuttle from left
to right. In gating the loom the batten is so hung,
that when at rest, the reed is just at the place where
the weft is to lie. THE QUALITY OF THE WORK
DEPENDS VERY MUCH UPON THE WAY IN WHICH THE
SHUTTLE IS CAUGHT AND THE THREAD DRAWN
THROUGH THE SHED. IN FACT, IT IS THE DELICATE
MANNER IN WHICH THIS CAN BE DONE WHICH
MAKES GOOD, HAND-SHUTTLE WEAVING SUPERIOR
TO ALL OTHER KINDS WHATEVER.

The Fly-
shuttle
The simple invention of the fly-shuttle, in the
eighteenth century, was an extremely important
event in the history and development of weaving.
Its effect will be referred to later on, but it will be
best to describe its construction in the present
chapter, in which the weaver's tools are especially
being dealt with.

The fly-shuttle differs from the hand-shuttle

114

Fɪɢ. 52.—Method of handling One, or Two, Shuttlès.
If more than two shuttles are used they are
laid in order on the web.

both in form and in the manner in which it is
thrown and caught. The shuttle itself is represented in fig. 53. The difference in its form will
be at once perceived. The fly-shuttle has both
sides curved exactly alike, and the metal points are
set exactly in the centre of the ends; they are also
heavier than those of the hand-shuttle. The shuttle
itself is longer, and deeper and broader in proportion

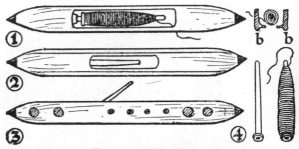

FIG. 53.—Fly-shuttle.

to its length. The weight of a fly-shuttle for silk-
weaving is from three to four ounces, but for heavy
work and power-loom weaving it is made much
heavier. The oblong hollow for the reception of
the quill, or spool, is in the same position as in the
hand-shuttle, but differs in that it is cut right
through. The opening at the bottom, however, is
not so large as at the top. It is shown in the
section between the runners b, b, and also in no. 2.
In the hollow at no. 1, instead of the bent wire
on which the quill is fixed, a thin metal spike is
securely fastened. This spike is hinged at the end
near where it joins the shuttle, so that it can be

116

turned up into the position shown in the side view, no. 3. For use, in this shuttle, the weft

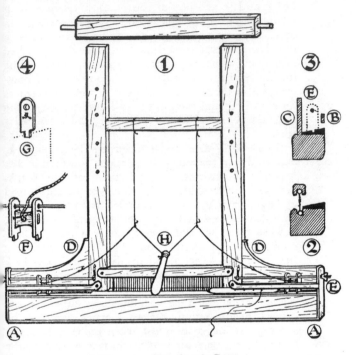

FIG. 54.—Fly-shuttle Batten.

is wound on to small hollow boxwood *plugs* (no. 4). When filled, these are pressed on to the spike, which is then turned down into the hollow. The weft, which is put on the plug in

117

such a manner that it unwinds uninterruptedly from
the end, is threaded through the endmost hole,
no. 3, and in and out of the other holes, according
to the degree of tension desired by the weaver. In
order to increase the weight of the boxwood, both
the fly- and hand-shuttles often have holes drilled
into them, which are filled with plugs of lead. The
ingenuity of the fly-shuttle invention does not, however, lie in the shuttle itself, but in the contrivances
for throwing and catching it. These consist of the
shuttle-box, the picker or propeller, and the picking
stick.

The *shuttle-box* is constructed on the race-block,
extended, for the purpose, to about fourteen inches
beyond the swords, on both sides of the batten
(fig. 54). The shuttle race in a box-batten, instead
of being merely a small rounded beading as in the
hand-batten, is a perfectly even strip of hard wood,
not less than two and a half inches wide, and long
enough to reach from A to A, fig. 54. It is slightly
bevelled, and when glued firmly to the race-block
the surface gently slopes toward the reed. It is
bevelled at such an angle that when the batten is
pushed back, the race cannot slope outwards and
cause the shuttle to fly off, as it passes along. The
shuttle race has to be most truly and evenly made,
as the least irregularity on its surface is fatal to the
action of the shuttle. No. 2 is a section of the race-
block, the race itself being indicated by solid black.

The shuttle-box is shown in section at no. 3.
It will be seen that it has a high back and a
low front, C and B. Also that a groove is cut in
the race. This groove extends from the end of
the box to the edge of the sword D, no. 1.

Immediately over the groove, and a trifle longer than the groove itself, a thin metal rod, having a small flat head, is fixed. It is passed through a screw staple which projects from the sword to a hole in the end of the shuttle-box, where it is fastened by a screw and wing-nut, E.

The *picker* is represented at no. 4. It is usually made of buffalo-hide, which is very tough and hard, qualities most necessary for the purpose. Two pieces of hide cut to the shape of G, no. 4, are joined together by a piece of hard wood, strengthened with twisted wire, as at F. The tongues at the bottom of the pickers fit easily into the grooves in the bottom of the shuttle-boxes. The iron rod E, no. 1, passes through the hole at the top of the picker indicated by the dotted line (no. 3). No. 1 shows both boxes fitted up, each being furnished with a picker. The pickers have to move freely and firmly from end to end of the shuttle-box to the fullest extent allowed by the iron rod.

The *picking stick* is represented at H, no. 1. It is simply a convenient handle attached to the centre of a strong cord, which is long enough to join the two pickers together loosely as in the drawing. It will now be readily understood that IF THE PICKING STICK BE PULLED WITH A SLIGHT JERK TO THE LEFT, THE SHUTTLE IN THE RIGHT-HAND BOX WILL BE DRIVEN OUT BY THE PICKER, ACROSS THE RACE, INTO THE OPPOSITE BOX. IT WILL THERE BE CAUGHT BY THE OTHER PICKER, AND ANOTHER JERK FROM LEFT TO RIGHT WILL BRING IT BACK AGAIN. This, roughly speaking, is the method of using the fly-shuttle.

119

The advantages of the use of the fly-shuttle are, mainly, two : (1) The weaving can be done with increased speed. One hand only is required to work the picking stick, the other being left free to manipulate the batten, the beat of which may consequently be made much more rapid. (2) Webs of great width, which would be impossible to weave with a hand-shuttle, can, by means of the fly-shuttle, be as quickly woven as narrow ones. It is very rare to find any woven stuff, more than thirty inches wide, made before the invention of the fly-shuttle. If ever such wide work were attempted, two weavers were employed, one to throw, and the other to catch the shuttle.

It should also be noted, that, the invention of the fly-shuttle rendered that of the power-loom possible. the throwing of the shuttle being the chief difficulty which the inventors, who attempted to apply steam-power to the loom, had to overcome.

The temple is an appliance that should not often be required in hand-loom weaving. If the warp and weft are properly proportioned one to another, the cloth, as it is woven, will not "draw in" narrower than the entering of the warp in the reed, to any appreciable extent. When, however, it is found that this "drawing in" takes place, it may be readily corrected by the use of the temple.

The temple for hand-loom weaving is quite simple in construction. Two pieces of hard wood are cut to the shape shown in fig. 55, no. 1. At the broad end of each of these a row of fine points is set. These, when joined together, are for the purpose of holding out the edges, of the material being woven, to the required width. The means of adjusting the length of the temple are shown at A and B, nos. 1 and 2. A is a loose metal band fitting closely to the two parts of the implement. B is a long pin, which may be put through any of the holes in the two members, in order to join them together. The pin is first inserted, and the temple placed on the cloth a few inches from the reed, with the end points catching the edges of the

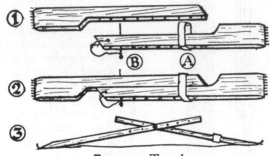

Fig. 55.—Temple.

material. This position is shown at no. 3. When placed thus, if the temple be pressed down it will slightly force out the edges of the web. The metal band A will keep it flat if slipped on as at no. 2.

When the weft is supplied to the weaver in skeins, a pair of reels, mounted on a stand in such a manner that the distance between them can be regulated, will be required (fig. 56). The upright of the stand has a slot cut in it for the greater part of its length. The reels revolve on elongated axles, and may be fixed in the slot, at any height, by means of a screw and collar. This is for the purpose of adjusting them to different-sized skeins. The weft is usually wound

121

first on to bobbins, and from the bobbins on to the quills or plugs ready for filling the shuttle.

Several threads of weft often have to be slightly twisted together in order to make up the required thickness for each shoot. It is seldom, indeed, that a weft is made up of less than two ends. The little contrivance generally used for this *doubling*, as it is called, is shown in fig. 57. It has a solid square stand, A, and an upright, B, from the top of which a short arm extends, having a smooth hook, C, at the end of it. About a foot above the stand there is a shelf, D, in the centre of which a thin tube of glass, or metal, is fitted into a hole. The tube is small enough to go through the hole in a bobbin when one is stood over it in the centre of the shelf. For example, let it be supposed that four threads of weft have to be wound together on a quill. Three bobbins must be placed on end, near together,

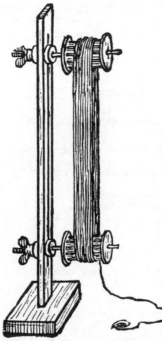

Fig. 56.—Skein-winder.

122

on the stand, in such a position that the silk upon
them all unwinds in the same direction. The three
ends of thread from these bobbins have to be carried

up through the
tube in the shelf
D, on which the
full bobbin, E, has
previously been
placed, as shown
in the drawing.
The ends of the
threads from the
four bobbins are
then taken over
the hook C, and
as the silk is
drawn off the
bobbins, that from
E gently winds
round the other
three threads and
loosely unites
them. No. 2
shows the shape
of the rimless
bobbins used for
weft.

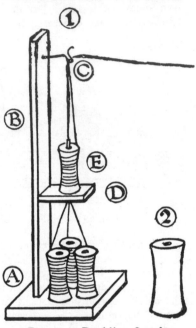

FIG. 57.—Doubling Stand.

The *quill-
winder* is a very important adjunct to the loom, as
good winding is very necessary for successful weaving.
This is especially the case when several threads are
wound together on the quills. A drawing of the
most useful kind of winder is given in fig. 58.

A small, low table, about two feet long, has two,

123

firm uprights fixed near the right-hand end. Between
these a small, heavy wheel, having a broad, shallow
groove on its edge, is truly poised on an axle, which
terminates in a small handle. By means of this
handle, the wheel can easily be made to revolve with

FIG. 58.—Quill- or Plug-winder.

great rapidity. At the opposite end of the table a
slot, A, is cut, and into this a shaped block is
made to fit. The large screw C, which, after passing
through the edge of the stand into the slot, runs into
the block, not only secures it firmly in position, but
is used to regulate the distance between the block
and the wheel. D, D is a pair of thick leather
bearings, in which a metal spindle, having a pulley in
its centre, is carefully fitted. The pulley is connected
by a cord to the large wheel, and the latter being
turned causes the spindle to revolve with great rapidity.
The elongated end of the spindle E is tapered, so that
the hollow plugs or quills can be fixed on it, and on
these the weft is wound very carefully as the spindle

124

revolves, and with perfect evenness (see Note 1 at end of chapter, p. 127).

Fig. 59 represents the weaver's shears, the picker

and nipper, and the rubber The shears and nipper are in constant requisition, but need no explanation. The rubber is made of sheet steel, with a wooden handle, and is used for rubbing the surface of the woven material after it has been cleared of knots and ends. Its

FIG. 59.—Shears, Picker and Nipper, and Rubber.

use is particularly needed in plain silk-weaving, the evenness and beauty of which it much enhances.

The hand-loom for plain weaving and all its appliances, as well as the necessary preparations for the work itself, having been described, the actual process of making cloth, both by hand-shuttle and fly-shuttle, will only require a very brief explanation. For this purpose reference must again be made to fig. 42, which fairly represents a gated loom, except in respect to the harness, which is placed too far from the batten. This was purposely done in order to show the headles quite clearly.

The weaver takes his seat in the loom, his feet

lightly resting on the treadles. He begins by
pressing with his left foot the treadle on which
it rests. This immediately raises the back headle
and depresses the front one. The result of this
action is the first open shed. On pushing back the
batten a few inches, by pressing the thumb of his
left hand against it, a part of the shed appears in
front of the reed, and if the loom be properly gated,
the opening will be found large enough for the
insertion of the shuttle. The method of throwing
the hand-shuttle has already been fully described at
p. 114, and should here be referred to, together with
fig. 52, which shows the hand-shuttle in use. It
must be added, however, that as soon as the shed
is free from the shuttle after every shoot, and the
batten is released in order to beat the weft into
place, the opposite treadle must simultaneously be
used and the shed changed. This prevents the
newly laid weft from springing out of position, and
makes all ready for the following shoot. It must
also be emphasized, that, when catching the shuttle
after the second and following shoots, the weaver
gives a slight pull to it, which causes the weft to lie
straight in the warp, and brings it exactly to the edge,
where it turns in, at the opposite side. Unless this
is properly done the *selvage* will be disfigured either
by a pucker or a loose loop.

As the weaving progresses the breast roller has to
be turned from time to time, in order to roll the
newly made cloth upon it. This is done by means
of a short, strong stick which fits into the holes in
the roller, one of which is shown near C, fig. 42.
(See *take-up motion*, note 2, at end of chapter).

With regard to the friction brake on the cane

126

roller, both the heavy and light weights must be kept suspended. Neither must be allowed to approach too near either to the roller or the floor, or their effect will be marred.

When the box-batten and fly-shuttle are used, the left hand of the weaver is kept on the cap of the reed (fig. 54), near to its centre, and the right hand holds the picking stick. The way the box-batten is balanced in the loom is rather different from that of the hand-batten. Instead of the weaver merely allowing the batten to fall against the weft to beat it together, in this case, he pulls the batten towards him with his left hand, with whatever force is required for the blow. The box-batten, therefore, is not hung so near to the front of the loom as the hand-batten. The quality of the work, when the fly-shuttle is used, depends, of course, mostly upon the way in which the picking stick is manipulated. The shuttle has not only to be driven by a jerk of the hand, but to be caught on the picker at the other edge in such a way as to cause it gently to slide into the shuttle-box without any rebound. The knack of doing this, as it should be done, by a simple drop of the hand, is only to be acquired after a great deal of practice. The evenness of the selvages of the web, which is the final test of good weaving, depends almost entirely upon the manner in which the shuttle is caught in the box.

NOTE 1.—The winding of the plugs or quills for the shuttle is most important. If it be badly done it is impossible to do good weaving. This is particularly the case with regard to winding for the fly-shuttle. Loose, uneven shoots, knots, loops, and all sorts of disfigurements in the web, are the result of careless winding ; to say nothing of breaking threads and the flying out of the shuttle from the loom. Fig. 59A will show the proper method of winding the weft. No. 1 is the correct shape of a wound quill. No. 2 shows the way it should be started. The thread must first be wound from A to B, and each layer should gradually diminish in length until the shape of No. 1 is attained, and is finished off in the centre.

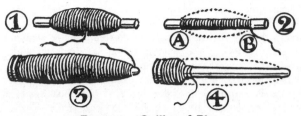

FIG. 59A.—Quills and Plugs.

The plug for the fly-shuttle (no. 3) must be so wound, that it will run off clearly from the point. It must be filled up at the thick end, to its full size, and the shape of no. 4 must be retained until it is finished off at the thin end. A well-wound plug will run off quite freely from the fixed plug, in a single thread, from beginning to end. A badly wound, soft quill or plug will come off in lumps, get entangled, and give much trouble to the weaver.

NOTE 2.—What is called a *take-up motion* is sometimes fitted to a hand-loom. This is an arrangement of cog-wheels, or worm and wheel, which causes the cloth to wind on to the breast roller automatically as it is woven. That this is not necessary is proved by the fact that weavers usually wind the motion by hand, instead of connecting it to their treadles or Jacquard machine, as is intended.

PART II
SIMPLE PATTERN-WEAVING

PART II

SIMPLE PATTERN-WEAVING

CHAPTER IX

TAPESTRY-WEAVING

A Definition of Pattern-weaving—Ancient Textile
Decoration—The Origin of Tapestry-weaving—
Tapestry a Variety of Plain Weaving—The Effect
of tight and loose Wefting—Tapestry-weaving
necessarily an Artistic Handicraft—Tapestry akin
to Embroidery.

THE art of pattern-weaving consists in the
mechanical repetition of a simple or a complex
ornamental design, wrought in as the fabric is
being woven, and occurring at regular intervals in
more or less obvious geometrical shapes and spaces.
With this kind of pattern-weaving there is no
evidence to prove that the ancients, with the
exception, perhaps, of the Chinese, had any acquaintance. The webs of Egypt were famous
throughout the ancient world, and the Egyptians
exchanged the productions of their looms for the
manufactures and other merchandise of neighbour-
ing, and even far-distant, nations; but amongst all
the examples of Egyptian webs, so many of which

Definition
of Pattern-
weaving

Pattern-
weaving
Unknown to
the Ancients

have been preserved to the present time, there have
been found no specimens of mechanical pattern-
weaving. It is true that a few trifling attempts seem
to have been made to vary the texture and appearance of these ancient weavings, by means of the use,
both in warp and weft, of different-sized and different-
coloured threads, but even these are extremely rare,
and in some cases may even be accidental.

Although the mechanical weaving of design does
not seem to have been practised by the ancient
Egyptians, it must not be supposed that the plain,
fine webs made by them remained undecorated, for,
on the contrary, many of them were highly orna-
mented. Such ornamentation, however, was not
produced in the loom automatically or in the actual
texture of the fabric. It was added to the
material either when in progress or after it was
finished, and was done by means of painting,
dyeing, stencilling, stamping, printing, or embroidery, with or without a needle. The designs
thus applied to these ancient textiles consisted, for
the most part, of bands of ornament and detached
spots powdered over the ground.

Towards the middle of the dynastic period in
Egypt (B.C. 2000) the fine linen mummy-cloths,
which had hitherto been quite plain, are found to
have stripes of different-coloured weft, occasionally
shot across them. They also often have short
spaces of warp left unwoven, forming bands across
the material. It may well be assumed that the idea
of darning in a pattern on these bare spaces of warp,
in imitation of the applied borders of ordinary needlework, would occur to some enterprising embroiderer,
and, being carried out, would be the beginning of a

132

new form of textile decoration. This in turn might
lead to the cutting away of the weft in spots and
spaces, as in drawn-thread work, and to these being
filled in with darning in a similar manner. At any
rate, whatever may have been its origin, there is
now evidence that such work was done in great
perfection as early as B.C. 1500. It was practised
as a traditional method for the ornamentation of
woven materials in Egypt until the Ptolemaic period
(B.C. 305), was continued through the Roman period
and during the early centuries of the Christian
era. The British Museum and the Victoria and
Albert Museum at South Kensington are particularly rich in specimens of the Egypto-Roman
work, but at present there are only three samples
of ancient Egyptian weaving of this kind known to
exist. These are in the museum at Cairo. They
were found in 1893, in the tomb of Thothmes IV.,
who reigned in Egypt B.C. 1450. The smallest
and oldest piece of the three has, worked into
it, the cartouch of Amenhetep II., who reigned
fifty years earlier than Thothmes IV. They
are fine, delicate pieces of workmanship, and must
be typical of the best textiles of that period
(plate VII).*

Ancient
Ornamental
Textiles
consist of
only Two
Sorts of
Plain
Weaving

With regard not only to Egyptian, but to almost
all ancient, ornamental textiles of earlier date than
A.D. 600, it may safely be said, that, however
elaborate they may seem to be, they exhibit only
two sorts of simple, plain weaving, and that these
two sorts of weaving only differ in the manner in
which the weft is laid in the warp.

* For a full and interesting description of these precious
fragments see Mr. W. G. Thomson's "History of Tapestry."

Ancient
Ornamental
Textiles
consist of
only Two
Sorts of
Plain
Weaving

In the plain ground of these ancient webs, the weft is passed across in the shed with sufficient tension to pull it straight, as has been fully explained in Part I., on plain weaving. The effect of this is, that the warp and weft show in almost equal proportion in the finished material. For the ornamental parts, however, the weft is placed quite slackly in the shed, with the result, that, when it is pressed down, the warp is completely covered up and hidden by it. For example, if a white warp be shot with white weft in the ordinary way, white cloth will, of course, be made. But if the weft be changed to black for, say, twelve shoots, a grey stripe or band, across the material, will be made by the mixture of the black weft with the white warp, each showing equally. If, instead of the black weft being shot in the usual way, it be put in quite loosely, the first shoot, when pressed down, will cover the first, third, and all the odd-numbered threads in the front, and the second and all the even-numbered ones at the back. The next shoot will cover the even-numbered threads in the front and the odd-numbered ones at the back, so that, the two shoots together will make a continuous line of black weft right across the cloth. If the loose wefting be continued for twenty-four shoots, the result will be a band of solid black, of about the same measurement as the grey band obtained by the ordinary manner of weaving.

In fig. 60, a piece of cloth worked, in the above manner, in two sorts of tabby weaving is shown. At A, A, A, A the white warp and weft are interlaced in the usual manner. At B, the white warp is shot in the same way, but with a black weft, thus

134

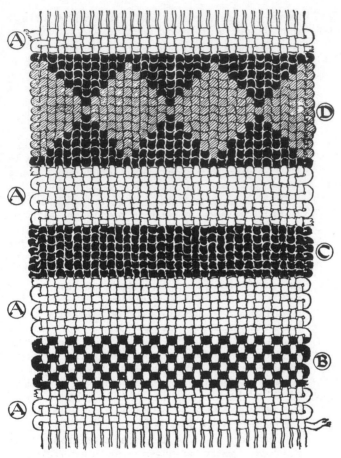

FIG. 60.—Bands of Tabby and Tapestry-
Weaving.

forming a grey band. At C the white warp is shot loosely with black weft, so that the warp is entirely hidden. At D the loose weft, instead of being carried right across, is worked up in pyramidal shapes, from their bases on nine threads to their point on one thread. Into the spaces between these pyramids, diamond shapes, in some other colour are fitted, still with loose weft. They begin on a single thread, and, after filling the space, are diminished again to a point. The triangular shapes now remaining, are filled in with black, until a line is reached at which the ordinary white ta by weaving again begins.

This is precisely the method in which all the beautiful textiles of ancient production, that remain to us, were woven. Figs. 61 and 61A are examples copied from the borders of a Coptic textile in the Victoria and Albert Museum. The exquisite designs of these tapestry-woven ornaments in plain linen webs, have often been commented on, but the technique of the work has seldom, if ever, been described. The spaces for the patterns were either left unwoven, or the weft was cut away, in the desired shapes, after the length of fabric was taken out of the loom, as in drawn-thread work. On the warp threads thus laid bare, the pattern, in two or more colours, was darned by means of a needle, or worked in with the fingers, the loose weft being passed backward and forward between alternate threads in the manner above described.

There are no examples remaining from classic times of tapestry hangings of any considerable size, but it may be assumed that the famous picture tapestries, so often referred to in Greek and Roman

136

Fig. 61.—Coptic Border.

history and poetry, were made in the same manner
as the textile ornaments of these Egypto-Roman
and Coptic webs—that is, they were a mosaic of many
coloured pieces of simple weaving with a loose weft,
the plain ground between the ornaments probably
being entirely dispensed with.   Whatever may have
been the technique of these ancient works, there is
no doubt that this was the simple method used in
weaving the wonderful Mediæval, Renaissance, and
later tapestries with which our museums and private
collections abound.   It is an interesting fact, that,
the loose weft cannot be put in by machinery, or

Fig. 61A.—Coptic Border.

137

Tapestry-
weaving
necessarily a
Purely
Artistic
Handicraft

Tapestry
akin to
Embroidery

thrown swiftly across the web in a shuttle.   As this must always be done with judgment, tapestry-weaving is likely to remain a purely artistic handi-craft as it has ever been.

Tapestry-weaving is really, as has been pointed out, akin to embroidery, and only differs from it, in that it is freely darned or woven in the simplest manner on a bare warp, instead of being wrought upon an already woven material.   It was therefore quite appropriate, that it should have been treated of in the volume of the present series devoted to needlework.   To that book any reader desirous of following out the subject in detail must be referred.* It was necessary, however, to give some little attention to the matter here, in order that the automatic weaving of repeated pattern might be clearly distinguished from tapestry-weaving.

* "Embroidery and Tapestry-weaving," by Mr. A. H. Christie.   Artistic Crafts Series of Handbooks (Pitman, publisher).

CHAPTER X

THE SIMPLEST WARP AND WEFT EFFECTS OF PATTERN

Further Definition of Pattern-weaving—Patterns possible on the Loom with only Two Headles—The Striped Webs of India—Ancient Use of Striped Cotton Hangings—Patterns resulting from striping the Warp—East African Woven Design—Various Simple Warp Patterns—Simple Weft Effects—Tartan Patterns—Inlaying or Brocading—Primitive Indian Brocading—Usual Method of Brocading—Binders or Ties—Brocading on Weaving Board—Extra Headle for Brocading—Long and Short Eyes of Headles—Cashmere Shawl Weaving—Origin of Brocading.

WE have seen how entirely dependent, in tapestry-weaving, is the working out of any ornamental design, on the artistic skill and taste of the weaver. We have seen also, that as the technique of tapestry is so simple, scarcely any tools or mechanical appliances are necessary in order to weave it. Ordinary pattern-weaving, on the contrary, whether simple or complex, is done by means of certain devices and appliances which have been invented from time to time in the course of ages. By their use the loom is *set up* or *tied up* under the direction of the designer, in such a way, that, when the weaver begins his shuttling, the design will be woven and repeated automatically, in the loom, as the work proceeds. This being so, the weaver's whole attention can be given to the keeping his loom and all its fittings in order, and his threads of fine silk, or other material, mended and even, both in warp and weft. In a fine silk loom, of thirty or forty thousand threads in the width, this is quite sufficient occupation for one man or woman.

Needless to say, the mechanism by means of which the pattern is worked out, which is often a marvel of ingenuity, was not all invented at one time. In fact, every weaver is continually devising little helps and dodges for his own use. But the most important contrivances were invented very early in the history of the loom, and succeeding generations of craftsmen have only extended and developed them. It must never be forgotten, however, that EACH STEP TOWARDS THE MECHANICAL PERFECTION OF THE LOOM, IN COMMON WITH ALL MACHINERY, IN ITS DEGREE, LESSENS THE FREEDOM OF THE WEAVER, AND HIS CONTROL OF THE DESIGN IN WORKING.

We must now return to consider the old English loom, fitted up as represented in fig. 42, and inquire as to the possibility of designing patterns which can be woven automatically upon it—patterns, that is, which will work out, as the weaver proceeds, shoot by shoot, as if he were making plain cloth. It is obvious that such designs must be very simple in character, and must depend entirely on some arrangement, or diversity of the threads, in warping. It is interesting to find that a great variety of patterns can be designed to work out in this simple way.

140

The Indian weavers of fine cotton fabrics have always been famous for warp pattern effects. They were perhaps the first to make use of broad and narrow stripes of contrasting colours in their webs. This is of course the simplest of all pattern effects to be obtained. Many of these Indian fabrics, by reason of their finely contrasted colours and the pleasant proportion of their stripes, are very beautiful in effect, and can be used with great advantage in personal and architectural decoration.

The Striped Webs of India

The garden court of the palace of Shushan, where the little drama of Esther and Ahasuerus began, was hung, no doubt, with material decorated with coloured stripes. The hangings are described as of "white, green, and blue, fastened with cords of fine linen and purple, by silver rings, to pillars of marble" (Book of Esther, ch. i. v. 6). This account of an ancient decorative scheme, furnishes us with another evidence of the frequently remarked unchangeableness of the East, for just such striped and coloured webs, are being made by the Indian weaver of to-day on his simple hand-loom, a counterpart of the ancient loom, on which, the hangings for the Persian palace court were woven so long ago.

Ancient Use of Striped Cotton Hangings

By means of striping the warp, in quite a different manner from the above, a large range of small patterns can be made which are very interesting. As these are constructed on the same principle as that on which suitings and homespun cloths are designed, it will be well to devote some little space to their particular consideration.

Patterns resulting from striping the Warp

A delicate and pretty example of this simple kind of pattern-weaving may be seen in a case of

"personal ornaments" made by the natives of East
Africa, exhibited in the ethnographical galleries of
the British Museum (see plate 1). The pattern is
in very dark blue (almost black) and bright red, on
a white ground. This design, in common with
those just referred to, is made by taking advantage
of the fact that in plain, or "tabby," weaving,
one shoot of weft has all the odd-numbered warp
threads above it and the even ones below, while
in the next shoot the order is reversed, the even
threads being above and the odd ones below.

The collotype illustration plate VIII is taken from
a woven copy of the edge of the East African web
just mentioned. It is shown in process of making.
The loom is simply a small board with a warp
stretched on it. The sheds are opened by a shed-
stick and leashes as described at p. 85. The actual
width of the web is an inch and a quarter, in which
space there are sixty threads, eighteen being black
and forty-two white.

It certainly appears curious that if white and
black threads are warped alternately rather close
together, so as to well cover up the weft, the effect
of black and white lines running, as might be
expected, in the direction of the warp, will not
result when the web is woven. Instead of running
longitudinally, the black and white lines will be
across the web, as in no. 1, fig. 62. In this
diagram the black vertical lines represent the odd
threads of a warp, and the white lines the even
ones. If a shed be made by raising the odd threads
and depressing the even ones, it is manifest that
only the black portion of the warp will show on
the front of the material. The next shed being

made, the position of the threads will all be reversed, and the white portion of the warp now being above the weft, no black will be visible at all. If, as is necessary for this kind of pattern, the warp be full enough to well cover up the weft, the latter will interfere very little with the colour of the latitudinal stripes.

No. 2 shows the warping of an even and odd, and an odd and even black thread, warped alternately at regular intervals in the whole width, the result of this warping being, when the stuff is woven, two vertical zigzag lines with opposing curves.

By warping the black and white threads in the order shown at no. 3 the latitudinal lines given by the warping of no. 1 are cut up into alternate squares, and form a common checker pattern.

The warping of no. 4, weaves into detached squares, and no. 5 forms quite an elaborate pattern, with border.

The warping represented by no. 6 is that of the border of the East African web, a copy of which is shown in plate VIII.

These diagrams give only a few of the designs which can be made for this simple form of pattern-weaving. The number possible is infinite, especially if threads of various colours are used in addition to the black and white ones.

By striping the *weft* an additional number of simple patterns can be made. But weft effects cannot be rendered automatic except by the aid of much more complicated machinery than the loom, as at present described, is furnished with. For weft effects, the weaver would have to count his shoots, or measure off spaces, in order to keep any

[margin note: Copy of East African Woven Design]

[margin note: Simple Weft Effects]

143

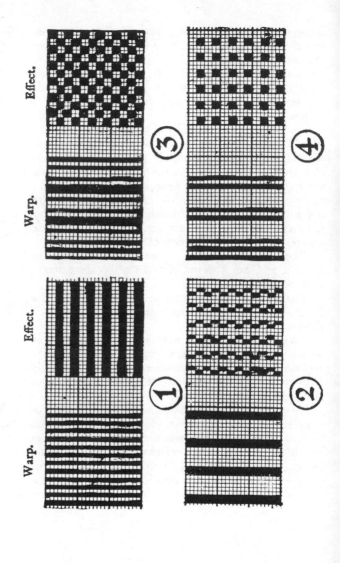

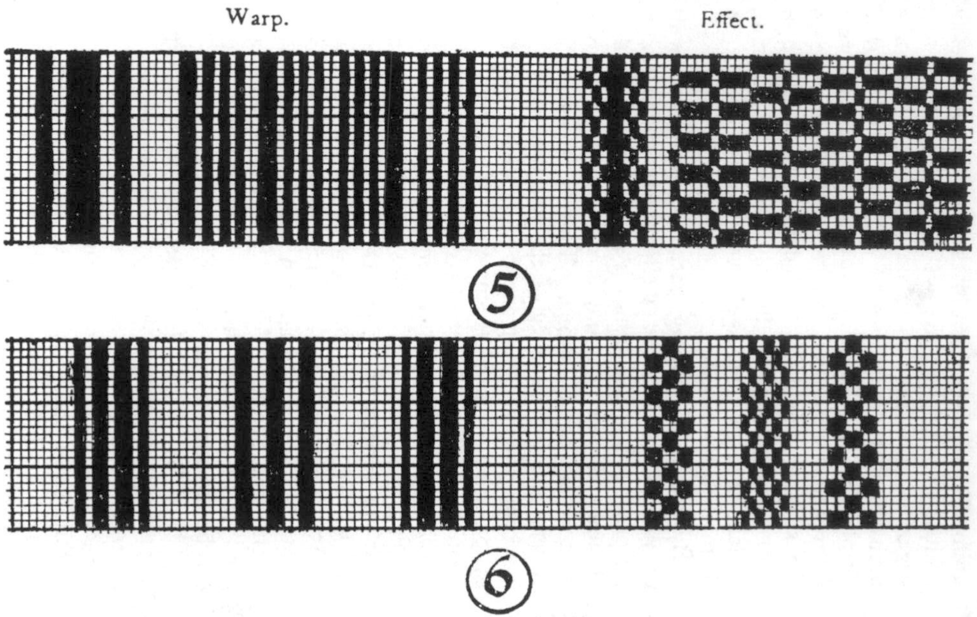

Warp.   Effect.

⑤

⑥

FIG. 62.—Warping Patterns.

uniformity or proportion in the stripes. As already noticed, by striping the weft, the Egyptians first began to ornament their plain weaving. It is quite probable that the stripes of red, blue, white, and purple, in the hangings made for the Hebrew tabernacle, were weft effects. If these were so the striping would be horizontal, and would form a fine background for the gold figures of cherubim, which, we are told, were wrought cunningly on them with the needle.

By means of striping both the warp and weft in various colours, the well-known *tartan* effects are produced. The tartan is a very ancient kind of ornamental weaving, and is capable of an infinite number of combinations. This is proved by the variety and individuality of the Scottish *plaids*. It has been supposed that the "variegated webs made by Sidonian women" mentioned by Homer, were a kind of tartan mixture of colour.

Fig. 63 shows the manner in which tartan striping is arranged. In this case both warp and weft are variegated by stripes of blue, red, yellow, and white.

At the crossing of the stripes the additional mixed colours made are, deep red, deep blue, orange, green, and purple. When fine, rich colours and good yarns are made use of, very gorgeous effects can be obtained in this simple manner.

There are many other easy methods for ornamenting plain woven webs, such as the use of different-sized threads, both in warp and weft, the use of different materials, such as glossy silk or cotton in contrast with linen or woollen yarns, the use of threads of different twist texture, &c., &c.;

146

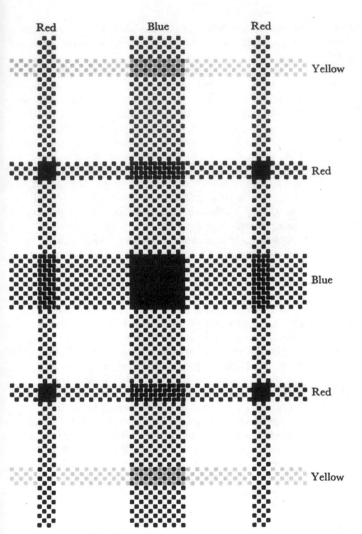

Fig. 63.—Tartan-weaving.

Other
Methods of
ornamenting
Simple Webs

Inlay or
Brocading
so that even with quite the simplest looms, plenty of scope is given for the exercise of ingenuity and design.

An ancient and favourite method of decorating woven fabrics was by inserting, in addition to the ordinary weft, secondary wefts of rich threads, such as gold, silver, silk, or rich coloured wools. These additional wefts were so arranged as to form spots, or detached ornamental shapes, distributed over the ground. This decoration is called *inlay* or *brocading*. At the beginning brocaded ornaments were not worked automatically in the loom, as they afterwards gradually came to be. It will be necessary, therefore, as well as advantageous, to trace, as nearly as possible, the manner in which the brocading process was developed. Especially as it led to some of the most important inventions in the history of weaving, and, moreover, many suggestions useful to the artistic craftsman may be gathered by the way.

A most primitive manner of brocading is described by Dr. J. Forbes Watson in his book on the textile manufactures of India, as follows :

"Two weavers sit at a loom. They place the pattern, drawn upon paper, below the warp, and range along the track of the weft a number of cut threads equal to the flowers or parts of the design intended to be made. Then with two small, fine-pointed, bamboo sticks they draw each of these threads between as many threads of the warp as may be equal to the width of the figure which is to be formed. When all the threads have been brought between the warp they are drawn close by a stroke of the reed. The shuttle, with ordinary weft, is

148

then passed by one of the weavers through the shed or opening in the warp, and the weft having been driven home, it is returned by the other weaver. The weavers resume their work with the bamboo sticks, and repeat the operation of the reed and shuttle in the manner above described, observing each time to pass the cut threads between a greater or less number of the threads of the warp, in proportion to the size of the design to be formed."

Although brocading is sometimes done in the way described above—viz., by using short pieces of coloured threads cut to the required sizes—it is much more usual to find a continuous thread, carried in a small shuttle, made use of for the purpose, each colour, and each separate piece of design having its own shuttle and being worked backward and forward to the shape of the ornament.

The working of brocaded ornament into a plain warp between the ordinary shoot, does very well so long as the warp is fine and very scanty, as is the case with that used for the gauze-like Indian muslins. These are open enough to allow the sparkling gold and bright-coloured silk to shine out from between their threads, but in denser warps the ornamentation would be buried and almost invisible if merely placed between the ordinary shoots of weft.

In order to make these inlaid ornaments have their proper effect in a close warp, the brocading weft must be made to pass under only one in every three or more warp threads, instead of being tied down closely like the ordinary weft. By this means the rich gold or coloured weft not only shows for all it is worth, but, being tied down by

149

only one in every three or more threads, stands clearly and boldly up on the surface of the cloth.

This effect can be tried on the weaving board, fig. 39, and a practical experiment will best demonstrate the theory of ties and binders. The mechanical contrivances for binding the brocaded ornament in the loom can then be readily explained.

For this experiment the board must be set up with thirty-one strings, and plain weaving with self-coloured weft begun on it as in fig. 64, AA. At B brocading commences. It will be seen that the brocaded form in the illustration is drawn in two shades, half-tone and black. These shades may represent any two colours that may be selected. Beginning with the lighter colour, and counting from the right hand, the weft must be brought from the back between the seventh and eighth strings of the warp, passed underneath the tenth, and over the eleventh and twelfth strings. The brocading weft must now pass at the back of seven strings and reappear in the front between strings nineteen and twenty. The coloured thread must then be carried over two strings, under one, over two more, and between strings twenty-four and twenty-five, pass to the back, and be left hanging there, while the ordinary weft is thrown twice across the warp, after the usual sheds have been opened for it. As soon as the shoot has been pressed down the brocading may proceed, beginning this time from the left. The coloured weft must now be brought forward between the twenty-fourth and twenty-fifth strings and taken back, over and under the same strings as in the first line, until it reaches the point of starting. Here it must be again taken to the back, and the two shoots

150

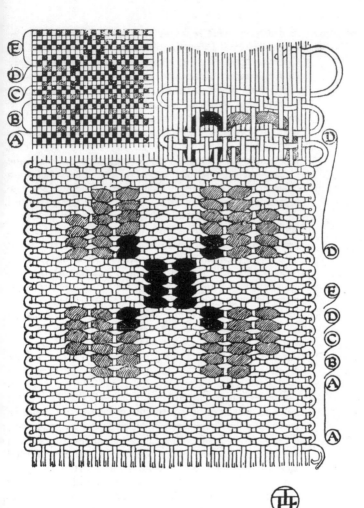

Fig. 64.—Brocading on Board.

of ordinary weft repeated. This will complete the space marked B in the drawing. It will be seen that the brocading in space C must approach three strings nearer to the right and left edges of the web than that of B. In all other respects the space C must be worked in exactly the same manner as B. In space D, however, two brocading colours are indicated. The new colour, represented by black, should be put in first. It will be seen that the black only covers four strings, two on each side of the centre, with a space of seven strings between them. As soon as the dark weft is in its place the lighter colour may be filled to right and left of it, and this being repeated twice, the space D will be filled. At E only the dark colour occurs, and that in the centre of the web, where it covers two spaces of two strings each, with one string between to bind them. From this point the brocaded figure can readily be completed without further instructions. In order more clearly to illustrate the process, at the top right-hand corner of the drawing, the portion D of the brocading is represented in progress, but without the web having been beaten together. At the top left-hand side of the illustration a part of the ground and figure is shown as it would be expressed or designed on weaver's ruled paper.

To return to the old English loom fitted up as in fig. 42. Brocading up to this point and in the above ways may be done upon it without extra appliances. The process, however, of picking up the threads for the binders and counting the spaces in the undivided warp would be a very tedious one. It will therefore be readily understood that it would be a great advantage if the binding threads necessary for the

152

brocading could be separated in the warp automatically when they were required, without interfering with the making of the plain groundwork of the cloth.

The facility of selecting certain threads can be secured if another headle be added to those already in the loom. This additional headle must be so arranged, that, after two or more shoots of plain ground have been made, the proper shed for the brocading may be opened. This shed may be so made as to act across the whole of the warp, or in particular spaces, such as borders of a certain width, at the centre of the web, or at any regular intervals that may be desired. This contrivance not only facilitates the binding of the brocaded figure, but by dividing the threads into small groups makes it much easier to *count in* the shapes of the ornaments, previously designed on ruled paper. The method of drawing figures for inlaying or brocading is shown by fig. 65.*

The extra headle required for brocading has to be fixed in front of the two already in the loom, and through the eyes of its leashes the warp threads must be entered, after they have passed through those of the ground headles, and before their entry in the reed. The new headle will only require one leash to every three of the warp threads for the production of the brocading suggested by fig. 65, and of

* In designing ornaments for brocading, on squared paper, it must be remembered that each square of the paper represents the group of threads between the binders, and also that the size the figure will be, when woven, depends on the number of ties to the inch laterally and the thickness of the weft longitudinally.

Use of
an Extra
Headle for
Brocading

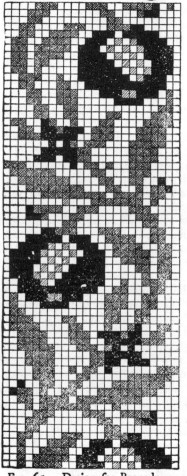

FIG. 65.—Design for Brocade, on
Ruled Paper.

these, two must
be entered to-
gether in one eye
and one drawn,
without entering,
between the
leashes. The
effect of this ar-
rangement will
be that, when the
new headle is
raised, either by
an extra treadle
or a hand-cord
and pulley, two
threads will be
raised and one left
down, right across
the loom, or
wherever, in
the width, spaces
to be brocaded
are arranged for.
Thus the neces-
sary shed for the
brocading weft is
made. When
one line of the
brocading has
been done and
the following
shoots of plain
tabby ground
have been made

the strips of coloured weft will be found slightly but firmly tied down on the under surface of the cloth, which is really the face of it. In a horizontal loom webs are generally worked face downwards, and, indeed, must be if brocaded.

Use of
an Extra
Headle for
Brocading

There must be an important difference between the leashes of the ground headles and those of the brocading headle. It will be at once perceived that if the leashes of the latter had *small eyes* similar to those of the former, the back headles could not work freely, as two out of three of the threads would be fixed by the new row of eyes standing in front of them. This difficulty is obviated by making long eyes in the leashes of the front headle, so that when it is at rest there is room for the ground headles to work without hindrance. It will be found that this arrangement does not interfere at all with the lifting power of the front headle.

Difference
in Eyes of
Leashes

By means of fig. 66 this important difference in the leashes of the two sorts of headles may be readily understood. Nos. 1 and 2 show in section the ground and the brocading headles. In no. 1 the headles of the ground harness are depicted one raised and the other depressed, whilst the brocading headle is at rest. In this position the front headle does not affect the warp at all, the long eye allowing the threads to rise and fall, as necessary for tabby weaving. In no. 2, however, the front headle being raised, takes up with it all the threads entered in it, and allows all those passing between its leashes, which are the binders, to remain at the level of the warp as long as the ground harness is at rest.

Two Sorts
of Leashes

This simple difference between the leashes of the headles, some having long and some short eyes,

155

Importance
of the Use of
Long and
Short Eyes
in Figure-
weaving

plays a very important part in the development of pattern-weaving. The invention of damask-weaving in particular is based entirely on it.

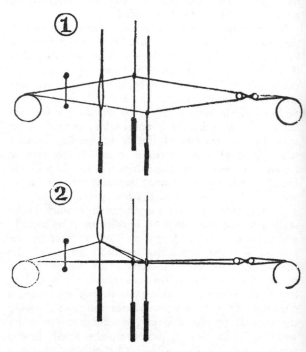

Fig. 66.—Section of Two Sorts of Leashes.

The exquisite work which may be done on a loom with mechanical fittings such as have now been described, is shown by the wonderful shawls for

156

which Cashmere has been famous for many centuries (see fig. 67).

The process of weaving the Cashmere shawls has been instructively described by a traveller in India : *

"The loom differs not in principle from that of Europe, but is inferior in workmanship, and the factories contain from three to three hundred of them, crowded together into very small spaces. About three weavers work at each loom. When the warp is fixed in the loom the pattern-drawer makes a design in black and white. He shows it to the colourist and the scribe, and they confer together. The colourist, having well considered it, points out the proportion of the colours, and, beginning at the foot of the pattern, he calls out the colour and number of threads to which each is to extend, that by which it is to be followed, and so on in succession until the whole pattern has been described. From his dictation the scribe writes down the particulars in a kind of shorthand, and delivers a copy of the document to the weavers.

"The workmen then prepare the needles by winding on each, coloured yarn of about four grains weight. These needles without eyes are made of smooth wood, and have both their sharp ends slightly charred to prevent their becoming rough through use. Under the superintendence of the colour-master, the weavers next knot the yarn of the needles in their proper places to the warp.

"The face or right side of the cloth is placed next to the ground, the work being carried on at the back, where the needles all hang in a row, making from four to fifteen hundred, according to the lightness or heaviness of the ornament. As soon as the designer is satisfied that the work in one line is completed the reed is brought

* Moorcroft's "Travels in Cashmere," 1841.

157

down upon it, with a vigour and repetition apparently very disproportionate to the delicacy of the material."

It is a grievous fact that this beautiful handicraft of shawl-weaving has almost died out in India, owing to the competition of the cheap, meretricious,

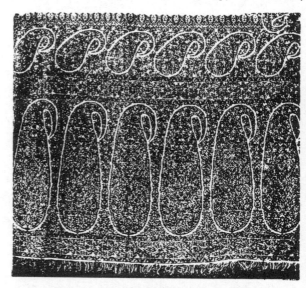

FIG. 67.—Border of an Indian Shawl.

European, machine made imitations of the Cashmere weaving and design, with which the markets of both the East and West were flooded in the last century.

Before leaving the subject of brocading, for the present, it may be interesting to remark that, no

158

doubt, like tapestry decoration, it was suggested at first by the work of the embroiderer, to which it bears even a closer resemblance than does tapestry itself. Brocading has been called "embroidering with the shuttle." There is a beautiful passage in the *Iphigenia among the Tauri* of Euripides in which the phrase is used :

"But now beside the ruthless sea I make my cheerless home, an alien, torn from home and friends, with none to call me wife or mother; never singing Hera's praise, my Queen in Argos, nor mid the merry whirr of looms broidering with my shuttle a picture of Athenia Pallas or the Titans."

CHAPTER XI

SINGLE-HARNESS PATTERNS

Ruled Paper and its Uses—Sketches of Entering and Tie-up—Designs possible on a Loom with few Headles—The Position of Cloth in Weaving—Tying up the Loom—Plan of a Tie-up—Simple Twills—The Broken Twill, its Importance—Origin and Peculiarity of Satin-weaving—The Four-headle Twill—Method of drawing Designs for Simple Looms—Simple Pattern with Tabby Ground throughout, its Advantages.

Single
harness
Patterns

AN important range of small patterns can be woven by the use of a single harness * composed of several headles, and the range may be very much extended by entering the warp in varying order instead of in regular succession.

Before giving a few examples of these patterns, it will be necessary to devote a little space to the explanation of three things. (1) The setting out and use of designer's *ruled paper* ; (2) the method of expressing on paper the order in which the warp is *entered* in the headles; and (3) the *tie-up* of the loom, as the connection between the treadles and headles is called, which renders pattern-weaving automatic.

* Leashes with short eyes have some advantages over those with long ones. A single harness, therefore, should be made with leashes having short eyes.

160

All designs for weaving, except those of the
very simplest description, have to be worked out
on ruled paper, and it is possible, after a practical
acquaintance with the principles of the craft has
been obtained, to arrange *all* the details of the most
complicated webs in this manner.   Fig. 68 will
show the manner in which the paper is ruled.
In the first place, the paper is always set out in
exact squares ruled in thick lines, and these squares
are subdivided both vertically and laterally.   To
the left of the line AA the partial ruling consisting of vertical lines only is shown, and the spaces
between these represent the threads of the warp, in
some cases single and in others in groups of equal
numbers.   To the right of the line AA the squares
are divided laterally as well as vertically.   These
lateral divisions are for the purpose of enabling
the designer to indicate the weft wherever it is
intended to show as it crosses a thread of the warp.
The proportional thickness of the weft in relation
to the warp is indicated by the size of the spaces in
the lateral divisions.   For instance, to the right of
the line AA the lowest squares, B, are divided into
four spaces, both vertically and laterally ;   this
indicates that the weft is of the same thickness as
the warp thread, or group of threads, indicated by
the vertical spaces.   If the weft be thicker than the
warp, as would usually be the case if single threads
of the latter were intended, the lateral spaces must be
larger in order to keep the right proportion in the
woven design.   In the case of the weft being one-
third thicker than the warp the squares would have to
be divided 4×3, as in the middle squares, C, instead
of 4×4.   If this were not so the design, when woven,

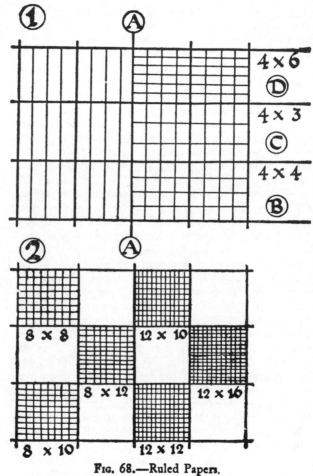

The Use of Ruled Paper for Designing

① Ⓐ

4 × 6 Ⓓ

4 × 3 Ⓒ

4 × 4 Ⓑ

② Ⓐ

8 × 8

12 × 10

8 × 12

12 × 16

8 × 10

12 × 12

Fig. 68.—Ruled Papers.

would be one-quarter longer in proportion to its width than the drawing as set out on the large squares. The general shape and proportion of the design, therefore, is sketched, in the first place, on the thick-lined, large squares, and the edges of the shapes, the details of ties, &c., are worked out correctly by means of the subdivisions. No. 2 shows some of the most usual ruled papers in use, but papers of all kinds of sub-division may be obtained. Un-less otherwise specified, in the illustrations throughout this book each verti-cal space, as well as each lateral one, may be un-derstood to represent only one thread respectively either of warp or weft.

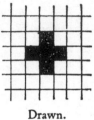 

Drawn.   Woven.

Fig. 69.

The filling in of a single space, in a ruled-paper drawing, indicates that in that particular spot the weft crosses the warp and covers it up (see fig. 69).

Fig. 70 shows the method by which the designer indicates to the weaver the way of entering the warp in the harness. The vertical lines represent the warp threads, and the horizontal lines the headles of the harness. The headles are numbered 1, 2, 3, and 4, beginning, as is generally the case, at the back. A tick or dot on the cross-line indicates the headle through which the thread is to be entered.

A HARNESS OF ANY NUMBER OF HEADLES MAY ALWAYS BE UNDERSTOOD TO BE ENTERED IN THE

163

REGULAR ORDER SHOWN IN THE SKETCH, FROM BACK TO FRONT. IF ANY OTHER ENTERING IS INTENDED SPECIAL INSTRUCTIONS ARE GIVEN FOR IT.

In order that the weft may cross the warp as shown in fig. 69, the cloth being made, as is

Cloth
mostly
woven Face
Downwards

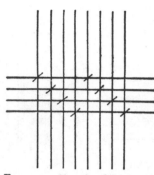

FIG. 70.—Sketch of entering in Harness of Four Headles.

usual, face downwards, it is of course necessary that the headle in which the warp threads covered by the black cross are entered must be raised, so that the shuttle carrying the weft may pass beneath them. It has already been explained that the headles are raised by means of treadles, which the weaver controls

with his feet, and the simplest way of connecting the headles and treadles for this purpose is shown by fig. 42. There are, however, various ways of doing this, which will be described later on, under the head of *Shedding Motions*, but they are all alike in one particular, which is, that they all pro-

Designs on
Ruled Paper
not affected
by Shedding
Motions

vide for the lifting of the headles as indicated on the ruled-paper drawing. This being so, the drawing out of the design is not affected by the particular kind of shedding motion with which the loom, on which the web is to be made, is fitted up.

Tying up
the Loom

Tying up the headles and treadles is a matter for the weaver to arrange according to the sequence of rising indicated by the design of the pattern on

164

ruled paper, and much ingenuity has often to be exercised in doing this in the most convenient manner for weaving. If, as he were working, the weaver had to think of the pattern, however simple, and the necessary succession of treadles to form it, the weaving would be slow and not automatic. He therefore has to arrange a plan for the *tie-up*, which will allow of his treadling in the order to which he is accustomed, and will, at the same time, cause the headles to rise in such a succession and combination as will work out the pattern correctly.

Tying up the Loom

The usual order in which a set of treadles is worked is from the outside right and left to the centre. For instance, with eight treadles, the outside right one is no. 1 and the outside left no. 2. Next to no. 1 is no. 3, and next to no. 2 is no. 4. No. 5 is on the right by no. 3, and no. 6 on the left by no. 4. No. 7 is the last trodden by the right foot, and no. 8 the last taken by the left. Some weavers prefer to begin with the left foot and others prefer to work right across, in which cases they make out their plan or draught to suit themselves; but this does not alter the method of tying up.

The Plan of Tie-up

Fig. 71 shows two plans of tie-up, together with the effect produced by them when woven. They also illustrate the simple method generally used by weavers to indicate the tie-up on paper. Both figures represent a set of eight headles, each harness being entered in the usual straightforward manner. This is shown by the ticks to the right of the diagrams above B. The vertical lines C, C are the treadles, numbered according to the above-mentioned sequence of treading from the right and left to the centre. The tie-up of the treadles

Examples of Tie-up

165

to the headles is indicated by the crosses, on the
several lines, at places where they intersect. In
diagram 1, where only two treadles are necessary to
produce the effect designed at A, each treadle is tied
up to four headles, no. 1 to headles 1, 3, 5, and 7,
and no. 2 to headles 2, 4, 6, 8, so that treadle 1

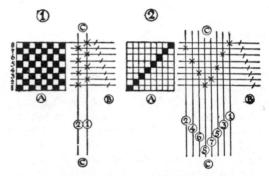

FIG. 71.—Plans of Tie-up.

will raise headles 1, 3, 5, and 7 and produce the
effect of the lowest and other similar lines in the
design A. The second treadle will in like manner
raise the headles for the four alternate lines of the
sketch, nos. 2, 4, 6, and 8. Diagram 2 has the same
headles and entering as diagram 1, but instead of
only two, there are eight treadles, C, C, one headle
being tied separately to each treadle. The result
of this tie-up, when the treadles are used in the
order in which they are numbered, is shown in the
sketch above A.

An amazing amount of ingenuity has been
exercised by weavers in arranging for the lifting of

Examples of Tie-up

large numbers and complicated systems of headles, and pattern-weaving was formerly done to quite an astonishing extent in this manner. The use of simple automatic contrivances has, however, quite superseded the use of an inconvenient number of treadles. But for small patterns, grounds, satins, twills, &c., there can be no doubt, that the direct tie-up of the treadles to the headles is better and more certain in action than any other contrivance whatever.

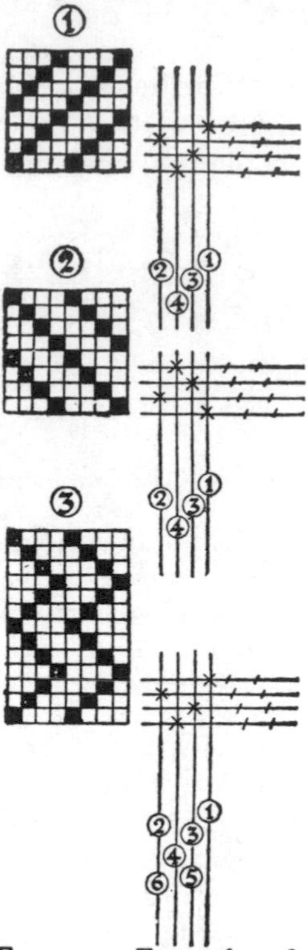

Fig. 72.—Examples of Simple Twill Patterns

Pattern-capacity of a Loom with Four Headles and Four Treadles

The principles of the use of ruled paper, the entering of the warp in the harness, and the connection of the treadles to the headles being understood, it will now be interesting to exemplify and examine a few of the patterns that can be woven on a loom with a single harness of only four headles, and an equal number of treadles. Fig. 72 gives examples of the simplest possible designs. The treadles for these are tied up singly to each of the four headles.

Simple Twills

At no. 1 a right-hand *twill* is given, with the plan of entering it and also the tie-up of the treadles. The numerals in the circles on the treadle lines show the order in which the treadles are to be worked. At no. 2 the tie-up is seen to be reversed, which throws the twill in the opposite direction, making it a left-hand one. At no. 3 a combination of both the above is shown, the result being a zigzag. This is made by extending the treading as indicated by the numerals in the circles of no. 3 itself, and

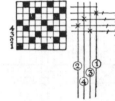

may be used with either the tie-up of no. 1 or no. 2 indifferently.

The next ground pattern to claim attention is sometimes called a *broken twill.* It is made, like the ordinary twill, on four headles and

FIG. 73.—Broken Twill treadles, but the tie-up is rather different; fig. 73 is a draught of it. It will be seen that the direct diagonal line of the twill is broken by missing headle 2, and making it rise between the fourth and the first headles. The result of this arrangement is that if a rich close warp is being used the weft will scarcely show at all, the tie being distributed so evenly over the ground that no ribs or lines are visible. This is a most ingenious invention, and shows the principle on which the various satins

are formed. It is said to be of Chinese origin, which is most probable, as it is particularly adapted for displaying the rich, glossy quality of silken thread, which the Chinese were certainly the first people to use for weaving. Before passing on, it should be noted particularly that IF COUNTED IN EITHER DIRECTION THE SAME NUMBER OF THREADS WILL BE FOUND BETWEEN ALL THE TIES OF THE BROKEN TWILL.

The Origin
and Cha-
racter of
Satin Ties

Extension of
the Four-
headle Twill

THIS IS THE SPECIAL CHARACTERISTIC OF ALL THE
SATINS. FURTHER REFERENCE TO THIS WILL PRE-
SENTLY BE MADE.

Several more extended designs may be made
on the same principle as the twill, with four headles
and treadles only, if the entering of the warp
be specially arranged for them. A sample group
of these designs is given in fig. 74, and many others
can be devised, both by alteration of the entering,
tie-up, or order of working the treadles. The
entering necessary for the designs illustrated, repeats
once in every twenty-four threads of the warp. It
will be seen that three courses of four threads are
entered from back to front, then one thread by
itself on the back headle, followed by three courses
of four threads, from front to back, the fourth
thread in the last course beginning the next repeat.
If the treadles are tied up and trodden as for
ordinary twill a large lateral zigzag will be woven
(fig. 1); by working the treadles in the order
shown by the numerals in the lower part of the
diagram no. 2 will be made; and on taking the
treadles in the following order, 1, 2, 3, 4, 13, 14,
15, 16, no. 3 will result.

With the same entering and tie-up plain cloth
may be made at will, so that lateral spaces or
panels of any of these small designs may be woven
by way of ornament at intervals in the plain
material. Very pretty effects may be arranged for,
especially if the bands are shot with gay-coloured
wefts. In order to make the plain cloth in alternation with the ornamental bands, it is only necessary
to depress the first and third treadles together with
the right foot, for one shoot, and the second and

169

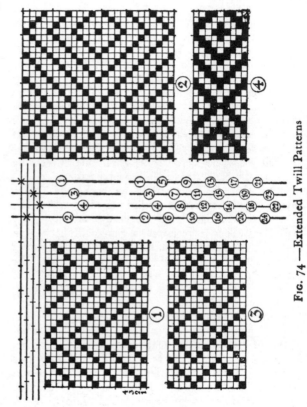

Fig. 74 —Extended Twill Patterns

fourth treadles together with the left foot for the next.

In order to produce the design shown at no. 4, fig. 74, the same entering and treading are required as for no. 3, but the tie-up must be different (see fig. 75). In this case two headles must be tied up to each separate treadle, in the following order : Headles 1 and 2 to treadle 1 ; headles 2 and 3 to treadle 2. Treadle 3 has headles 3 and 4 tied to it, and treadle 4 must be tied up to headles 4 and 1. The effect of this tie-up may be seen in the diagram, and requires no further explanation.

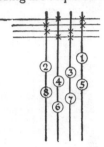

FIG. 75—Tie-up for fig. 74, no. 4

It will have been gathered from the last illustration that more than one headle may be tied

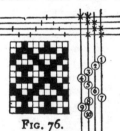

FIG. 76.
Pattern with unequal Tie-up.

up to each treadle. This being so, a much greater variety of patterns is possible than would be the case if only single tie-ups were practicable. The tie-up may really be of any number of headles to one treadle, only short by one of the number that would raise the whole of the warp. If four headles are used, one, two, or three of them may be tied to any one treadle, it not being necessary that an equal number be tied to each treadle, as is the case in fig. 75. Fig. 76 is

171

Extension of
the Four-
headle Twill
an illustration of a pattern and tie-up in which one, two, and three headles severally are connected with single treadles, as will be seen by the plan.

The curious diagonal design fig. 77 requires six treadles tied up to four headles, as shown in the

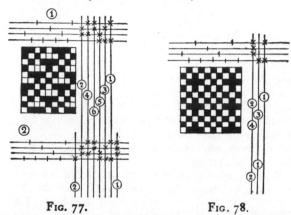

FIG. 77.   FIG. 78.

plan. The entering in this case is remarkable, as half the warp is raised by means of the fourth headle and the other half is distributed equally over the other three. Plain ground cannot be woven with this tie-up of six treadles, but two extra ones, one on each side of the six, will render it possible. These tabby treadles must be tied up as shown in the plan no. 2.

With the same entering as that of the last design, and a tie-up to three treadles, the pattern fig. 78 can be made, and by the use of treadles 2 and 3 plain tabby ground can also be woven in alternation with broad bands of ornament.

172

Fig. 79 gives the plan of one of the most elaborate **Extension of**
designs workable by this simple method of weaving. **the Four-**
It requires the use of a harness of ten headles and a **headle Twill**
set of ten treadles to produce it. The entering is

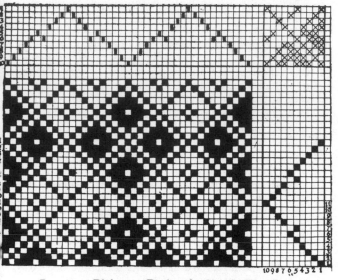

FIG. 79.—Elaborate Design for Simple Weaving.

on twenty threads of the warp, and the tie-up is
rather complicated, as will be seen by the plan.

It will have been noticed that this design and **Setting out**
plan, (fig. 79) are worked out entirely on ruled **Complete**
paper. This is a convenient method of setting out **Plans on**
complicated weavings, as the order in which the **Ruled Paper**
treadles follow can be marked in the line of the
design they each govern. A careful study of the

173

drawing and a comparison of the numerals will elucidate the relation of the various parts one to another. The final arrangement of the position of the treadles for working is always left to the weaver, and is, indeed, quite immaterial, so long as it causes the headles to rise in the order set down in the design. In setting out such a drawing, the entering must be indicated first, and then the design filled in below it on the same number of squares as one repeat of the entering contains. The number in this case is twenty. The scope of this design is also further limited, by the nature of the entering, to a figure having its centre line on the eleventh thread, and both its halves alike except that they are reversed and point in different directions. In weaving this is technically called a *point* design. The length of the design is not limited, as its breadth is, by the entering of the harness ; this is decided to some extent by the number of treadles employed. Any treadle, however, may be made to rise and repeat the same lateral line of the design any number of times, and the whole number of treadles, or any portion of them, may be worked backward and forward or in any sequence necessary to form the pattern.

After the design and entering are set out, the design must be dissected, in order to find how many different lateral lines there are in it, as the several headles forming each different line have to be tied up to a treadle. In fig. 79, for example, there are ten different lines, which necessitates the use of ten treadles. By repetition, however, their scope is extended to twenty lines. Many designs will allow of even a great deal more repetition than this.

174

Designs of the kind exemplified by figs. 71 to 80 are particularly adapted for weaving on small looms such as may conveniently be used in the home. They are very suitable for linen and cotton fabrics intended for domestic use, such as table linen, bed furniture, and simple garments of the kind for which linen and cotton materials are required. These simple woven patterns are for the most part only effective when the yarns from which they are made are not very fine. They should generally be not more than forty to a reed space of one inch, and not less than thirty. The best effects also are to be obtained if good, even, hand-spun yarns are used, especially in the weft.

Setting out Complete Plans on Ruled Paper

It will be remembered that good cloth requires the weft to be thicker than the warp (see p. 5), and it will be at the same time observed that in order to weave most of the patterns illustrated, in the same proportion as the drawings, the warp and weft should occupy equal spaces. This difficulty is to be obviated by using a warp made of fine threads half the size of the weft. If these fine threads are warped and entered double, the condition of the proportion of the warp to the weft can be kept, and as the two warp threads will only count as one, the proportions of the design will also be maintained.

The Use of Double Threads in the Warp

When designing these small patterns for simple weaving, care must be taken to break up the spaces by intersection of the warp and weft as much as possible. Not more than five threads either way should ever be left to cross each other without interlacing, or the cloth will be found to be too weak for good wear. Even five loose threads must not occur too frequently

Frequent Intersection of Warp and Weft necessary

in the design. If broad spaces of ornament are desired in this kind of weaving, some means must be used to strengthen the cloth without interfering with the effect of the ornament. This can be done, and a similar effect obtained to that of brocading, except that the ornaments, instead of being in

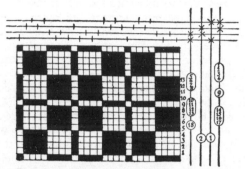

FIG. 80.—Pattern with Tabby Ground

detached spots, will be repeated in a close geometric pattern all over the cloth. Fig. 80 is a type of the design suitable for weaving in this way, and will clearly exemplify the weaving together of the ornamentation and the ground cloth. This design requires only four headles, entered in the order shown above the sketch, and four treadles, two of which are used for the tabby groundwork and two for the pattern. On the two outside treadles the pattern is tied up, and on the two inside ones the tabby ground is tied. An extra shuttle and richer weft must be used for the *design* part of the weaving, and it is better for this purpose to use several fine threads together as a weft, than one

176

coarse one, as they will lie flatter and cover the ground better. Ordinary plain cloth is woven by using only the centre pair of treadles, but as soon as it is determined to introduce the design one of the outside treadles must be brought into use after any one of the tabby shoots, and the pattern weft introduced in the shed made by it. The next shoot of tabby ground must then be made, and after it the same pattern treadle again depressed and another pattern shoot thrown. These alternate shoots of ground and pattern must be repeated until the first row of squares is complete, in which there will be found four shoots of ground and four of pattern. When this point has been reached, the opposite pattern treadle will have to be used, in the same alternation with the ground ones, for the same number of shoots, thus making the second row of squares. After this the first pattern treadle must be depressed for one shoot only, in order to make the thin strip dividing the squares. After four more shoots in the shed, made by the second pattern treadle, the first one is returned to, and after four more shoots and a single one, the first repeat of the design will be found to be complete. It will be readily understood that the squares of this pattern may be made of any size desired, by extending the entering in the harness and the number of sheds made by the pattern treadles. At the same time this will not weaken the cloth, as the same tabby ground will run throughout, whatever size the squares may be. Whilst weaving this kind of design it will be found necessary to beat the weft together with more force, or with a double blow, in order to keep the ground as close as the plain parts of the web, if there are to be any such. If properly beaten together the pattern woven by this method should appear quite solid, and entirely hide the tabby ground which is beneath it.

The great importance of the satin ties in the development of weaving, especially of fine silk, renders it necessary that the next chapter should be set apart for their exclusive consideration. But at the same time it must be noted here, that many useful and beautiful satin and partly satin webs may be designed for weaving on small domestic looms in which either linen, cotton, woollen or spun-silk yarns can be used.

CHAPTER XII

THE SATINS AND DOUBLE CLOTH

Construction and Utility of the Satin Tie—
Meaning of the Term *Satin*—Peculiar Quality of
the Satin Tie—Various Satins and the Number of
Headles required for weaving them—Reasons for
weaving Webs Face Downwards—Exceptions—The
Selvages of Satin and other Webs—Separate Selvages
and their Fitting up—When Separate Selvages are
necessary—Contrast of Colours in Satin Webs and
its Limits—Double Cloth, its Advantages—Preparing and entering the Warp for Double Cloth—
Weaving Double Cloth.

THE construction of the broken-twill has already
been explained (p. 168, fig. 73) and its importance
as an example of the principles of satin-weaving
commented on. Its reputed Chinese origin was
also mentioned. It is remarkable that, apart from
Eastern influence, there seem to be no traces of
this tie in ancient weaving, although there are a
few examples of the ordinary twill. The earliest
known specimens of weaving in which the use of
satin ties is a feature belong to the fourth or fifth
centuries of the Christian era, and even of that date
the fragments that remain are very few in number.

The satin tie for plain webs is not much used,
except in the case of warps of fine silk, the richness

179

of which it is peculiarly fitted to display. But it is in the weaving of the extensive and elaborate pattern webs known as damasks that its chief utility consists, and that not only for the weaving of silk, but for the weaving also of linen, cotton, and woollen ornamental fabrics.

The name satin is generally misunderstood. It is usually taken to signify some kind of silk material. This is no doubt owing to the fact that this tie is for the most part restricted to silk in the case of plain materials. The term, however, has no reference to the yarn employed in the web, but only to the manner of weaving it.

There are various kinds of satin in use, all being based on the same principle. They are distinguished according to the number of headles required in the harness used for weaving them. The broken twill, which we have seen requires a harness of four headles, is not always called a satin, but is often designated a satinette.

Peculiar value is given to the satin tie because of its throwing a very large proportion of the warp to the face of the material woven, so that if the warp consists of fine rich silk and the weft of common silk, linen, cotton, or wool, the rich silk, in the case of a very rich satin of, say, sixteen headles, will almost entirely cover up the poorer weft. The latter will in its turn show almost entirely at the back of the cloth. Fig. 81 represents the front and back of such a satin-woven material, very much enlarged.* In the actual cloth

* The square of sixteen-headle satin represented would repeat from nine to twelve hundred times in a square inch.

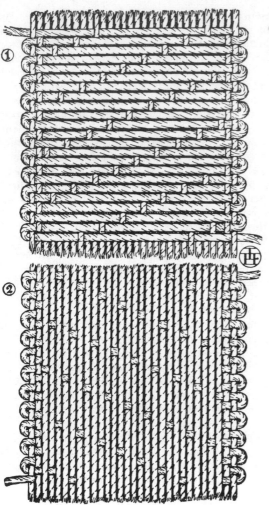

FIG. 81.—Satin Cloth (much enlarged).

represented the sixteen threads between the ties would probably not occupy a space of more than thethirtieth part of an inch. At no. 2 the face of the cloth is shown, and it will be seen that fifteen threads of warp intervene between each intersection of the weft laterally, and also that the warp threads each float over fifteen shoots of weft between the ties vertically. In the actual stuff when loose and out of the loom these infrequent ties would scarcely be seen at all, and the glossy surface of the silken warp would appear to be unbroken. At no. 1 the back of the stuff is shown. Here the weft only for the most part shows, held together at regular though infrequent intervals by the intersection of the fine warp.

Satins may be made on harnesses of almost any number of headles from five to twenty-four. The satin most generally used is that made on eight headles, and is called *eight-headle*, *eight-lam*, or *eight-shaft* satin. In some respects this is the best of all satins, as in it the ties are most evenly distributed, and the twill from which it, in common with all satins, is derived is less in evidence. (See no. 3, fig. 82.)

Five-headle satin is more used for linen damasks and other coarser woven ornamental fabrics than for silk. A great many of the mediæval silk damasks were, however, made with this tie, which gives the dry and more subdued effect often to be seen in them. (See no. 1.)

In fig. 82 are given ruled-paper drawings of all the satins. Many of them, however, are not in general use, as nine, seven, eleven and other odd numbers of headles would be inconvenient in a

182

harness, as plain tabby cloth could not be made on it. Five-headle satin (no. 1) is generally made

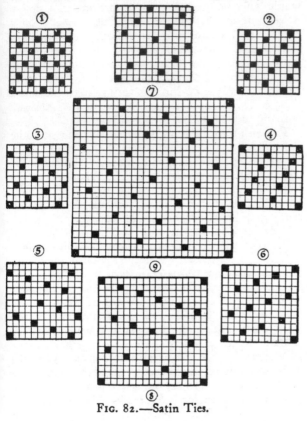

Fig. 82.—Satin Ties.

on a harness of ten headles, for the above reason, and tied up so that two of the headles rise at each tread. Such a harness can also, of course, be used for the ten-headle satin (no. 5). Nos. 2, 4, and 11 would only be used as ties on portions of a design woven on a different principle, as if made on a harness they could only be worked with an awkward number of headles, although the eleven-headle satin is perhaps the most well-distributed of them all, not excepting the eight-headle one. Nos. 7, 8, and 9 are only used for the very richest and finest silks, or as ties in portions of designs in fancy-silk weaving, which will be treated of later on.

Returning to the representation of sixteen-headle satin, fig. 81. It will be noticed that the back of the cloth, no. 1, corresponds more closely with the sketch of the same satin in fig. 82 than no. 2 (the front of the cloth) does. The reason of this resemblance is that the black squares of the sketch represent the lifted threads of the warp. It has already been stated that most weaving is done with the face of the cloth downwards. This is particularly the case with satin webs. Obviously the lifting of one headle out of many instead of the lifting of all but one, makes the work lighter for the weaver. The raising of one thread instead of many causes also much less friction and wear, not only in the warp itself, but in the harness and general fittings of the loom. There are several other minor advantages, so that, taking all into consideration, the inconvenience to the weaver caused by not seeing the front of the web as, the work proceeds, is more than compensated for. Moreover, the difficulty of weaving webs face downwards is not so great in most cases as would at first appear, for if the back is right and the loom in all its parts is seen to be

184

working properly the weaver need have little doubt that the surface of the material will be satisfactory. Although weaving is usually thus done face downwards, it is not absolutely necessary that it should be. In the case of some complicated fancy webs, where two or three thicknesses of cloth are woven together, and it would be impossible to judge from the back if the surface were weaving properly or no, it may be possible and advantageous to so arrange that the fabric may be made face upwards. This is effected by tying up in accordance with the white spaces of the ruled-paper design, instead of the black ones.

Exceptions to weaving Webs Face Downward

When a piece of cloth is being inspected by an expert one of the first points to be examined is the edge of the web, generally called the *selvage*. It may be pretty confidently expected that if the edges are straight and even, and at the same time neither tighter nor looser than the body of the stuff, the cloth will prove to be well woven throughout. A good selvage is the finishing grace in a woven fabric, and none but good weavers can keep perfect the edges of their work.

The Selvages of Satin and other Webs

In tabby or plain weaving, when the warp and weft are properly proportioned, there is not much difficulty in keeping a perfect edge, and it is only necessary to fortify the warp by making a few of the edge threads double ; but in the case of the looser satin, or the various kinds of fancy webs where two or three different warps and wefts are used, an arrangement of the selvage warps to work independently of the main warp becomes necessary, and often requires a good deal of ingenuity on the part of the weaver to devise. Another reference to

The Necessity for Selvages

185

fig. 81 will be sufficient for the purpose of explaining the necessity and working of the selvages on the edges of satin webs. Although there are only two threads shown in the drawing, it is quite clear that they make a straight tabby edge and prevent the weft being drawn back, by the returning shuttle, as far as the first tie of the satin. This might be any distance from the edge up to the space of sixteen threads of warp. Without these tabby-woven threads the edges would be extremely un-even, however carefully the weaving might be done. The defective edge can be avoided if a few strong threads are so arranged that a narrow strip of tabby weaving may be made along each side

of the web. There are various ways of arranging for the separate tabby shedding of the selvages, but the simplest way is to provide two extra pairs of headle shafts at the back of the harness, at the ends of which the selvage leashes are fixed, so that the extra threads passing through them, by the sides of the main warp, may be entered close to it in the rather wider dents usually provided for them in the reed. These selvage headles are each tied up to half the treadles in such a way that they will be raised alternately as one of the right or left half of the treadles is depressed. In the case of satins and other loosely tied webs it is found necessary to warp the selvages and weave them off small rolls, separately

fitted up and weighted, as shown in fig. 83. This separation from the main warp is necessary, because the more frequent intersection of the warp and weft, in tabby weaving, causes the warp to be used up more quickly than is the case with the less frequently intersected threads of the satin ground. If the

186

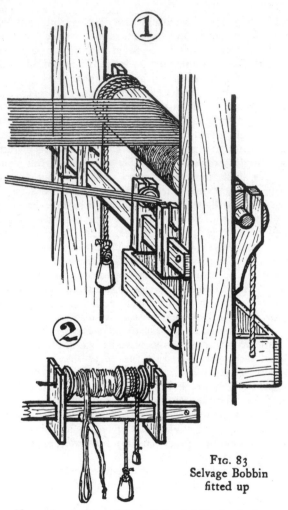

Fig. 83
Selvage Bobbin
fitted up

No. 1 shows the position of the bobbin in the loom.
No. 2 : Details of the bobbin, with warp and method
of weighting.

Why
separately
Warped
Selvages are
required

Contrast of
Colour on
the Back
and Front
of Satin
Webs

tabby selvages, therefore, came off the same roller as the satin warp, as soon as about half a yard of stuff had been woven, the edges would get so strained that the work could not go on. They would then break out altogether and spoil the web.

It will be readily understood from the foregoing description of satin-weaving, that the back and front of a web may be made different in colour, to a very large extent, providing the warp and weft used are distinct in that respect. The colour of the warp will predominate in the front, and that of the weft at the back in similar proportion. In five-headle satin, for instance, the warp colour on the face of the cloth will be in the proportion of four parts to one part of weft, and at the back the proportions will be reversed. With richer satins the difference will be greater, but however great it may be the colour of the weft will always tinge that of the warp in the front, and at the back the weft colour will be modified by the ties of the warp in the same manner. In satin-weaving, therefore, the colours of back and front can never be quite distinct.

There is another system of weaving, however, by means of which two separate webs, of perfectly distinct colours, joined at the edges may be woven at the same time, from the same warp, in the same loom. A great deal of pattern-weaving has been done by taking advantage of this possibility.

It will now be best to describe the method of weaving this double cloth, but its utilisation for pattern-weaving must be left for consideration in a future chapter.

Double tabby cloth of separate colours can be woven on a loom with a harness of four headles,

188

but the warp must be specially arranged for the
purpose. If it be decided to make one cloth black
and the other white, the warp must be made
throughout with alternate threads of those two
colours. The warp of black and white threads
being entered in the usual way, if the first thread
be black the whole of the first headle will be found
to contain all black
threads, the first, fifth,
ninth, &c.; the
second headle will
carry all white
threads, the second,
sixth, tenth, &c. The
third headle will be
all black, with threads
3, 7, 11, &c.; and the
fourth headle will take
the rest of the white

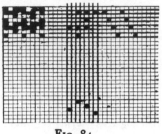

FIG. 84.

threads, 4, 8, 12, &c. In other words, all the odd
threads, which are black, will be found in headles 1
and 3, and all the even ones, which are white, in
headles 2 and 4.

With such a warp separate selvages would be
fitted up to work in the same way as for satin,
so as to bind the double cloth together at the
edges.

When all is ready, in a loom so arranged, weaving must begin by raising half the black threads by
means of headle 1, and throwing the shuttle carrying
the weft through the shed so formed. The next
shed is to be made by raising headle 3, which raises
the second, half of the black threads for the second
throw of the shuttle. This completes two shoots of

189

the black face of the double cloth. For the next shed, headles 1 and 3 must rise and lift all the black threads, and headle 2 must rise with them to lift half the white threads. The third shoot of weft having been made, the fourth headle will have to rise, as well as the first and third again, and the fourth shoot of weft will complete the second shoot of the white face of the double cloth. This order of shedding must be repeated, and when a few shoots have been made, it will be found, that, two distinct webs united at the edges have been woven. In order to make the colours distinct two shuttles must be used, one for the black and one for the white face of the cloth, and when this is done the double cloth will be found to be perfectly black on one side and perfectly white on the other. Fig. 84 gives the sketch on ruled paper with the plan and tie-up for double cloth.

CHAPTER XIII

SHEDDING MOTIONS

The Simplest Shedding Motion—Two Typical
Shedding Motions—Differences between the Two
Kinds of Shedding Motions—Choice of Shedding
Motion left to Weaver—Suitable Design for
Shedding Motion No. 2.

THE name *shedding motion* is given to any contrivance by means of which the opening or shed
is made in the warp, in front of the reed, for
the passing through of the weft. The shedding
motion shown on the old English loom, fig. 42,
consists of two treadles and two pulleys connected
with the headles of the harness by cords. A similar
motion, having precisely the same effect, in which
two short pieces of bamboo take the place of the
pulleys, is shown in the Indian loom, fig. 41.
Needless to say, these are the simplest forms of
shedding motion possible, but it now becomes
necessary to describe the rather more complicated
arrangements by means of which headles may be
lifted for the grounds and small figures exemplified
in the preceding chapters.

The
Simplest
Shedding
Motion

Only two distinct shedding motions need to be
described and their differences pointed out, as all
others are for the most part modifications of them,

Two Typical
Shedding
Motions

191

and will present no difficulties to the student if their
principles are perfectly understood. Figs. 85 and
85A represent these two typical motions.

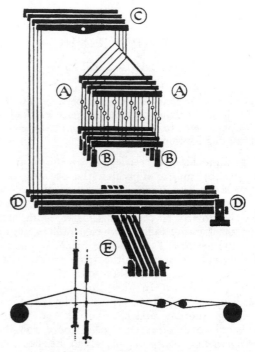

FIG. 85.—Shedding Motion.

In order to keep the diagrams of these shedding
motions as distinct and simple as possible, the harness
to which they are attached is only represented as

one of four headles. This is all that is necessary for the purpose of illustration, but any number of headles up to twenty, or even more, might be

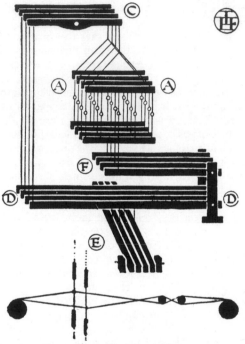

FIG. 85ᴀ.—Shedding Motion.

governed in the same way, providing that the number of levers and treadles was increased in the same proportion. In the diagrams, also, only the

193

headles and the shedding motion are shown; all the
supporting parts of the loom, which would only
complicate the drawing and render it less clear,
are omitted. The position of the harness in the
loom is, of course, the same as in fig. 42, with its
harness of two headles.

In fig. 85 it will be seen that the headles, A, A,
have long lead weights, B, B, on their lower shafts,
instead of their being tied directly to the treadles as
in fig. 42. If any of the four headles, therefore, be
raised, as soon as it is released, the weights on its
lower shaft will bring it down again to its normal
position. Strong wire spiral springs are sometimes,
for some purposes, preferred to lead weights, but these
have the same effect as regards the mechanism of the
shedding motion.* At letter C four short, strong
laths are shown, having a hole somewhere near their
centres, through which an iron rod is passed. The
ends of the rod are fixed in a long, wooden frame,
which rests on the top of the loom in the position
occupied by the centre cross-piece, from which the
harness is suspended, in the old English loom, fig. 42.

From one end of each of these laths, just above
the centre of the headles, a double cord descends,
and, being divided, in the manner shown in the
drawing, is attached to both ends of the top shaft
of headles. This attachment is made by the use
of the adjustable slip-knot, described in Note 2
to Chapter VII., p. 106, in order that the height
of the headles in the loom may be adjusted to
a nicety. At the opposite ends of the levers C

* The effect of the dead weight is to close the shed
rather more quickly than the spiral spring, and therefore
it is generally preferred.

194

long cords are firmly fixed. These descend, and
are tied, by the same kind of slip-knot, to the ends
of four long laths, D, which, reaching right across
the loom at the height of about a foot from the
ground, have their other ends hinged to a strong
support, which is fastened to the ground, or to the
framework of the loom itself. It will now be seen
that the four treadles, E, placed under the weaver's
feet, as he sits in the loom, only need to be tied up
to the long cross-levers to enable him by pressure
of his foot to pull down at will one end of any of the
levers C. This will raise the other end, from which
a headle is suspended, and open the shed. By this
means the headles can be raised in any order or combination necessary for the formation of the pattern.

In fig. 85A the arrangements for raising the
headles are the same, but the weights on the
bottom shaft are dispensed with. In place of the
weights, four levers, long enough to reach from
the side of the loom to beyond the centre of the
harness are fixed, between the long levers and the
bottom laths of the headles, and tied to each of
the latter (see letter F, fig. 85A). If, with the
motion arranged as at fig. 85A, the first treadle be
pressed down, the first headle will rise, and the
first lever F will rise with it. The second, third,
and fourth headles, having no weights to keep
them down except the light weight of the levers
themselves, will neither be held firmly down nor
raised. To rectify this, levers 2, 3, and 4 must be
tied firmly by cords to the first treadle. The result
of this additional tie will be, that, when treadle 1
is again depressed headle 1 will rise as before, but
headles 2, 3, and 4 will be drawn down at the

195

same time. This cording has to be carried all
through; thus, the second treadle must be connected with the levers 1, 3, and 4, the third
treadle with levers 1, 2, and 4, and the fourth
treadle with levers 1, 2, and 3. When all these
connections are made the raising of any one of
the four headles will cause the remaining three
to sink. If when this motion is used two headles
are required to rise at one time, the treadle must be
connected with two long levers in order to raise
them, and the remaining two levers must be tied
to the same treadle. By this means two headles
will rise and two sink. In short, no matter how
many headles the harness may consist of, each must
be connected with all the treadles either by means
of the long levers which raise the headles or by the
short ones which sink them.

The section of the sheds below figs. 85 and 85A
will show the important difference between the two
shedding motions. Fig. 85 is called a *rising shed*,
because, while the bulk of the warp is stationary, the
required threads rise from it. Fig. 85A is called a
rising and sinking shed, because when certain threads
are raised all the others sink down at the same
time.

Each of these shedding motions has its advantage,
according to the kind of weaving it is used for.
When only a few threads require lifting, as in the
case of satins, a rising shed is preferable, but when
about half the threads of the warp are raised, a rising
and sinking shed may be advantageous, although
there is always more friction when the latter is
used.

There are various other shedding motions in use,

196

but they are all based on one or other of these two principles, and the above may be taken as types of all.

Difference in the Two Kinds of Shedding Motions

Also, by connecting the treadles to only certain of the remainder of the headles instead of all, another variety of shed may be made. This connection will be described later on, as it is required in a particularly important class of pattern-weaving.

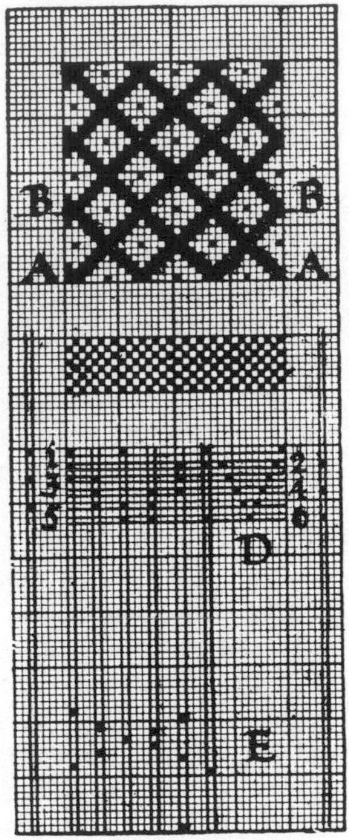

Fig. 86.

Choice of Shedding Motion left to Weaver

The sample patterns already given can be woven with either of the above shedding motions, and the use of one of them would not affect the design on ruled paper or the indicated tie-up of the treadles. The rising of the headles would be the same in both, but in the second motion after the tie-up for raising the headles had been made, the headles corresponding to the vacant spaces in the tie-up plan would have to be connected by means of the short levers to the several treadles. The kind of shedding motion most suitable for any particular design is a point for the weaver to settle to his own satisfaction.

Fig. 86 is an example of a small design suitable for weaving with the shedding motion no. 2—that is, with a rising and sinking shed—as the ground and figure are exactly equal in weight.

Between A and B, in the design, one repeat or the pattern is shown drawn out on the ruled paper. At first sight it would appear to require ten headles and ten treadles to make one repeat of the design. But on analysing it, it will be found possible to weave it on six headles, governed by six treadles provided the entering of the warp in the harness be done as indicated in the sketch above letter D. The real design is only a quarter of one repeat, but it is turned over or "pointed" both laterally and vertically. Instead, therefore, of containing ten different lines of squares, the design has only six, four lines being repeated twice in it. The lateral turnover is effected by the entering of the harness, the vertical one by reversing the order of treadling. The tie-up for this design with no. 2 shedding motion must first be made, as shown in the sketch, to the long levers, or *long marches*, as they are more correctly called. When this is done it will be found that there are three connections to each treadle, and three headles will still remain unconnected with each of them. These unconnected headles must, by means of the short levers, be connected with the treadles, as indicated by the unmarked crossings. The effect of this second tie-up has already been fully explained in the description of the second shedding motion, fig. 85A, p. 193.

CHAPTER XIV

DOUBLE-HARNESS PATTERN-WEAVING

THE name diaper is now usually understood to signify any small design which is repeated geometrically over the surface which it decorates. The term diaper-weaving, however, does not really refer so much to the kind of pattern woven as to the method of weaving it. This ingenious method, although invented in Asia, was as early as the eleventh century practised in England, especially for weaving the silken groundwork of the embroideries for which the ladies

Diaper-weaving

199

of England were famous at that time. A great deal
of quite large pattern weaving was formerly done in
this way, but on account of its being, except for simple
designs, difficult to set up as well as to manage, it
was superseded by less complicated contrivances.

For small patterns, however, especially in linen
and cotton materials, it may still be used with
advantage. It must therefore now be described.

In diaper-weaving, the harness is divided into sets
of equal numbers of headles. There may be any
workable number of sets, and these may contain any
equal number of headles. The treadles also are
divided into sets, but each set of treadles acts on
more than one set of headles, so that, whichever set
of treadles is used the whole of the warp is acted
upon, and no gaps remain in the weaving.

Fig. 87 is a simple design which will serve well
to explain the method. Here the harness is divided
into two sets having four headles in each (nos. 1
and 2). There are also two sets of treadles, each
set consisting of four. The entering shown to the
right of the plan corresponds with the proportions
of the square and oblong forms of which the design
is composed. For instance, if the design be compared with the plan of entering, it will be found that
the warp is entered in the spaces where dark pre-
dominates. The second division of the harness
and the bottom line of the design agree, while the
first division of the harness and the fifth line of the
design agree also. Before proceeding it may be
remarked that the size and proportion of the squares
and oblongs laterally is determined by the entering.
In the present case four courses are entered in no. 2
harness and two in no. 1, which makes the oblong

200

twice as wide as the square.

The plan of tie-up for the headles, shows the second harness connected with the four treadles of the first set. The connection is made in the order necessary to form the twill tie on the portion of warp entered in the second harness. To the same treadles the first harness is tied up to make the reverse twill. The second set of treadles is tied up with the reverse twill in front and the figure tie at the back. The effect of this arrangement is that if weaving be done, using

①

②

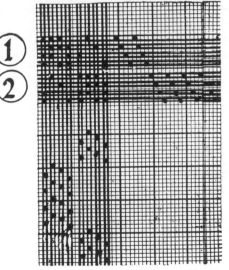

Fig. 87.—Example of Diaper-weaving.

201

Plan of
Tie-up for
Diaper-
weaving

Extended
Diaper-
weaving

Pattern-
weaving
with Two
Harnesses

the first set of treadles only, a broad and narrow stripe of light and dark reversed twills will be made; on the contrary, if the second set of treadles only are used the broad stripe will be dark and the narrow one light (see top and bottom of fig. 87A). By the alternate use, then, of the set of treadles 1 and 2 the changes from light to dark spaces, required for the pattern, can readily be made.

By adding to the number of sets of headles and extending the entering through them, with or without adding to the number of the treadles, a great variety of intricate designs can be arranged for; and, indeed, this used to be done, but since the same effects have been found to be attainable by less intricate means, the more elaborate forms of diaper-weaving have been discontinued, and the ingenious contrivances for working large numbers of sets of headles, are only interesting from an antiquarian point of view.

FIG. 87A
Variations of
Fig. 87

A great advance was made in the weaving of pattern when the idea occurred of passing the warp threads through two or more sets of headles, each set having its own separate function to perform, such as making the ground, forming the pattern, or binding a portion of the design separately, as is sometimes necessary.

A good example of the action of two separate harnesses working together, is afforded by the Indian

202

double-cloth pattern, fig. 88. The making of plain double cloth and the advantages such cloth possesses have been fully described at the end of Chapter XII., p. 188. That description should be referred to at this point. It may be noted in addition, that, while cloth is being woven from one half of the warp for one or two shoots, as the case may be, the other half-warp is either lifted out of the way or left below, but that THEY NEVER REVERSE THEIR RELATIVE POSITIONS. Now in double-cloth *pattern*-weaving while the tabby cloth of one colour is being made the warp of the other colour is lifted in some places and remains below in others, according to the design, but whether above or below it does not interfere with the tabby

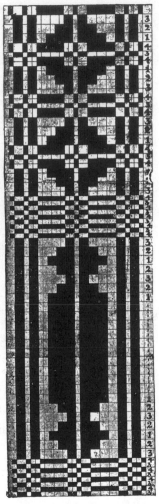

FIG. 88.—Indian Double Cloth.

203

weaving of the opposite colour. When the web is
finished the separate cloths will be found to be quite
distinct from one another, except at the edges, or

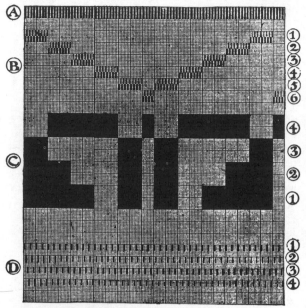

FIG. 89.—Plan of Indian Design.

outline or the shapes of the design, where the
threads will be found to cross or intersect one
another.

Fig. 89 is a portion of the working plan of the
Indian design fig. 88. The warp, which has alternate threads of black and white, is shown at A, at
the top of the diagram.

204

In front of the loom, as near to the reed as it can conveniently hang, the tabby or ground harness must be placed. This consists of four headles having long eyes on the leashes as described at p. 156, fig. 66. The warp must be entered in the harness in regular order from back to front, beginning with a black thread (fig. 89D). When the entering is finished all the black threads should be found on headles 1 and 3, and all the white ones on headles 2 and 4. Although thus mentioned first, as appeared necessary, the ground harness would not be fitted up or entered until the figure harness, which will presently be described, was in its appointed place with the warp ready entered in it.

In order to find the requirements for the figure harness the design fig. 88 must be dissected. The result of this dissection is shown at C, fig. 89. The design consists of only four different groupings of a few squares of eight black and eight white threads, arranged in lines and repeated in different sequence. These lines are numbered 1, 2, 3, and 4 in the design, fig. 88. It will also be seen that laterally there are five squares and two half-squares. The first figures indicate that four treadles will be required for the black portion of the design, and four more for the white portion. The second figures show that twelve headles will be wanted, six for lifting the white threads and six for the black. These twelve headles are shown at letter B in the diagram, and their construction and entering is as follows:

Unlike any of the enterings shown up to the present, this harness is entered in groups instead of single threads, the groups consisting of eight threads,

Mounting the Loom for Double cloth Indian Design

The Ground Harness

Dissection of the Design

Construction of the Figure Harness

205

except in the cases of the first black and first
white headle, which are entered in groups of four.
It will be at once seen that if any one of the
headles be lifted, all the black, or, all the white
threads in two squares of the design, will be
raised; also that by raising two, three, four, or
five, or even six headles together various groups
of squares can be formed; in the last case—that is,
with six headles—solid black or solid white will be
lifted.

If this harness were made specially for this
pattern the leashes would only be hung on the
shafts of the headles in the places required for the
groups of threads. This is called spacing the harness. By thus spacing the leashes, not only is time
and thread saved in making the harness, but the
inconvenience of having unnecessary empty leashes
hanging about is avoided. This spacing of harnesses will often be referred to as we proceed in
the subject of pattern-weaving.

The Work
of the
Tabby
Harness in
Double-
cloth
Pattern-
weaving
It will be remembered that in making plain
double cloth with a tabby harness of four headles
one half of the warp was raised by two of the
headles, while the plain weaving was being done by
the other two. In the case of double-cloth pattern-
weaving this lifting out of the way is effected by
means of the figure harness, and the tabby harness
is only used for making the black and white plain
cloth in regular alternation.

The province of the figure harness is to form the
design *in large* without regard to the binding or
weaving it together. If only the figure harness
were used, the design would be formed, but the
threads of both warp and weft would only interlace

206

where the black takes the place of the white or the white that of the black.

By using two harnesses, one for the formation of the design and the other for the details of the weaving, the scope of pattern-weaving is immensely extended, and IT WAS BY THE DEVELOPMENT OF THIS TWO-HARNESS METHOD THAT THE MOST SPLENDID RESULTS OF THE WEAVER'S ART WERE ACHIEVED.

The plan, tie-up and treadling of the Indian design are given in fig. 90. An examination of these will show that only some portions of the black warp are raised above the surface at the one time, and the same thing occurs in regard to the white warp. Those portions remaining below, however, do not get woven into the tabby, because they are of the opposite colour to that which is at the moment being made. For example, when the black threads are some, right up, and some, down, the white cloth, is being woven by two headles of the tabby harness and in like manner when some white threads are held up by the figure harness, and some left down, the black plain cloth is being woven and cannot interfere with them.

It will be sufficient, in order to make the working quite clear, to analyse one line of the design as a key to the whole. In the first line, beginning at the left hand, three squares together are shown black, one white, one black, half a white, one black, one white, three black together, and half a white. In order to form this series of squares headles 1, 2, 3, and 5, entered with black thread, must be lifted. While these are held up the second headle of the front harness is raised, and one shoot

207

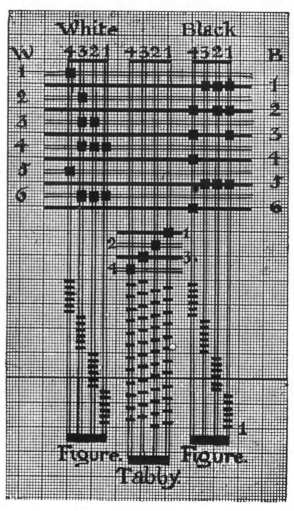

FIG. 90.—Plan of Tie-up.

of white weft thrown in.   This shoot being pressed close, the white figure headles 4 and 6 must be raised, and together with them the first tabby headle.   This being black must be shot with black weft.   The same black headles must again rise, but this time the fourth headle of the front harness must be raised with them, for the second shoot of white tabby. The same white figure headles again rise, and the third tabby headle makes an opening for the black weft.   After this order of proceeding has been repeated six or eight times, according to the size of the wefting, one line of squares will be woven. The upper and under surfaces of the cloth will be found to be exactly the same in design, but the colours will be reversed.

The first line of the pattern being complete, the second line will proceed as indicated in the plan, which need not be further described.

As will be gathered from the above, two shuttles must be used if the effect of clear black and white is desired.   If only one shuttle were used, the form of the design would be quite correct, but the colour of the weft would tinge the black and the white and modify them.

The treadles are shown in the plan and tie-up, arranged in three groups for the sake of clearness, but the weaver would no doubt rearrange them to suit his own convenience.   He would probably mix the white and black treadles up so as to bring the first white next to the first black, in order to work them with his toe and heel.   This rearrangement, however, will not affect the order of rising in the least if the tie-up be made correctly in accordance with it.

Another method of small-pattern weaving with two harnesses, by which what are known as damask effects are produced, is perhaps more generally useful than that for the weaving of double-cloth patterns. The material woven is also lighter and more perfect in texture. It owes its effect to the fact, already pointed out, that on one surface of a satin or twill web, the warp threads are for the most part exposed, and on the other surface the weft threads predominate (see Satin, p. 184). The result of this peculiarity is, that, if the weaving be arranged in such a manner as to bring both warp satin and weft satin, as the two surfaces may be called, together, side by side, in certain shapes, on the front of the material, the design so worked out will be quite distinct. This will be so, even if the warp and weft are of precisely the same size, colour, and material. This most subtle and charming of all effects of woven design results from the threads of warp and weft running, as they needs must, in contrary directions ; so that the light strikes and reflects differently on the different parts of the pattern, according as the vertical warp or lateral weft threads, most preponderate.

Fig. 91 is an example of a simple design which may be woven in the damask manner—that is, by means of two harnesses, one for raising the figure, or design, and the other for making the ground. The ground harness must be fitted up with leashes having long eyes, the same as in double-cloth pattern-weaving. The entering of the figure harness is shown above the design. The harness must have eight headles and four threads must be entered in each leash. This is indicated, in the sketch of the entering, by the filling in of four small squares to each entry (A, fig. 91). The entering of both harnesses would probably be done at once, the hook being passed through the eye of the leash of the ground

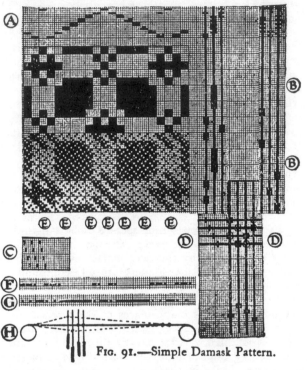

Fig. 91.—Simple Damask Pattern.

harness first, and then through the eye of the figure harness. If entered singly, the cross must be preserved by drawing the threads over and under a rod, alternately. Only six treadles are required for

211

working the figure harness to form the whole design, although it consists of sixteen lines in the one repeat. This is possible because one line is used six times over, one four times, and three lines twice in the one repeat.   The sequence in which the treadles are to be depressed for weaving the pattern is indicated by the black oblongs, placed on the treadle lines at B, and level with the spaces with which they agree. If it were woven with this harness alone, the white warp and black weft would only intersect at the places where the black shapes join the white ones, as shown in the upper half of the drawing.   The white spaces would simply consist of long loops of warp threads, and the black spaces of loops of weft.   In the lower half of the drawing a broken twill tie is represented binding the loose loops of warp and weft together.   In the case of damasks the threads of the weft satin (see black spaces in drawing) are tied down by the warp threads crossing them at regular intervals (see white spots on black figure), and the threads of the warp satin (white spaces in design) are bound by the occasional crossing of the black weft (see black binders on white ground). This effect is the same both on the back and the front of the material, except that the white spaces of one side will be the black spaces of the reverse.   It must now be carefully explained how this ingenious result is obtained.   After passing through the figure harness, in groups of four, the warp threads have to be entered singly in the long-eyed ground harness. As the tie, in this case is a broken, four-headle twill (p. 168), this harness must consist of four headles. The ordinary entering of the warp in the ground harness, is shown below the design at C.   This harness will require four treadles, and these would be placed in a group between the six treadles of the figure harness. They are so shown in the plan, D, D. The twill tie-up and order of treading are also there given. In this case the usual order of working the treadles for the twill ground may be departed from, because the weaver will only have one foot to spare for the ground, as the other foot will be occupied in treading and holding down the figure treadles. We have already noted the effect of weaving with the figure harness only. If in like manner we now use the ground harness by itself, the web will be a plain satin. The front, or under surface, will be like the white spaces in the design, warp satin with black weft ties. The back or upper surface will be just the reverse, being black weft satin with white warp ties.

Having now a clear idea of the effect of the two harnesses when used separately, and all being ready, let us suppose that the weaver places his left foot on the first treadle of the ground harness. This will raise the first of every four threads of the whole warp. If now, still holding the ground harness treadle down, the first figure harness treadle be depressed with the right foot, groups of threads will be seen to rise, similar to the black spaces E, E, E of the first line of the design, but more correctly shown at the line F, which represents the back or upper side of the web, whilst G gives the reverse or under side. The line G should correspond with the drawing, but it will be seen that it does not quite do so. The white ties are missing from the black spaces, although the black ties are to be seen on the white ground. At F, on the

213

contrary, the white ties are in their places on the black portions, but there are no ties on the white spaces. In order to rectify this omission and complete the damask fit-up of the loom, the ground harness must be furnished with the shedding motion similar to 85A, so as to cause the missing binder threads to sink, and be held down at the same time as the others rise. The counter-marches, or short levers, to which the lower shafts of the treadles are tied must be exactly the same as at fig. 85A. The connection with the treadles, however, must in this case be somewhat different, as what we now require is to sink and hold down, only one thread out of the three stationary ones left, when one is raised as we

Rising and
Sinking
Shed with
Stationary
Bottom
necessary
for Ground
Harness

have seen it. The shed now wanted is represented at H, fig. 91, where the dotted lines show the rising and sinking threads and the thick line the stationary bottom. We must therefore tie up treadle 1, to the short lever connected with the lower shaft of the first headle. The second treadle must be connected with the fourth headle, the third treadle with the second headle, and the fourth treadle with the third headle. This second tie-up for the sinking headles may be shown on the tie-up plan by circles, to distinguish it from the first or rising tie-up, indicated by crosses. The new arrangement being complete, if another trial be made it will be found that the sinking threads will make the required ties both for the warp and weft satins.

Contrary
Action of
the Two
Harnesses
further
explained

In order to make this contrary action of the two harnesses quite clear fig. 92 is perhaps necessary. It is a most important point, and must be perfectly understood, for, simple as it may appear to be, on it the whole system of damask-weaving depends.

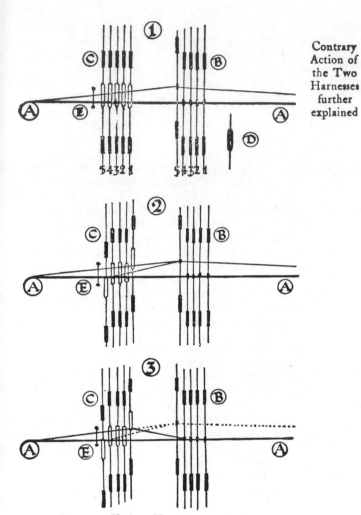

Contrary
Action of
the Two
Harnesses
further
explained

FIG. 92.—Various Two-harness Sheds.

Further
Description
of Shed-
making for
Damask
Patterns

In no. 1 of this figure the warp, represented
by the thick horizontal line AA, is seen to pass
through a figure harness (B) of five headles having
short-eyed leashes.   The entering in this harness
may be of any reasonable number of threads ; for
this instance let it be four ; and if it be deemed
desirable to keep the threads separate, although this
is not essential, the figure harness leash eyes may
consist of mails having four holes, as shown in the
enlargement at D.   Beneath letter C the ground
harness is shown, also consisting of five headles, but
these have long-eyed leashes.   Between this harness
and letter A on the left, a shed, E, is shown opened
by the rising of the fifth headle of the figure harness.
The rising of this headle has lifted four threads
together ; these are represented by the line drawn
from the eye of the raised headle to the letters A, A.
Although each of these five threads may pass through
the eye of one of the five ground harness headles C,
the latter will not be affected by them because of their
long eyes.   This allows for the formation of the
design without ties, as described at p. 212.   At
no. 2 the same line of warp, AA, and the same
harnesses, B and C, are depicted.   In this case,
however, the shed is much more complicated.   The
fifth headle of the figure harness is still up, but its
line of our threads is divided.   The thread passing
from it through the fifth headle of the ground
harness is not allowed to rise, as it is held down
by the sinking of the headle.   The effect on the
front of the web of this contrary action is similar to
that shown at G, fig. 91.   At F, in the same figure
is the back of the web as it would appear to the
weaver, providing the warp were white and the

weft black. Although one of the lifted threads passes through the first headle of the ground harness, it is not affected by its rising, as it is already up, so that it does not have any influence on the portion of the design raised by the figure harness headle. No. 3 will explain the action of the first headle (shown raised) of the ground harness on the parts of the warp not raised for the figure. Here the holding down of headle 5 will have no effect, as all the threads of the figure harness are down as well, but the first headle being up, will tie the figure at the back and at the front as at E, E, fig. 91. The dotted lines between the two harnesses are not really essential in no. 3, but are merely put in to make easier the comparison between nos. 2 and 3.

The great scope given to pattern-weaving by means of the above ingenious invention will now be realised. It will also be understood, from the foregoing examples, that all the most astonishing developments, to be seen in the more or less modern ornamental textile fabrics, are based on this principle whether they be woven by hand or by power, on the draw-loom of the seventeenth and eighteenth centuries, or by means of the Jacquard machine and appliances of the nineteenth century.

It has already been shown that the tabby selvage of a satin web will use up a greater length of warp than the body of the material, and that this is due to the fact that in tabby weaving there are more intersections of the warp and weft than there are in satin-weaving. The same thing occurs sometimes in a pattern web. A large space or stripe of satin, running longitudinally in the web, would, on account of this difficulty, require special consideration.

217

For example, let us examine fig. 93. Here we have a stripe of satin in a tabby ground. This pattern would be woven on eight headles, entered

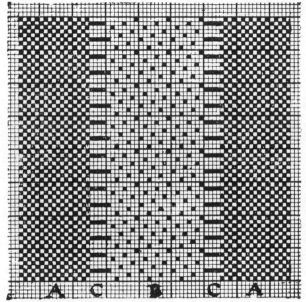

Fig. 93.—Stripe of Satin and Tabby Ground.

and tied up to eight treadles. If only one warp were used for this web, it would soon be found, that the tabby woven portion of the warp would begin to get tighter than the satin stripe, and ere long the difference would be so great that the weaving could not proceed. This inconvenience can be obviated by the use of a separate roller for the warp of the satin

218

stripe. This second roller would be fixed either above or below the one for the tabby ground. It would also be weighted separately from it. By this means the take-up of the two warps would be rendered quite independent one of the other. In making the two warps, the whole number of threads in the collection of satin stripes would be counted and warped together, and the same would be done for the tabby ground. In turning on to the rollers, the satin stripes would have to be set out and wound on in their proper places on the one ; and on the other, corresponding spaces left vacant for them. This being done, the two warps could be entered in the harness and reed as one. Very often in fancy weaving, especially when there is brocading, a separate binder is required, and it is generally necessary to have the warp for it wound on to a separate roller. This will be explained later on in the book, when the subject of *brocatelle* and other *tissue* webs, as they are called, is dealt with.

Plain velvet-weaving requires the use of two warps on separate rollers, while figured velvet needs for its production the use of many warps for the pile, sometimes to the extent of needing a separate warp roller or bobbin for each group of threads in the repeat of a design, and there are sometimes as many as four, or even eight hundred, of these tiny warps arranged in a figured-velvet loom.

For plain velvet-weaving, the two warps required are, one for the groundwork, which may be an ordinary tabby, twill, or satin, and one for the pile. The difference in the take-up of these two warps is astonishing, the pile warp having to be made at least six times the length of that for the ground. In order to make one yard of velvet, the ground will take up about one and one-sixteenth of a yard of warp, but for the pile, not less than seven yards will be required. The reason of this enormous take-up of the pile warp, in velvet, is owing to the method of weaving peculiar to this sumptuous material. Velvet-weaving also requires the use of two harnesses, and the two warps are each entered in the harnesses

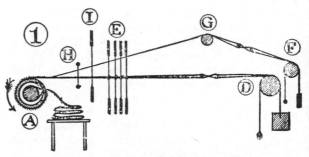

Fig. 94.—Section of Velvet Loom.

independently. Fig. 94 will assist in the explanation of the arrangement.

The Velvet
Breast Roller

In fig. 94 A is the breast roller, a section of which, so enlarged as to show its details of construction, is given on the next page (fig. 94A). This construction of the roller is necessary because the cut pile surface of the velvet cannot be wound and pressed on the roller without injury, as other materials may be. The roller is hollow, and generally much larger in circumference than ordinary breast rollers. It has a wide, hinged lid, running its entire length, so shaped on the outside as not to interfere with its cylindrical form when the lid is closed (fig. 94A, D). The edge of the lid is cut away and carefully rounded in the centre, so as to leave, when it is shut, a narrow opening wide enough for the velvet to pass in and out again, without crushing the pile together. Inside the roller, which must be perfectly smooth, a second roller, B, is fitted in such a manner,

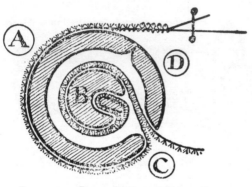

FIG. 94A.—Breast Roller of Velvet Loom.

that the velvet, after entering at the narrow opening C, fig. 94A, may pass round it and out again in the same opening. The inner roller has a wide and deep groove in it, and is covered with some material to which the velvet clings, so that very little pressure by a lath in the groove, is sufficient to prevent its slipping. This, together with the slightly rounded edge of the narrow opening, holds the velvet tight enough to allow for the strain of weaving.*

* When the inner roll is covered with the velvet it is prevented from turning by pins or buttons at the ends.

The Velvet Breast Roller As soon as enough velvet has been made to allow of passing it round the inner roller, the lid is opened, and after the end of the velvet is in the right position it is closed, fastened down, and the weaving proceeds. When the narrow opening in the roller, C, nearly reaches the under surface of the velvet, the work is loosed, the roller moved round, the lid

FIG. 94B.—Velvet Roller with Lid Open.

opened, and the velvet, being separated from the small roller, is drawn round it and carried under the loom, to be hung on a rack, or gently laid in loose folds on a low shelf placed conveniently to receive it (see fig. 94). The greatest care has to be taken to keep the material straight and true while it is being thus moved along. As the roller is about ten or twelve inches in circumference, it will be seen that about one yard can be made between every shift. One yard of fine velvet is about a day's work for a good weaver, so that this operation of moving the

222

web does not hinder the weaving to any great extent.

The Velvet Breast Roller

Referring again to fig. 94, D is the roller for the ground warp. This warp is indicated by the strong line passing from D to A. E are the headles of the ground harness ; four are shown here, but the harness may consist of any number of headles required to make the ground tabby, twill, or satin, as the case may be. F is the roller for pile or *pole* warp, as it is often called. This is usually placed above the ground roller, and is very lightly weighted. Sometimes the roller itself is fixed very high in the loom, but more generally a second small roller, G, is fitted high up, at about the centre of the loom, and over this the warp passes as in the diagram. This arrangement is made in order to keep the two warps as separate as possible, and is placed by the weaver himself so as to suit his own peculiar method of work. The line drawn from the roller F over G through the headle I and the reed H to join the ground warp, near the roller A, is the pile warp. Only one headle, I, is shown, and it may be that only one is necessary, as for plain velvet, with one pile warp, the pile threads all rise or sink together If, however, the pile is too rich to be all entered in one headle, two or more may be required. The pile harness is hung as near to the reed as the working of the batten will allow.

The Warps for Velvet-weaving

The Ground Warp

The Pile Warp

As regards the warps themselves, the ground warp is by far the richer, the number of threads in it being usually three or four times as great as that of the pile. All the other fittings of the loom for weaving velvet are the same as those for the ordinary hand-woven materials.

Proportion of the Warps

223

The special fittings of the loom for velvet-weaving
being now all described, the actual process claims
our consideration. Everything being, so far, in
order, the weaver would begin by making a few
inches of the ground, raising and depressing the pile
harness, in regular order, as may be indicated in the
plan. The pile thus woven in, has little visible
effect on the ground, especially if the latter be a rich
satin. It will only give a slight, lateral, ribbed appearance to the material, and thicken the ground to
a certain extent. When all is working properly
the pile is raised by itself, and its raising forms a shed
in front of the reed. Into this the weaver, instead
of weft, inserts a finely made, smooth, flat brass wire,
called a *velvet rod*. This rod has a fine groove cut
in one edge, which, when the rod is placed in the
shed, should be on top. It is held by the weaver
until the next shoot of ground is made with the pile
down ; this will fix it in position. Two or three
ground shoots are then made, the pile rising and
falling between them as may be arranged by the
designer ; this binds the pile to the ground more or
less securely. After these few shoots of ground, the
pile is again raised by itself and another rod inserted,
being followed up in the same manner. When five
or six rods are thus woven in, the most delicate
operation of velvet-weaving begins, viz., the cutting
of the pile. This is effected by the weaver, with a
tool called a *trevette*, in which a fine, sharp, peculiar-
shaped blade is most accurately fitted. The necessary perfection and accuracy of this tool, according to
some authorities, gave rise to the proverb "As right
as a trevette," and the suggestion seems quite reasonable. A drawing of this implement is given at fig. 95.

It is taken from a trevette of the simplest construction, and is therefore of the kind which in skilful hands is capable of the nicest adjustment. The trevette is made in two parts, the upper part, which carries the knife, shown open at no. 1, being hinged to one end of the lower part, and grooved at its bottom edge so as to fit quite firmly on to one side of it

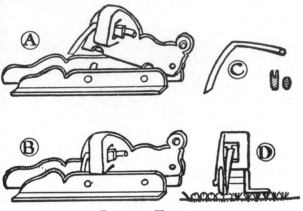

FIG. 95.—Trevette.

when the instrument is closed for use, as at letter B and at letter D, where the end view is given. The knife, C, is shown at A fixed in the strong staple, by small hardwood or metal wedges, and it is in the adjusting of the knife with these, and keeping it sharp, that a great deal of the art of velvet-weaving consists. It is for the purpose of adjusting and sharpening the knife that the two parts of the trevette are hinged together. When closed, ready for work, the knife is so placed that its sharp end is very near to the

225

inner edge of the straight steel side of the lower part of the tool. This may be seen in the end view, D. The brass front of the lower part, letter B, is for the purpose of steadying the instrument when in use.

We must now return to the loom, where we left the first rod ready to be cut out of the pile. The weaver, taking in his right hand the trevette, rests it on the left-hand side of the web in such a position, that, the sharp edge of the knife fits into the groove of the *first* rod woven into it. Making sure that it is rightly placed, by a firm, steady, rapid movement, he draws the trevette right across the web to the other side, and, if the knife be sharp and has been kept in place, the rod will spring out and the line of pile will stand up, like a row of delicate little, silk brushes in its place. Having cut out the first rod successfully, the pile shed is again opened and the cut-out rod inserted, ground is woven as before and the second rod cut out, and so on in regular succession. As may be imagined, great care has to be exercised in cutting out the rods, as an unfortunate slip may result in cutting out more or less of the ground warp, which is most disastrous. If properly cut, the velvet made by hand should require but very little finishing when out of the loom, beyond what the weaver himself can do.

Terry velvet is simply velvet woven in the above manner, but uncut in the pile. Smooth, grooveless wires are used in this case, and when half a dozen have been woven in, instead of being cut out the rod is drawn out from the same end at which it was inserted.

Velvets, woven and cut by hand in this ancient

226

manner and made of good silk throughout are un-
equalled, both for texture and durability, by any imitations that can be produced by modern means. A
comparison of the many specimens of ancient velvets,
with the most perfect and ingenious productions
of the power-loom, will verify this statement.
Power-loom imitations smoothly shaved and highly
finished present a hard, inartistic, shining surface
when thus compared with the rich, glowing and
slightly varied texture of hand-loom woven velvets,
either of mediæval or modern times.

With regard to small-pattern weaving in velvet,
a great deal might be done by quite simple means,
such as varying the colour of the pile warp, or
spacing it out so as only to come up in spots or
lines, vertical or lateral. The use of terry and cut
pile in the same pattern is also quite easy to produce. Many of the ordinary small designs, too,
could be made in velvet quite readily if the pile
were entered in a harness which would lift it in the
separate portions required, and the warp were distributed over the requisite number of warp rolls.
The necessary arrangements for small velvet patterns will, however, be better understood when the
description of figured-velvet weaving, which will be
found in Part III. of this book, has been read.

The edges of stripes in striped materials such as that
shown at fig. 93, p. 218, and taborettes, as well as the
grounds of rich brocades, are often decorated with
little squares, oblongs, or lines, composed of warp
threads floating over two or more shoots of ground
weft and dipping below it at regular intervals. These
form bright edges and embellishments, and often
have a very pleasing effect. This simple kind of

227

ornamentation is called *tobine*, and requires a separate warp spaced out and entered in one headle, in the same manner as a velvet pile warp. Fig. 96 is a ruled-paper drawing of a taborette stripe, and will

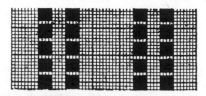

Fig. 96.—Tobine Stripes.

sufficiently explain the method of introducing the tobine edges. Plate ix is a good example of the use of tobine stripes, which, being graduated in colours, form the sole but very effective ornamentation of a seventeenth-century silk.

CHAPTER XV

AUTOMATIC MACHINES FOR SHEDDING MOTIONS

Automatic Shedding Motions and their Use—
Disadvantages of the Jacquard Machine for Home
Weaving—Comparison of it with Simpler Machines
—The Jack-in-the-box—Its Inventor—Character
of Old Hand-loom Weavers—Tie-up and Working
of the Jack-in-the-box—The Drawboy Machine,
its Details and Use—Examples of Pattern-weaving
with Drawboy.

IT now becomes necessary to describe two ingenious automatic contrivances, by means of which the inconvenience of managing a large number or treadles, required for lifting the headles in the formation of some patterns, may be obviated to a great extent. At the present time the ingenious invention, the Jacquard, and the various machines made on the same principle, have taken the place of all other automatic machines for pattern-weaving. But the Jacquard machine, although admirable in its capacity and adaptability, has certain disadvantages for hand-looms, especially if these be in a private house, a small workshop or a studio. Not the least of these disadvantages is that the Jacquard machine requires the constant attention of a skilled

machinist to keep it in working order. It also requires to be continually in use. For the weaving
of simple designs, therefore, on an isolated hand-
loom, the less delicate and complicated machines,
invented by weavers themselves for the purpose of
simplifying the shedding of the loom, are preferable.
They have the advantage, too, that the weaver himself
can repair and keep them in order, as, like the loom,
they are chiefly made of wood and string. They
are also less heavy and noisy in working than the
Jacquard machine, and, being placed by the side of
the loom instead of at the top, no extraordinary
height is required in the place where they are set

up. For rapid commercial work in a factory, where
a great number of looms are set up and in constant
use, the Jacquard machines are, of course, superior
and offer many advantages, but it can be readily
understood that different qualities are desirable in a
machine for home weaving.

The two machines we have to examine are the
Jack-in-the-box, or Jennings shedding motion, and
the *Drawboy* machine, which latter was intended
for drawing the cords of the draw-loom, but was
found to be equally useful for drawing up any
number or combination of headles required for
small-pattern weaving.

The Jack-in-the-box was chiefly used for making
rich satins and very small figures. For this purpose
many hand-loom weavers prefer it to a small Jacquard
machine, it being so perfectly reliable in its action.

It was invented about 1840 by a working silk-
weaver of Bethnal Green named Theodore Jennings;
and it is interesting to notice, by the way, how many
of the valuable inventions of weaving appliances in

the old days were made by the actual workers, who not only understood the working of the loom when al! was prepared for weaving, but could build harnesses, contrive alterations of design and methods of working, tie up new patterns, and do all the necessary preparation of the loom, themselves. This required for its accomplishment much judgment and skill, and we find that many of the old hand-loom weavers possessed these qualities to a very great extent. Some of them, indeed, were quite famous in their day, not only for weaving, but in various branches of science. Mathematical, entomological, botanical, and other clubs were common amongst them, and several were corresponding members of the learned scientific societies of the eighteenth and early nineteenth centuries.

In Chapter XIII., where the typical shedding motions are described, it was pointed out, that as many treadles were required as there were headles or groups of headles to be raised in succession to form any particular pattern. In an eight-headle satin, for instance, the eight headles required eight treadles to raise them in the following order : 1, 4, 7, 2, 5, 8, 3, 6. The Jack-in-the-box provides the means for raising any number of headles in any sequence by the use alternately of two treadles only.

Fig. 97 is a general view of the shedding motion of the loom, with this simple machine in its relative position to the treadles and headles. Fig. 98 gives the details and construction of the various parts. Fig. 98, no. 1, AA, is a strong oblong wooden box, without back or front, set on end and perforated at the top end with two rows of holes,

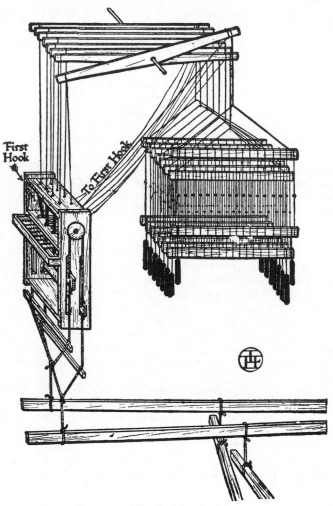

First
Hook

To First Hook.

FIG. 97.—The Jack-in-the-box.

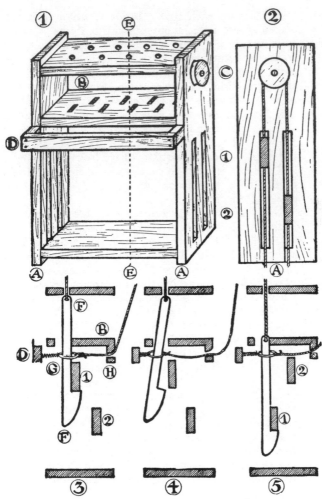

FIG. 98.—Details of the Jack-in-the-box.

Description
of the Jack-
in-the-box
four holes in each row. Inside it has a shelf, B, placed across it, at about one-third of the distance from the top to the bottom ends. This shelf has transverse slots cut in it, to correspond with the eight holes with which the top is pierced. These transverse slots are cut in such a position, that one of the top holes is over the centre of each slot. The box has also two long slots cut in each of its sides, and above these pulleys are fixed. One of these is shown in the drawing and marked C. Just below the shelf, in front, a bar, D, is fixed from side to side, and this bar is made to stand an inch or two in front of the box, by means of two short arms which project from its sides.

No. 2 shows an elevation of one side of the box. Both sides being exactly alike, the description of one will suffice. Here we have again the two long slots and the pulley C. In addition to these, the elevation shows the sections of two, long bars, numbered 1 and 2, which are fitted to the slots and are long enough to reach from side to side of the box, and, after passing through the slots, to project not less than three inches beyond them. To the top of one bar a strong cord is tied, carried over the pulley C, and then fixed to the other bar. The cord is of such a length, that when one bar is near the top of its slot, the other bar will be at the bottom of the other slot. Two other cords are fastened to the bottom edges of the two bars, and connect them with the two treadles of the loom in a manner which will presently be explained. It will now be perceived that when one bar is pulled down, the other must rise and reverse the position shown in the drawing. Also, that, by working the two treadles, with which

234

they are connected, this action of the bars can be repeated in alternation.

Nos. 3, 4, and 5 represent a section of the box no. 1, taken at the place indicated by the dotted line EE. The parts which will be recognised severally are : (1) the bottom board of the box ; (2) the top board pierced with holes, one of which appears in the section ; (3) the shelf, with one of the transverse slots shown ; (4) the front bar attached to the sides of the box; and (5) the two sliding bars. In this figure three new and important features are shown : (1) The large hook FF, made of hard wood and suspended from a cord passing through the hole in the top board. The hook itself hangs through the corresponding transverse slot in the shelf, and when held in the position shown, is caught by the bottom edge of the sliding bar 1, which is represented up. A metal ring, placed just below the slot, is connected with the front bar D by a strong piece of elastic, or wire spring, G. The ring encircles the hook F, and would pull the hook towards the bar D were it not held, in its present position, by the tight cord tied to it, which passes through the perforated narrow board H. This board is fixed to the back edge of the shelf B. The position of the hook set free by the slackening of the cord is shown in No. 4.

In order to complete the machine it must be fitted up with eight hooks, springs, rings, and cords. A greater number of hooks can be used, and the capacity of the machine much enlarged, but the details of the construction would remain the same in any case.

Turning back to fig. 97, where the Jack-in-the-

Description
of the Jack-
in-the-box
box is shown fitted in the loom, the eight headles suspended from the eight levers, will be recognised as similar to those seen in the illustration of the shedding motions in Chapter XIII. The cords, however, which in those passed down from the ends of the levers and were fastened to the ends of the long marches, are now seen to pass into the box and terminate in the hooks hanging there. In this case only two long marches and two treadles are needed, instead of as many of each as there are headles in the harness. The long marches are connected with the two rising and falling bars, whose ends project from the side slots in the box.

The machine itself is now complete, and, if the treadles of the loom are worked alternately the result will be, that, the two sliding bars will rise and fall regularly, but nothing else will happen, as the hooks at present are all held back by the rings and springs as at No. 4, fig. 98.

Tie-up of
the Jack-in-
the-box
The tie-up to the headles, in accordance with the design, must next be effected. From the ends of the levers, just above the headless, even loose cords and one tight one are seen to pass into the back of the box, and it is by means of these cords that the tie-up is made. As the tie-up has to be made with very great nicety, all the strings must have adjustable loops, as well as the cords by which the hooks are suspended.

Although any tie-up can be arranged for, it will be best, for the purpose of illustration, to take the simplest one possible, which is that for an eight-headle twill. For the formation of this, the headles will have to rise in regular succession from back to front. The cord from the first or back lever, therefore, must be tied to the ring of the second hook, which is the *first* in the back row of hooks. The second lever cord must be tied to the third ring, the third lever to the fourth ring, and so on till the last lever is reached. This cord must cross over and be tied to the first ring in the box. Now if the cords are all of the proper length—which can only be ascertained by experiment—the result of drawing down any one of the hooks will be that the lever to which it is suspended will be drawn down with it, and its other end, to which the headle is suspended, will be raised, raising the headle with it. The lever rising will also tighten the cord which is connected with the ring of the next hook to be drawn down and pull it forward, so that it catches on the sliding bar, which is at present up. When this bar is drawn down by the treadle, it carries the hook down with it ; this raises the headle and draws forward the next hook, and so they all follow, in succession, till the last is reached, which, being connected with the first ring, draws it forward, and the same course is repeated again and again. All that is now required to start the motion, is, for any one of the hooks to be placed under the sliding bar and drawn down by one of the treadles ; all the others will then follow in proper order if the tie-up be correct. The tie-up always has to be arranged so that each succeeding hook is in the opposite row, in order that it may be drawn down by the alternating bar. This can always be provided for by altering the tie-up of the hooks to the levers above the box, if it cannot be done without.

The action of this little machine, especially when

Tie-up of
the Jack-in
the-box

237

Working
the Jack-
in-the-box

The
Drawboy
Machine

used for the weaving of light webs, such as twills and satins, is most neat, cheerful, quiet, and altogether admirable.

The *Draw-boy machine* is of much greater capacity than the Jack-in-the-box, and more adapted for heavy and complicated work. Any number of headles or cords, singly or in groups, up to as many as four hundred or more, can be managed by its means, and only two treadles are required to keep it in motion. It was originally intended for use with the draw-loom, in place of the boy employed by the weaver to draw the cords necessary for the successive lines of the design, as will be explained later on. It was, however, soon adopted for the purpose of drawing the complicated systems and sets of headles for pattern-weaving, which had till then been drawn by a large number of treadles, brought in and out of action by various levers and cords. It is said that "when introduced in Spitalfields the weavers hoped to reap great advantage from them ; for instance, they would save the draw-boy's wages. But they began to find that they had adopted a mistaken notion. They found that if they had not to pay the draw-boy they had to pay the manufacturers for the use of the machine, and, moreover, the work itself was heavier." The complaint that the work was harder would refer only to the draw-loom, as the simple management of two treadles must be much easier and lighter than that of twenty.

Fig. 99 is a representation of a drawboy machine. It is shown attached to a set of cords, A. These cords may, in their turn, be connected with any system or sets of headles. Twenty cords are shown, but there might be any number attached, the number of headles only being limited by the space in the loom where they could hang and be efficient

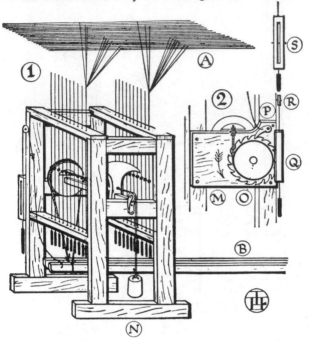

Fig. 99.—The Drawboy Machine.

for opening the shed.   The machine is worked by the long marches of the loom, B, which, in their turn, are governed by the two treadles.

Fig. 100 gives all the parts of the machine in

239

detail. No. 1 is the framework, which consists of four strong wooden uprights, about two feet six inches long, D, D, D, D. These are set firmly in

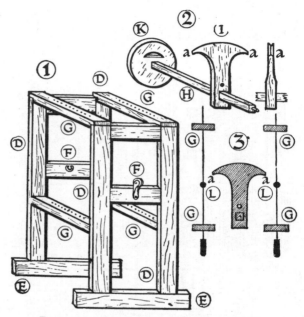

Fig. 100.—Details of the Drawboy Machine.

pairs on two cross-pieces, E, E, which are screwed to the ground at the side of the loom near the front and about two feet apart. Each pair of uprights is joined together at the top by a strong cross-piece, and there are also cross-pieces, F, F, just above the centre. In these centre cross-pieces, on the insides,

240

there are sockets, made to hold the end pins of a rocking shaft, which when placed in them reaches from one end of the frame to the other. On the centre of the outside of the cross-piece F, at the end shown in the drawing, a pulley may be seen raised a little above its top edge. The two pairs of uprights are joined together by four side cross-pieces ; G, G, G, G. Two of these are fixed at the top and two at the sides a little lower than the end centre cross-pieces F, F. The cross-pieces G are made of hard wood, and have a number of holes (in this case ten in each) accurately and smoothly drilled in them, not more than an inch apart, The row of holes must begin and end about six inches from the four uprights.

At H, no. 2, a rocking shaft is shown, which fits into the sockets on the inside of the cross-pieces F, F. The shaft is made of hard wood, and must be exactly the same size, and perfectly square from one end to the other, so that the pecker, I, when fitted on it, may be made to slide easily backward and forward along its whole length. At one end of the rocking shaft a large, strong, deep-grooved pulley, K, is firmly fixed. Through the pulley a segmental hole is cut, just above the centre, where the shaft joins it.

The pecker, I, no. 2, shown in position on the shaft and in side elevation on the right, is also generally made of hard wood, although sometimes partly of metal. The points a, a, and the top edge, have a deep but narrow groove cut in them, just large enough to allow a fair-sized cord to slip in them. The pecker has also a hole pierced through it, just above the shaft, as well as the square hole through

The Pecker which the shaft itself passes. When the rocking shaft is in its place (see fig. 99) the pulley K is near the end of the shaft towards the back of the loom. In the groove of this pulley a strong cord is placed, its ends being tied separately to each of the two long marches of the loom, B, which are made long enough to enter the frame beneath the end of the shaft where the pulley K is fixed.

The Cords No. 3, fig. 100, shows a section of the machine, with the pecker, also in section, in position. G, G, G, G are the perforated side cross-pieces; the pecker is seen mounted on the rocking shaft; L, L are two, of twenty cords, having weights at their ends which are seen, in fig. 99, to hang in the holes of the side cross-pieces, a row of ten being on each side of the machine. Near the points of the pecker, a, a, a hard knot, or bead, is so placed, that, when the rocking shaft is set in motion by the long marches being pulled down alternately, the pecker will rock from side to side, and, catching the cords in the groove at its points just above the beads, will pull the cords downwards, first on one side, and then on the other. It will now be seen that if the pecker be caused to slide along the bar, rocking as it goes, its movement being properly regulated, as it comes opposite to each pair of cords, they will be pulled down as described, and that by the time the pecker has passed the twenty cords, they will all have been pulled down in regular succession. If then the side cords of the drawboy machine are tied up to a set of twenty headles, the latter may be caused to rise in any grouping and sequence desired.

In order to complete the description of the draw-

242

boy machine, it only remains to explain the means
by which the pecker is caused to travel along the
rocking shaft. No. 2, fig. 99, represents the back
end of the machine where the pecker motion is
placed.

M is a strong board firmly screwed to the
uprights. Above the board, between the uprights,
a part of the pulley of the rocking shaft, with its
segmental hole, may be seen. Opposite the centre
of the hole, and projecting a little from the board,
to the top edge of which it is fixed, a small metal
pulley matches the pulley at the other end of the
machine above letter F, fig. 100. Over the pulley
F in fig. 99 a cord with a weight, N, attached to
it is seen to pass, through the pecker, and along the
shaft to the segmental hole in the large pulley, where
it disappears. Turning to no. 2, the same cord,
coming through the hole in the rocking shaft pulley
and passing over the small pulley on the edge of the
board, is seen to be attached to another large pulley,
which is riveted to a ratchet wheel. The combined
ratchet wheel and pulley turn loose on their axle,
which is a stud strongly bolted to the board M.
Now, if the ratchet wheel be turned in the direction
of the arrow, the cord will be wound on to the
large pulley and drawn through the hole, drawing
with it the pecker along the rocking shaft, past each
pair of cords, until it reaches a stop, fixed on the
shaft near the rocking shaft pulley. Also, if the
distance between the beaded cords, be made equal
to the teeth of the ratchet wheel, the pecker as it
travels along the shaft will stop between each pair of
drawing cords, and, as it rocks, pull them down first
on one side, and then on the other. When the

243

pecker has drawn all the cords, if the ratchet-pulley be released, the weight N, fig. 99, will bring the pecker back to its original position in the machine.

The ratchet wheel itself is governed by means of two catches, P and Q. The catch P, is to prevent the ratchet wheel turning back before the pecker has finished its course. The other catch, Q, is to move it gradually, one tooth at a time. The catch P has a thin cord attached to it, which may easily be guided by pulleys to the front of the loom and enable the weaver to release the ratchet at the completion of one repeat of the pattern. This, of course, coincides with the pecker's arrival at the stop on the rocking shaft. The catch Q, which moves the ratchet, is connected with one of the marches by the cord which passes over the pulley R, and its length is so regulated as to raise the catch just enough to move the ratchet one tooth at a time, or as may be desired. The mechanism of the catch Q, is shown above no. 2. It is simply a piece of hard wood having a long slot, into which the ratchet wheel partially enters. It is so hung that the pin S, will be, when the catch is at rest, just underneath one of the teeth, and as the catch is raised by the cord attached to the march, it will move the wheel, which, when moved, is prevented from returning, as the catch Q falls, by the second catch, P.

Any of the designs previously given could be woven with two treadles if the drawboy machine were used. Fig. 101 is, however, an example of the kind of design for which it is specially adapted, and the way of tying it up to the cords is shown

244

above the machine (fig. 99).* This design might
be woven in various ways, but it will only be
necessary to give two of the most useful workings
as specimens.

Utility
of the
Drawboy
Machine

Examples
of the Use
of the
Drawboy
Machine

(1) The warp might be fine cotton or linen,
entered in the back or figure harness in the order
shown above the design, two threads being entered
together in each headle eye for each square of the
drawing. If in the reed there were forty threads
to an inch, the woven design would be about twice
the size of the drawing. The kind of weaving
suggested in this case would have the same effect
as that described at p. 176, fig. 80, being a tabby
ground with a floating figure woven by alternate
shoots with two shuttles. In addition to the figure
harness, a ground harness having long eyes must
be used. It would be advisable to make it of eight
headles, as such a harness would be most generally
useful, and it could just as well be used with only
two treadles as a harness of smaller capacity.

The warp would be entered in the front harness
singly, in regular order, and the eight headles would
be tied up to the two treadles in the usual way
(see fig. 71, no. 1, p. 166).

The length of the design would be regulated by
the number of times the depression of each treadle
was repeated. Probably two treads for each line
of the design would be sufficient, but this depends

* The tie-up of two lines of the design to two draw-
cords of the drawboy only are shown (fig. 99, p. 239).
There would, of course, be a much greater space between the top of the draw-cords and the headle cords
than it is possible to show in the limited space at
disposal.

entirely on the size of the warp and weft used in the weaving. Either a fine coloured, tussah silk or

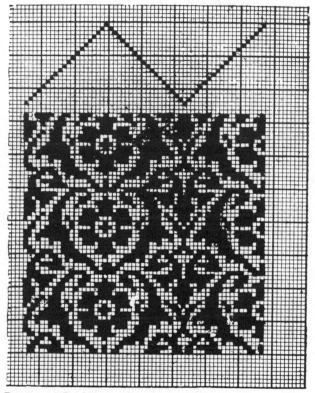

FIG 101.—Design for Floating Figure on Tabby Ground.

fine wool, would be a very suitable weft for the pattern shoot of this material.

246

(2) This would be a very suitable design for a
fine silk damask, the arrangements for which would
be as follows.   The headles would have to have
eyes or mails of glass, with separate holes for eight or
ten threads to be entered in.   (See fig. 92, letter D).
These eight or ten threads are represented in the
drawing by one small square of the ruled paper.
The headles, too, would of course be spaced, so that
leashes were only placed on the shafts where required (see top of fig. 101).   In addition to the
twenty pattern headles, a front or ground harness of
eight headles with long eyes will be required, in
which the fine silk threads must all be separately
entered.   The number of leashes to the inch must
agree exactly with the spacing of the figure harness.
It is not necessary that the number of threads lifted
by each mail of the figure harness should agree
with the number of headles in the ground harness,
but only that the whole number of threads must be
entered evenly and come out to the same total width
in both.   The satin made on eight headles may
either be eight-headle satin or four-headle broken
twill.   In the latter case it would only require four
treadles for the ground harness, but in order to
make a fine, rich-looking damask, eight-headle satin,
requiring eight treadles, must be used.   The method
of tying the treadles up for the satin has already been
explained in the chapter devoted to their consideration, and that of damask-weaving in connection with
fig. 91, p. 211.
  In damask-weaving it is not necessary to drop the
pattern headles between each shoot of the ground
weft.   The two treadles of the drawboy machine
can therefore have a hook near them screwed in the

247

Examples
of the Use
of the
Drawboy
Machine

floor, which will allow of their being conveniently held down, while the necessary number of ground treadles are worked over.   In this pattern each line of the design would require about six shoots of weft between the change of figure treadles.   In damask-weaving the length of a design can be perfectly regulated by the number of times each line of the ruled paper is worked over.   It is necessary to add that in the case of damask-weaving the drawboy machine only acts on the figure harness, the ground harness having to be governed by treadles in the usual manner.

PART III
COMPLEX PATTERN-WEAVING

PART III

COMPLEX PATTERN-WEAVING

CHAPTER XVI

THE DRAW-LOOM AND THREAD MONTURE

Ancient Origin of the Draw-loom—Its Importance in Weaving—Description of Draw-loom—Building the Monture—The Two Kinds of Repeating Patterns—The Comber-board—The Pulley-box—The Tail Cords—The Simple and Guide Cords—The Term *Cords* in reference to Design—Rigidity of Lateral Repeats on a Loom—Freedom of Vertical Repeats—The Drawboy—The Drawboy's Fork—The Most Perfect Loom—The Thread Monture—Various Uses of the Thread Monture—Examples of Silk-weaving on Thread Monture.

THE number of headles it is possible to hang effectively in a loom must necessarily be limited, because of the space they occupy, no matter how closely they may be crowded together and how thin their shafts may be made. This limitation renders it impossible to weave any large design with a figure harness composed of headles. The small

251

capacity of the headle harness led, no doubt, to the invention of the *draw-loom*, in which, in place of the headles, a narrow perforated board is fixed across the loom, in the holes of which, separate leashes are hung. They are so arranged, that a design which occupies the whole width of the loom for one lateral repeat, takes up no more space than a harness of eight or ten headles, on which number only the very smallest patterns can be woven, as we have already seen.

It is impossible to fix the date of this ancient invention. The earliest specimens of, what are without doubt, draw-loom webs, are of about the sixth century, and are of Asiatic origin. But when, or wherever it may have first been made, THERE CAN BE NO DOUBT THAT THIS INVENTION IS THE MOST IM-

PORTANT IN THE WHOLE HISTORY OF TEXTILE DEVELOPMENT. All the finest pattern-weaving of the Eastern, as well as the Western world, ancient and modern, has been done on the draw-loom principle, and even the invention of the Jacquard machine, which is often supposed to have superseded it, did not alter the essential principle of draw-loom weaving in the least. Jacquard's invention only rendered the tedious process of tying up the design on the cords of the loom itself unnecessary. Jacquard substituted for the tie-up, an endless band of cards, on which the pattern to be woven was punched line by line. The design for the tie-up of the cords of the draw-loom was worked out, or draughted, on paper, ruled out in squares, in exactly the same way as is requisite for the punching of the cards used in the Jacquard machine. In some of the early accounts of its introduction into this country, Jacquard's invention is called the " new draw-loom engine."

252

The essential part of the draw-loom is the per-forated *comber-board*, in and about which the *monture*, as the draw-loom harness is called, is built.

Fig. 103, is a representation of a draw-loom monture very much simplified for the sake of clearness. A headle harness is drawn below it for comparison. A is a harness of six headles, entered, in the way before de-scribed, as neces-sary for a design having equal sides pointing different ways, and which re-quires eleven threads of warp for one lateral repeat. B is the comber-board of a draw - loom, perforated with eleven holes in a

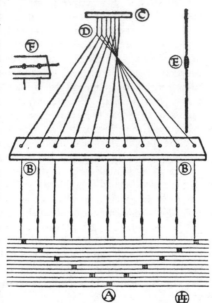

FIG. 103.—Diagram of Monture and Harness, Point Repeat.

single row. C is the bottom board of a box pierced with six holes, through which the cords D are seen to pass. These answer to the cords from which we have hitherto seen the headles suspended. We need not trouble at present about the means of

253

governing them, whether by treadles, drawboy, or Jacquard machine. All that concerns us now are the details of the monture below the board C.

Hanging in each of the eleven holes of the comber-board a separately weighted leash may be seen. The weight itself consists of a thin strip of lead wire, having a hole at one end, by which a loop of harness thread about six inches long is attached to it. These strips of lead are called lingoes, and vary in weight from an ounce upwards, according to the kind of material to be woven in the loom when completed. As in some cases there are as many as three or four thousand of these lingoes in a monture, the accumulated weight is considerable when a large proportion are drawn up, especially as the weight is nearly doubled by the friction at various points of the monture. At the other end of the thread loop, to which the lingo is attached, a glass eye or mail is tied, having at least three holes in it, through the centre one of which the future warp will be entered. The holes at the ends of the mail are used, one for attaching it to the loop of the lingo, as we have just seen, and the other for tying it to another loop about nine inches long. When this has been done the leash is complete as shown at E.

When preparations are being made to build a monture all the loops of one size are, of course, made together of exactly the same length. They are then tied up in bundles ready for slipping on to the mails and lingoes, as required.

In building a monture the top loops of the leashes are hooked up through the holes in the comber-board, and a cord temporarily threaded

254

through them in order to keep them suspended while the upper cords are being attached. This is shown, still in place, in the separate diagram F.

Referring now to the plan of entering the harness shown at A, the first, and the eleventh leashes, are found on the first headle. Accordingly the corresponding leashes in the comber-board, must be joined by threads passing from them to the end of the first cord at D, in the bottom board of the box C. The second and tenth leashes are on the second headle ; the corresponding ones to these in the comber-board must be joined in the same manner to the second cord D. The third and ninth, fourth and eighth, and the fifth and seventh leashes, must be connected in like manner to the cords D, while the sixth, the only remaining leash, is to be connected singly with cord 6, which corresponds with the sixth headle, on which only one leash is found to two on each of the other headles.

It is now obvious that if any of the cords D are pulled upwards, singly or in combination, it will have the same effect on the warp, entered in the mails, as the similar raising of any one or more of the harness headles. Thus we have in a single row in the comber-board, equal facility for selecting and raising particular threads of warp with that afforded by the six rows of headle-mounted leashes. But this example, owing to the necessary simplicity of the drawing, is very inadequate to show the enormous advantage obtained, for suppose the row of holes in the comber-board extended to eleven hundred (quite a moderate number) instead of only eleven, the effect would be the same as if the harness consisted of six hundred headles, which is, of course, an impossible

255

Monture Capacity

number. A linen table-cloth was woven at Dunfermline, about sixty years ago, which required a comber-board with four thousand two hundred leashes, each under separate control, so that one, or any combination of them, could be raised as indicated on the draught.

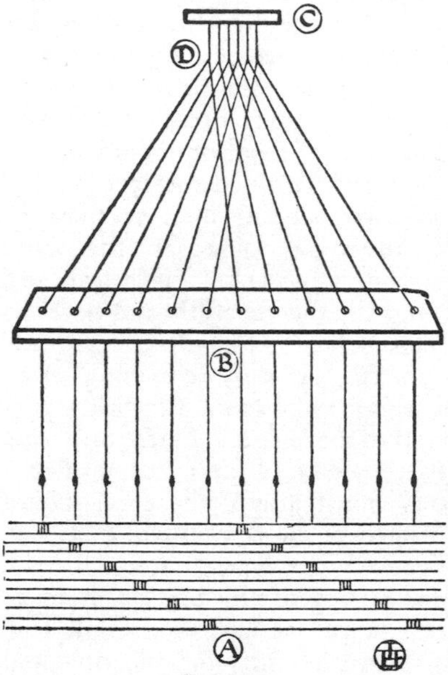

FIG. 104.

The Comber Repeat

Fig. 103 shows the comber-board arranged for the *point* repeat, the valuable qualities of which, to the designer, will have to be dealt with later on. Fig. 104 is the same in all respects as the previous one, except that it is what is now called a comber* repeat. It has the same effect as the ordinary straightforward entering of the harness, indicated at the bottom of the diagram. Two exact repeats, or combers, on six threads, are shown in the harness, and these require twelve holes in the board, instead of the

* Originally *camber*.

eleven required for the turnover point repeat. Any design for this arrangement would have to be made so as to repeat on every six threads of the warp. For comber repeats, the necking of the monture is tied up differently. The first and seventh leashes are connected to the first cord D. The second and eighth, the third and ninth, the fourth and tenth, the fifth and eleventh, and the sixth and twelfth are all likewise joined to the top cords in regular order. This difference between the point and comber repeats of woven designs must always be borne in mind, as they will now very frequently be referred to.

Fig. 105 represents a draw-loom complete enough for the purpose of explanation. In this drawing the comber-board is pierced with three rows of holes. It will also be observed that it is not simply a single board, but is composed of several slips of thin, hard wood. This is a great convenience when a very large number of holes is required, as the perforated slips can be spaced out slightly, and thus enable the builder to regulate the number of holes to every inch of the entire width, which must be done with great accuracy.

The comber-board in the illustration is made up of eight slips, each containing nine holes. The board is therefore pierced with seventy-two holes in all.

These seventy-two holes are divided into four repeats of eighteen holes each. It is usual in England to hang the first leash in the first row, at the back left-hand side, as indicated in the drawing. To prevent confusion, only the first six leashes which begin the repeats and the last one in each repeat are shown, these being all connected in the diagram by dotted lines. The first leash of each

257

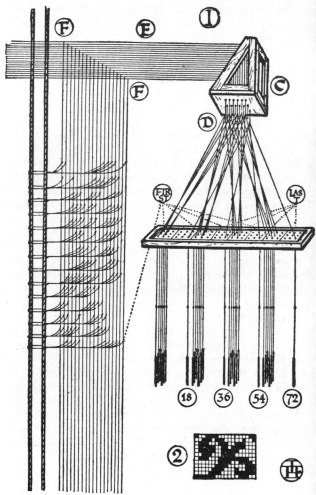

FIG. 105 —Mechanism of the Draw-loom.

repeat is attached by the necking cords to the first
pulley cord D, which is seen to enter the pulley-
box, C. Six pulley cords only are shown, but it is
evident that there must be eighteen of them, as
eighteen sets of four necking cords each have to be
tied to them. The attachment of the six sets of
necking cords is shown, and from these the principle
of the whole arrangement will be readily understood. It must be noted that the height of the
pulley-box, above the comber-board, must be much
greater than could be shown in the drawing without
making all the parts inconveniently small. It may
vary from four to six feet. As much height as possible is necessary here in order to avoid friction in
the working.

The *pulley-box* itself (C) now claims attention.
The bottom board of the box, looking upwards,
shows the eighteen holes through which the pulley
cords pass. Inside the box an arrangement of the
eighteen pulleys is fitted up. They are so placed
as to be immediately over the holes in the bottom
board. The box has to be very strongly framed
together, and to be very firmly fixed in its place on
the top of the loom. The comber-board also has
to be very firmly fixed close to the ground harness
in the exact position required for the proper opening of the shed. In gating the loom all these details
of position require a great deal of consideration and
experiment.

The pulley cords D, after passing over their
several pulleys, are carried to the nearest wall or
beam, and tied there in regular order, being accurately
adjusted as to length, in a horizontal line, as shown
at E, fig. 105. These cords, between the pulleys

259

and the wall, are called the *tail cords* of the loom. When a drawboy machine is used the design is tied up on them, and they are simply pulled down in the requisite order to form the pattern. The pulling down of a tail cord pulls up the corresponding necking cords, and raises the several leashes depending from their ends. By this means the necessary shed is opened.

When a real drawboy, not a machine, is employed, another set of cords, equal in number to those of the tail, is required. These are called the *simple*, and on it the design is tied up. In the illustration the simple is shown joining the tail cords at F, F, and from that point its cords are carried vertically to the ground. In front of the simple two very strong cords called *guides* are stretched vertically, between the ground and the roof of the workshop. The groups of ties to the simple cords, making each separate line of the design, are gathered together and passed round these strong guiding cords in succession as they are formed. By this means they are kept in regular order and free from entanglement. In the drawing the small design no. 2 is shown tied up on the simple, and its formation will be readily traced out.

The above description of the draw-loom, although complete as to its mechanism, must not be taken as a sample of its capacity. It is only intended to show the construction and purpose of the various parts of the machine, as well as their relation to each other. In a very ordinary silk-loom the space occupied by the design no. 2 would not be more than three-quarters of an inch, so that there would be in the narrowest loom, say twenty-one inches

wide, twenty-eight repeats to be allowed for in the
comber-board. The latter would have to be pierced
with five hundred and four holes, and require to
be furnished with the same number of leashes.
Twenty-eight leashes would have to be attached to
each of the pulley cords, and by their means the
pattern would be exactly repeated across the whole
width of the web. WITH THE SAME COMBER-
BOARD AND THE SAME NUMBER OF LEASHES ANY
KIND OF REPEAT THAT CAN BE DESIGNED ON FIVE
HUNDRED AND FOUR LINES OF RULED PAPER COULD
BE ARRANGED FOR. The most ordinary repeat is,
perhaps, two combers or one repeat point. Either
of these would require two hundred and fifty-two
cords in the simple for working out the design on,
and, of course, the same number of tail and pulley
cords. In this case each pulley cord would only
have two leashes attached by the necking to it.

The Term
Cords
used in
describing
Width of
Design

The technical method of describing the number of
lines in the width of a design is, to say that it is
draughted on, two hundred and fifty-two cords, or
four hundred cords, as the case may be ; the cords
referred to being those of the simple. The same
term is used now in connection with the Jacquard
machine, but it would be more correct to say,
draughted for so many needles or hooks, as these have
taken the place of the *simple*, in modern weaving.

It may be well here to call attention to the
fact, that, in all weaving, but particularly in draw-
loom, and Jacquard weaving, the *width* and
number of repeats in a loom is most rigid, and
cannot be altered without rebuilding the whole
monture. The designer and draughtsman must
know exactly the number of cords and the kind of

261

repeat the loom has, which he is designing for. This is not the case with regard to the *length* of the design ; here the artist is at perfect liberty. The only objection to a very long, vertical repeat is, that the tie-up for the draw-loom, or the endless band of cords for the Jacquard machine, has to be more extensive. No alteration is required in the loom, whatever length the design may be, nor is the weaver's work affected by it to any appreciable extent.

The work of the *drawboy*, as the weaver's assistant was called, must now be described. He had to pull forward, by means of the loops on the guide cords in front of the simple, each set of cords, in regular order, as they were required to form the successive lines of the design. He not only had to pull them forward, but downward, in order to raise the leashes ; and not only this, but to hold them down while the weaver worked over three, four, or more shoots of the ground, as explained in the chapter on damask-weaving. We have seen that the lingoes often weigh an ounce each, and also that in a not over-rich silk-loom, such as that described at p. 261, twenty-eight leashes had to be raised by each cord of the simple.

When several of these cords were drawn together, and the frictional resistance added to the actual weight of the lead, it is obvious that the boy must need some mechanical assistance in drawing the cords down, and holding them as long as required. The heaviest line in no. 2, fig 105, is the sixth, in which twelve cords have to be drawn together. The lingoes for these would weigh three hundred and thirty-two ounces, or twenty-four pounds, so that, taking into consideration the frictional as well as the dead weight on this line, the cords have to raise thirty-six pounds at least, and the boy has not only to lift that weight, but, as just explained, hold it for about one-third of a minute while the ground is woven. For

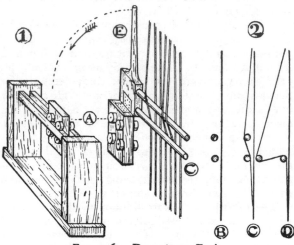

FIG. 106.—Draw-loom Fork.

his assistance in this arduous work the boy is furnished with a fork and lever (fig. 106).

This drawing shows a solid stand, no. 1, having two broad uprights. This is fixed by the side of the simple, but a little in advance of it. At the top the uprights are joined together by two parallel bars. A, is a block of hard wood which fits between the two bars, and is kept in position by four small wheels, or runners, being fixed on both sides of the block, two above and two below, as shown in the drawing.

These runners allow the block to move freely along
from end to end of the bars.   The fork and lever,
shown separately at A, E, are hinged to the top of
the sliding block in such a manner that they can be
easily moved from a vertical to a horizontal position,
and will remain in either.

When about to be used, the block is moved back
until the points of the fork are by the back edge of
the simple, and in the upright position as shown in
section at B, no. 2.   The boy, by means of the loops,
next draws forward the simple cords necessary for
the formation of one line of the design.   He carefully
inserts the upper prong of the fork in the opening
made, gradually drawing it forward as he does so.
When this has been done the position is represented by C, no. 2.   Grasping the end of the lever,
the boy now draws it down and holds it in a horizontal position, the result being that the required
cords are drawn down as shown at D.

The most perfect pattern loom possible, is one in
which the leashes are entered with one thread of
warp only, and every leash is under separate control by means of the tie-up.   On such a loom every
imaginable form of design and variety of tie can be
woven without the use of any other mechanism what-

Large
Designs
Unpractical
in Silk with
Thread
Monture

ever.   The extensive tie-up in the case of the draw-
loom, and the unmanageable quantity of machinery
required if Jacquard machines were used, would, in
the case of silk at any rate, render this unpractical.
Silks warps, of twenty-one inches wide, sometimes
contain, as we have seen, as many as eight thousand threads, which would involve the building
of a simple with eight thousand cords, or the use of
twenty Jacquard machines, with four hundred needles

and hooks in each.* As regards the comber-board and the loom itself, there would be no difficulty; in fact, the weaving on such a monture would be as simple as any pattern-weaving could possibly be.

Large Designs Unpractical in Silk with Thread Monture

If linen, cotton, or wool warps are used, such an arrangement for a fine bold design is quite practical. A design draughted on eight hundred and forty lines in the width of the ruled paper gives forty threads to an inch in the reed. This is sufficient for a massive pattern, where great refinement of detail is not required. Weaving with a thread monture gives the designer liberty to use any variety of texture, form, and detail that he can get in on the eight hundred and forty threads at his disposal. He may make the ground of tabby, twill, or satin, and he may ornament parts of the figure with tabbies of double, treble, or any number of threads, and fill the different spaces of it with any of the various twills or satins he may wish. IN FACT, HIS ONLY LIMITATION IS THE NUMBER OF THE SQUARES INTO WHICH HIS SPACE IS DIVIDED.

Practical for Cotton, Linen, or Wool

A Large Design on Thread Monture

It will be seen that the preparation of the draught, particularly for this kind of weaving, is a most important work, as on it the whole of the success of the finished web depends—that is, with regard to its ornamental shapes and texture. It also requires a thorough knowledge of the effect that weaving has in modifying or exaggerating edges, angles, and outlines generally.

Preparation of the Draught needs Technical Knowledge

Fig. 107 is a portion of one of the finest of the traditional Italian damask designs. Various versions of it are to be found amongst sixteenth- and

Example of Italian Design

* This might be possible if electricity were applied to the draw-loom.

FIG. 107.—Italian Damask.   Point Design.

seventeenth - century weavings. Some of the earliest wall-papers in imitation of silk damask were copied from it. There is some such paper remaining in the mansion of Christchurch Park, Ipswich, copied from one of the finest versions of it, the length of its longitudinal repeat being about nine feet.

This design will also illustrate the great advantage gained by using the point repeat. All the effect in scale of a design drawn on eight hundred and forty cords, is by its use obtained on a simple of four hundred and twenty cords. This was no doubt the reason for the frequent adoption of this plan of design in the early work. It will be observed that nearly all the old designs of greater width than ten or twelve inches are constructed in this way. We must notice in passing that in the Sicilian and early Italian designs (fig. 108), which are so admirable, narrowness of repeat is a chief characteristic of their construction, and there can be no doubt that the reason for this peculiarity is the desire for economy in tying up the design on the loom.

Fig. 108.—Sicilian Damask.
Point Design.

Modern
Treat-
ment of
Traditional
Italian
Design

In this case, then (fig. 107), the simple would need four hundred and twenty cords, and the monture would have to be built in *point* as in fig. 103. The first, and the eight hundred and thirty-ninth leashes, would be drawn by the first cord, answering to the first, and the eleventh, in that diagram.* All the other cords would also draw the leashes from opposite sides until the centre cord 420 was arrived at. This, like the centre cord of the diagram (fig. 103), would only support one leash.

Effect of
Point
Repeat
on Tabbies,
Satins, and
Twills in a
Thread
Monture

If the centre cord only has one leash attached to it, a tabby ground will not be affected by it. This is one reason for building the monture on eight hundred and thirty-nine cords instead of the even number. All the other ties, satins, twills, &c., will be thrown in opposite directions by the point repeat. This will make little difference in the general effect, and will only require a little extra care at the centre line of the design, where the change of direction in the ties is most obvious.

The damask effect depending on reversed satins can quite easily be woven on a thread monture. Fig. 109 shows a small portion of the design draughted for this effect. For the coarse texture at present under consideration a five-headle satin, shown in the sketch, is the most suitable one. A linen or cotton warp, not too fine in size, shot with wool of a contrasting colour, would bring the design out well. This kind of web used to be largely used for furniture and curtains, and was called *union damask*. It was very useful and artistic, as

* One hole in the comber-board would remain empty, as the centre cord only requires one leash instead of two.

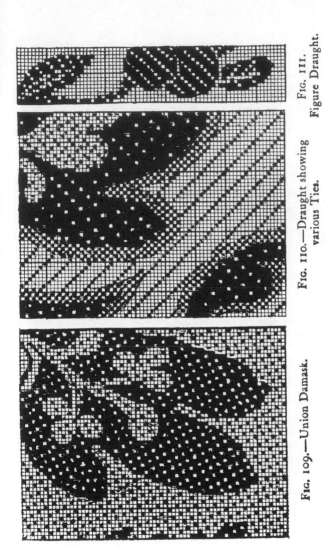

FIG. 109.—Union Damask.

FIG. 110.—Draught showing
various Ties.

FIG. III.
Figure Draught.

well as durable, if the colours were well chosen and
the yarns good and well dyed.

Perhaps a still better effect would be gained by
making the ground tabby and the figure a looser satin
or a four-headle twill and shooting a coarse-spun or
tussah silk into the warp instead of wool.   Of course,
endless suggestions might be made in this connection,
but it is in such details as this that the designer and
craftsman must exercise his taste and invention.

Fig. 110 is a draught of a portion of the same
design in which a different treatment is adopted. The
field or background of the design is a twill, while the
figure is shaped and brought out by means of a tabby
outline and the use of different ties for its various parts.

If a tabby shoot of weft, similiar to the warp,
were made between each opening of the figure shed,
and an extra shuttle carrying a different weft used
for the figure, the strength and solidity of the cloth
woven would be much enhanced. This separate
treatment of the design would also make it stand
out from the ground in a bolder and much clearer
manner both as to form and colour. The easiest
way to do this would be to fit up a harness with
long-eyed leashes in front of the monture and enter
the warp in it as well as in the leashes of the
monture. This would enable the weaver to work
the tabby ground independently of the drawboy, by
means of two treadles. The draught of this effect
would not need the tie on the ground to be
indicated, but would be drawn as in fig. 111.*

* If a Jacquard machine to govern the thread
monture is being used, the tabby can be made by
inserting an extra card between each of the figure cards,
and the extra harness would not be necessary. The

If the thread monture be used for silk-weaving without any additional harness or other appliance for making the groundwork, very perfect webs, full of variety and detail, can be made. The designs certainly must be very limited as to size, but that is practically their only limitation. They may be as fine as the finest engraving, for any lines and spots down to the three-hundredth part of an inch may be woven with the greatest ease and certainty. Such delicate little designs as fig. 112—which is reproduced the exact size of the original—are examples of thread-monture weaving. The example illustrated was made in Spitalfields about the end of the eighteenth century, most probably on a draw-loom with a draw-boy machine. A few weavers are left in Bethnal Green who still make this kind of silk, which is mostly used for ties and scarves. The Jacquard machine is, of course, now used for lifting the threads, but the monture itself is exactly the same as in the old times. This Spitalfields sample is woven about two hundred and eighty threads to an inch. The design repeats fourteen times in twenty-one inches, and is drawn for four hundred cords. The comber-board would have to be pierced with five thousand eight hundred and eighty holes, and the same number of leashes and lingoes would, of course, be required to fill it up. The repeat of this design is comber. Although the figures are turned over to extend them, they do not turn over on the same lines ; they are

work, however, would be much heavier, and the number of cards necessary would be doubled. The front harness would probably be used even in this case, especially as it would allow of the ground being changed at will.

271

FIG. 112.—Spitalfields Silk. Size of Original

therefore what designers now call *drop turnover* Silk-weaving
repeats. This is of no advantage in regard to the on Thread
Monture

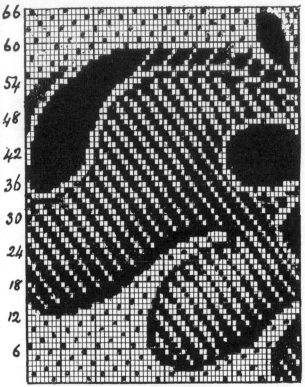

66
60
54
48
42
36
30
24
18
12
6

FIG. 113.—Part of Draught for Fig. III.

weaving, but is an easy way of getting balance in
a design, and is often resorted to.

273

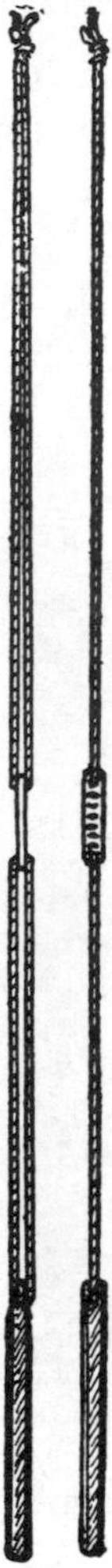

FIG. 114.—Leash fitted up for Damask.

Fig. 114 is taken from a portion of a ruled-paper draught for fig. 112. It represents the twenty-fifth part of a square inch of the finished silk, and shows the amount of detail required in such designs, as well as the freedom with which the textures may be varied in designing for this most perfect loom.

The manner of weaving damask webs with two harnesses has already been fully explained in Chapter XIV., but it is necessary just to describe the making of damask on the monture of a draw-loom, which takes the place of the figure harness. Such large designs as the traditional Italian pattern given in fig. 107 or the beautiful Louis XIII. damask of plate XI cannot be made on a thread monture, and, indeed, would lose a great deal of their beauty if they were. The fine sharp edges which result from the lifting of every thread would make such large designs hard and uninteresting. A great deal of the charm of woven ornament results from the mystery given to the edges of the forms by the more or less evident steps of their outline.

Both the large designs referred to are made on from four hundred to four hundred and fifty cords of the simple, acting on ten and a half inches of the warp, and as they are point designs, one repeat fills the whole twenty-one inches of the width of warp, and requires eight hundred or eight hundred and fifty holes in the comber-board. If

274

the count of silk in the warp were four thousand
eight hundred threads, each mail in the monture
would have to lift six threads at least. In order to
do this the mails of the leashes must be perforated
with six holes in addition to the two required for
the construction of the leash. Fig. 114 shows a
leash fitted up with its lingo, and a mail having
the required number of holes. It will therefore be
seen that THE RICHNESS OF THE SILK IN DAMASK-
WEAVING DOES NOT DEPEND ON THE SCALE OF THE
DESIGN, BUT ON THE NUMBER OF THREADS LIFTED
BY THE LEASHES. After passing through the mails
the threads of warp are entered separately in the
long eyes of the front or ground harness, which
is worked by treadles, and the process of weaving
is the same in all respects as that described in
Chapter XIV.

CHAPTER XVII

THE SHAFT MONTURE

Invention of the Split or Shaft Harness—The Comber-board for Shaft Harness—Building a Shaft Harness—Description of Various Parts of the Harness—The Shaft Harness in Use—Note on regulating the Length of Designs—Draughting Designs—Examples of Shaft-harness Weaving.

Important Addition to the Thread Monture

A VERY important improvement was made in the monture about the middle of the last century by Mr. James Gough, a weaver of Bethnal Green. By means of this invention separate grounds, satins, twills, and tabbies can be made without a separate front harness, the use of which was explained in the last chapter. At the same time the design can be worked out in a larger repeat on groups of two, four, or more threads, while the ties are made with single threads. This facilitates the weaving of fine silk in large designs, and gives freer opportunity, when a separate binder is provided, for making the large and important class of webs known as *tissues*, of which the *brocatelle* is a member.

Invention of the Split or Shaft Harness

The invention was not made until after the Jacquard machine had come into general use, and was therefore never used on the original draw-loom. It would, however, have been a very useful addition

276

to it, and have made the wonderful tissues of the seventeenth and eighteenth centuries much less laborious to weave.

Invention of the Split or Shaft Harness

This invention is called the *split* or *shaft* harness. One name is as good as the other, but each by itself only describes the invention in part, for the leashes are split, and they are also suspended on shafts.

The comber-board for this description of harness requires the same number of holes as the thread monture, but each cord of the simple raises several leashes together for the formation of the design, just as the glass mails lift several threads together in the damask monture.

The Comber board for the Shaft Harness

Let us take such a warp of silk as the sample of Spitalfields weaving examined in the last chapter, and see what can be done with it on a shaft monture. The count was five thousand five hundred and eighty threads, one thread being entered in every leash. We will at once decide that each square of the ruled paper, on which the design is to be draughted, shall represent four threads. This gives us one thousand three hundred and ninety-five groups of four, in the whole width, which shall be twenty-one inches. Three comber repeats, of seven inches each, would be a convenient size for a design ; we decide, then, on this, and divide one thousand three hundred and ninety-five by three. This gives us four hundred and sixty-five cords on which to form the design. The ruled paper must also have four hundred and sixty-five squares, counted laterally, for the draught.

$5580 \div 4 = 1395 \div 3 = 465$

The number of rows of holes in the comber-board must next be decided, and if the most usual satin, viz., eight-headle satin, is intended to be used there must

277

be eight, sixteen, or twenty-four rows. Twenty-four rows would no doubt be decided on, two hundred and thirty-three being in twelve rows, and two hundred and thirty-two in the remaining twelve.*

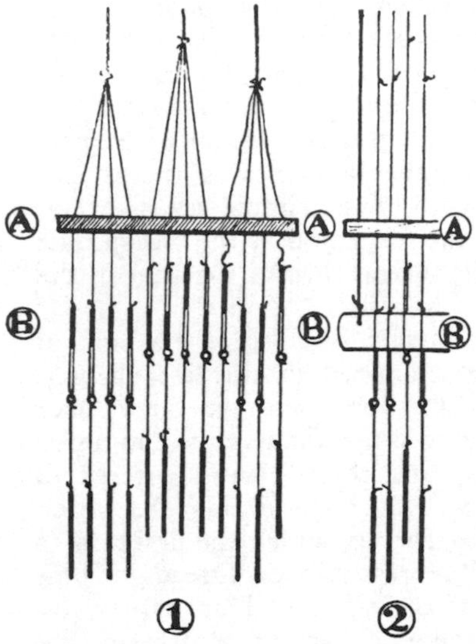

FIG. 115.—Section of Split Harness.

Before the leashes are gathered up in groups and joined to the pulley cords by the necking they must be carefully examined, for it is in the leashes below the comber-board that the peculiarity of the shaft harness is to be seen.

Fig. 115 shows the formation and arrangement of the leashes. A, A, no. 1, is the section of a comber-board having twelve rows of leashes suspended through its holes. The lower parts of the leashes have lingoes and mails, and are made in the usual manner. But between the mails and the comber-board the leash is much longer than usual in the ordinary monture, and part of this length is occupied by a long loop, which begins at, or a little above, the mail and reaches

* For description of comber-board and illustration see p. 308.

278

about half-way between it and the comber-board.
The upper part of the leash to which the loop is
attached is made of stouter cord. This passes
through the comber-board and is gathered together
with another, or it may be, several other leashes,
and knotted to a necking cord, which in its turn is
attached to the cord coming from the pulley-box
above the loom. The twelve leashes of the illustration are shown joined in fours to three of the
necking cords of the monture. No. 2, B, B, shows
the end of one of a set of twelve shafts of stout
hoop-iron, made perfectly smooth, and enamelled.
The shafts are a little longer than the comber-board,
and are passed through the loops as shown at B,
no. 1, in section, one shaft passing through all the
loops of the leashes in each row. The shafts are
hung from strong cords, which pass through an
extra row of holes drilled in the frame of the
comber-board, which is made wide at the ends for
that purpose. The shafts are hung at such a
height that the leashes just hang on them when the
loom is at rest. This is the state of the four leashes
on the left. If one of the cords of the simple, on
which the tie-up of the design is made, be drawn,
it will draw up with it the four leashes with which
it is connected, but the shafts will remain stationary.
If then the shafts were raised they would have no
effect, as their particular loops are already drawn up.
This position will be made clear by the centre group
of leashes in the illustration, which has been raised by
the figure cord. The third shaft in the group is seen
to be raised, but has no effect on the leash. In the
third group of leashes on the right the result of raising
two of the shafts, while the figure cord is left down,

279

Description
of the
Shaft
Harness

The Shaft
Harness
in Use

is shown. The shafts have raised the two leashes, with which they are connected, but the other two members of the group are unaffected. It will now be seen that any ground or figure can be made with single threads by means of the twelve shafts independently of the figure harness. Also that any pattern made by the figure harness raising the four threads in groups may be made without affecting the shafts, so that in spaces where the figure is not raised the shafts can be filling in a background of satin or twill, as may be arranged.

Fig. 116 will make the whole arrangement perfectly clear. The large sketch is a portion of a ruled-paper draught, and represents the face of a figured silk made on a shaft harness. The warp is fine white silk, of which the drawing shows one hundred and sixty threads. The weft is black silk, for the sake of contrast. The twelve shafts shown in section at fig. 115, each carrying a twelfth part of the warp, have to make a ground of twelve-shaft satin. This is indicated by the fine black dots powdered over the background of the draught. One shaft has to be lifted for each shoot, and each shaft must rise in the necessary order to form the satin. The mechanical method of raising the shafts will be described presently.

The effect of the figure harness is seen in the bold black squares of the design. These consist of weft, which crosses in front of the lifted white threads. The shaft satin has no binding effect on the figure, for the reason already explained; accordingly it follows that the smallest intersection of warp and weft in the pattern must be four threads wide. Such intersections are shown working a tabby

280

edge to the square in the centre of the flower. If
all the odd- and even-numbered cords of the simple

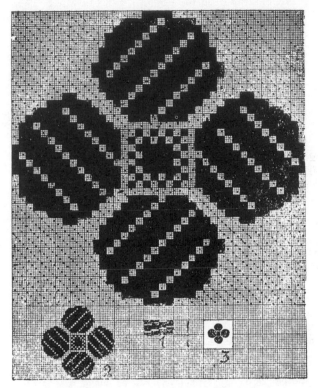

FIG. 116.—Draught for Shaft Harness.

were drawn alternately, this tabby effect, with a
single-thread tie occasionally appearing in the

281

white portion only, would cover the face of the cloth.
It will now be apparent that any ties on the figure,
must be drawn on the design ; and that these when
woven will be four threads wide.   These quadruple
ties are seen on the petals of the flower, arranged in
diagonal lines.   Much care is necessary in designing
these ties, in order to prevent undue length in the
floating loops of weft.   The draught being made on
ruled paper with squares divided equally 8 × 8, the
ties in this case are square and need more than one
shoot of weft to build them up. If the designer
had wished, he might have made them only one shoot
high instead of four, as shown in no. 1 below the
flower.   This would, however, involve the drawing
of the figure cords every shoot, and make the tie-up
four times as long as at present. If a Jacquard
machine were used, the number of cards required
would also be increased fourfold.

It is perhaps necessary to pause and specially note
here that in order to bring any design to the
required length, the cords of the simple have to be
held down over two or more shoots, according to
the size of the weft and the nature of the pattern.
The draughtsman makes his design on the number
of lines he deems necessary for the effect he wishes
to obtain, but the number of shoots to each line
required to bring the woven pattern to the same
proportion as the draught, has to be settled by
experiment, when the web is ready for starting.
Some designs, especially for damasks, need each
separate line to be repeated as many as eight
times.   In the draw-loom the figure harness is
left up while the requisite number of shoots of
ground are made, but with a Jacquard machine

the shed is closed every shoot, and opened again by keeping the same card on the cylinder of the machine, until the requisite repetition has been completed.

Returning to fig. 116, no. 2 shows the manner in which the design would be worked out on the ruled paper. The ground would be left plain, being woven independently by the shafts. The pattern for the tie-up would have to be drawn with all its ties and subordinate effects, such as little diaper patterns and different-sized tabby fillings. Any shapes and details that can be got in on the available four hundred and sixty-five squares are weavable. In making the draught, care must be taken to avoid long loose floats of weft. The design may be of any length desired, but it must be remembered, that, great length of design needs a long tie-up on the draw-loom, or an expensive and unwieldy set of cards for the Jacquard machine.

No. 3 of the illustration shows the proportional size of the flower in comparison with the draught, and its general effect when woven in fine silk.

Plate XII is a copy of an eighteenth-century French silk. It was photographed from the woven silk reproduction, and is the same size as the original. The illustration only shows a part of the design, which is seven inches wide and repeats four times in a web of twenty-eight inches. The count of the warp is about the same as that of the Spitalfields example, fig. 112, p. 272. The groundwork is eight-shaft satin, woven on a split harness, and the lace-like pattern is formed by raising the threads two together instead of four as in fig. 115. The draughting is on eight hundred cords instead of the four hundred and fifty. This increase of size in the draught is rendered necessary by the fewer number of leashes raised by each cord of the simple. In all other respects the draughting and weaving of this silk are the same as described in connection with fig. 115.

CHAPTER XVIII

BROCATELLE AND TISSUE WEAVING

The Technique of Brocatelle Webs—Weaving Brocatelles—Draughting for Tissue weaving—Two Methods of mounting Binders—Old Spitalfields Tissue—Broché Tissues—General Utility of Shaft Harness—Shaft Harness for Coarse Materials—Tissues of Wool, Linen, and Cotton on Shaft Harness—Examples of Modern Wool Tissues—Old Method of Tissue weaving without Split Shaft Harness.

BROCATELLES and other webs, which weavers call by the general name of *tissues*, cannot be made on the shaft monture, described in the last chapter, without some arrangement being added in order to work a separately warped binder. The reason for separate warping generally, was given in Chapter XIV. But it will be necessary to examine a sample of these webs and ascertain the reason why a separate binder is specially required for brocatelle and tissue weaving ; and afterwards the fitting which has to be added to the loom, for this kind of weaving, can be explained.

The chief characteristic of a brocatelle web is the raised satin figure, which gives such a rich appearance to the fabric (see plate XIII). In a damask web the background of the figure is a satin, made by the long floating threads of the silk warp, while the figure itself is the reverse satin, in which the weft chiefly shows. In the brocatelle, on the contrary, the warp floats rather loosely in the figure, and a special weft entirely covers it up in other places. The second weft is tightly bound down by a separate binder, and forms the background to the design.

Fig. 117, no. 1, shows a portion of a brocatelle as it would be draughted by the designer. The weaver, in tying up the design on the simple cords, in this case, would not tie up the figure, shown in white, as he would for a damask web, but would tie up the ground, represented by the black portion of the draught. In like manner, on cards for a Jacquard machine the instruction to the card-puncher would be, "Cut the ground, not the figure." No. 2 shows the effect as far as it could be woven on the shaft harness as described in the last chapter. Plain satin has been woven all over by the shafts, the warp being white and the weft, as is usual in brocatelles, an undyed linen.* The satin ties, shown on the figure are of linen, but the ground having been raised by means of the simple cords, a black silk weft has been shot across the spaces so lifted. These ground spaces are thus only covered by unbound loops of the second weft, and the separate binder is required to tie them down securely in their places. In brocatelle weaving the characteristic raised effect of the satin figure is obtained by

* The first or satin shoot of a brocatelle only binds the satin, and does not show on the face of the cloth. Linen gives solidity of texture, and on that account is usually employed.

lightly weighting the roller of the main satin warp and heavily weighting the binder roller, and the effect is further enhanced by the harshness of the linen back.

No. 3 shows the ground weft bound down by a four-headle twill, and it is in order to enable this to be done that an addition of some kind has to be made to the monture. This may be arranged for in two ways, as follows : (1) The number of shafts may be increased by four, the extra ones being fitted up in front of those used for the satin ties of the main warp. This will make twenty shafts in all. On these shafts, four extra rows of leashes are hung by their long loops. These leashes have no top member

Damask and Brocatelle Effects compared

Plan of making a Separate Binder

Fig. 117.—Illustration of Draughting.

287

passing through the comber-board, as the others
have, but are complete when hung upon the shafts.
The warp for the binder is brought through the
main body of leashes, one between every four, and
entered in regular order in the binder. This completes the arrangement, and the brocatelle effect of
no. 3, fig. 117, is obtained by the following procedure.

The first shoot of flax thread is made with the
binder all lifted, and one shaft of the main warp
lifted as well. The second shoot of weft (black
silk in this case) is made with one shaft of the
binder down and the ground of the design raised by
the drawing of the cords of the simple. When
this has been done the effect of one line of no. 3,
fig. 117, will have been woven. The next and
following shoots proceed in their proper order, first
the flax and then the silk, in regular succession. A
set of four additional treadles and levers will be
required to lift the binder shafts, or if an automatic
machine such as a drawboy or a Jack-in-the-box
are used to lift the grounds, the necessary additions
will have to be made for them.

In draughting for brocatelles, and other tissues,
it is necessary to be more careful in selecting the
ruled paper, in regard to its proportion ; as the length
of the design of a brocatelle cannot so easily be
regulated in the loom as can that of a damask. It
is true the same *simple* cords can be drawn twice
or thrice over, but as there are two wefts to be
shot in, the space occupied by one line of the design
is much greater than is the case in fine damask.
The draught has to be made on paper ruled
8 × 12, or 8 × 10, and the final regulation of the
length of the woven pattern must be made by the

alteration of the size of the wefting used, as well as by the closeness with which the weft itself is beaten together. In the case of some tissues in many colours, where several shoots of weft go to make up each line, the ruled paper has to have fewer lines in the height than the width. It may be necessary, therefore, to use paper ruled 8 × 6 or 8 × 4. Anyway, all these points must be carefully calculated before the draught is commenced.

2. Another arrangement of the binder, required for weaving brocatelles, is to mount an ordinary harness, of the proper count, in front of the shaft monture in the same position as for damask-weaving, and to enter the second or binding warp in it. The warp, however, unlike that of the damask harness, is not entered in the mails of the monture leashes, but passes between them. It is also not necessary that the binder leashes should have long eyes. This kind of binder harness is sometimes preferred to the shaft harness, but the latter takes up less space and is in the position to receive another improvement, which will be noticed presently. As far as the brocatelle and some other tissues, which now claim our attention are concerned, one of the above plans of fitting up the binder harness is as good as the other. For a temporary work perhaps the binder could be more easily added in the second method.

The weaving of a great variety of fabrics is possible, with the draw-loom at the stage of development to which we have traced it. A volume, or perhaps many volumes, might be filled with descriptions and dissections of such webs, but a very few

289

typical specimens must suffice for the present hand-book.

First we must examine two very different ex-amples of tissue weaving, which might, however, have been woven on the same loom, with the same count of warps and precisely the same fitting up.

Plate XIV is taken from a fine piece of tissue-weaving made in Spitalfields probably at the be-ginning of the nineteenth century. The colours are green and gold. The ground is green satin, both rich in colour and in texture. The design is in green, lighter than the ground, and gold, and repeats *point* once in the width. Both the green and gold portions of the figure are tied by the same twill binder. The warp of the satin ground was not lightly weighted, as in brocatelle weaving, but is peculiarly flat, which would suggest that it was more heavily weighted than is usual even for a damask. The binder warp of the figure, on the contrary, is rather lightly weighted. This tissue has no linen shoot, but is all pure silk throughout, the weft of the ground satin being fine and rather harder than usual. The green and the gold weft used in the figure are both, rich, lightly twisted silk, known by the name of *tram*, as distinguished from *organzine*, which is the harder-twisted silk always used for warps. Three shuttles are required for weaving this web, one for the ground satin, which is the first shoot. The ground satin, as we saw was the case in the brocatelle, is made on the main warp, with the figure cords at rest and the binder all lifted out of the way. At the second shoot, the green part of the figure is lifted, and one shaft of the binder left down while the other shafts

290

are all raised. The shed for the second shoot being thus made, the shuttle carrying green weft is sent across, and passes behind the satin ground until it comes to the lifted figure. Here it goes in front of the satin and all the binder warp threads, except those entered in the one left down. These remain in front of the weft to tie it. When the shed has closed on the second shoot the gold figure cords are

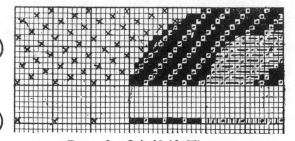

FIG. 118.—Spitalfields Tissue.

drawn, the same binder shaft left down, and the shed being open the third shoot is made, the weft now being gold-coloured silk. This shoot also passes behind the satin ground, and behind the green figure as well, until it reaches the opening made by the raised ground warp and all the binder threads except the first. Here it shows on the face of the cloth, and when the shuttle is drawn out and the shed closed one line of the ground and figure will be completed, and is represented on ruled paper in fig. 118, letter A. In this draught the white squares stand for the main warp threads of green silk, the dots for the green binder warp threads, the crosses for the first shoot of green ground

291

weft, the black squares for the green figure shoot, and the lined squares for the third shoot, the gold weft.

The draughting of the separate colours on the ruled paper must always be done very carefully, as a separate tie-up has to be made for each. If, for instance, two shuttles have to be used in forming one line of the figure, as in the above case, there have to be two rows of loops in the tie-up on the simple, in order that the cords may be drawn in proper succession. If as many as seven shuttles had to be used for one line of the figure, the same number of rows of loops would have to be tied up for it.

The next example, fig. 119, is of quite a different character. In this design, a part of which only is shown, a great variety of colours are used, which have on the face of the material almost the effect of brocading in many coloured silks. Four shoots have to be made in each line of the weaving, one for the plain ground, and three for the figure, and they are all thrown right across the web in the ordinary manner. A glance at the back of the material would show that the colours are all arranged in lateral stripes of different widths, and also that the colour effect is obtained by changing the weft used for the figure, at certain intervals, as arranged for on the draught by the designer. In many designs of this class great ingenuity is displayed by the artist in distributing the coloured ornament in such a way, that, the lateral stripes of the weft are altogether lost sight of. This at first was no doubt the aim of the designer, who wished to obtain the effect of brocaded ornaments in a quicker way. But although this deception is quite possible, after all, some of the most successful of such designs show the method of working quite

292

Ⓖ
Ⓕ
Ⓔ
Ⓓ
Ⓒ
Ⓑ
Ⓐ

FIG. 119.—Rococo Tissue.   Broché Weaving.

frankly. It will be seen that the chief difference between this example and that of the tissue previously given is a matter of design. The working out is very similar, except that the ground is a tabby with a thick weft, such as used to be called a *lutestring*, or *lustring*, as it is often spelt on old designs. The three figure wefts are all thrown into the same shed of the binder, which opens, in different parts of the web, according to the drawing of the simple cords at three successive shoots. In order to show clearly the method of changing the colours of the weft, the sketch is ruled laterally from letter A to G. At A the architectural feature is coloured yellow and shaded with dark brown; in the yellow there are small touches of dark green, represented by the solid black. The foliage above the vase is mostly dark green, and the yellow shuttle is changed for one having light green weft in it, so that in the space marked B, only light and dark green show. In the space C the light and dark green are continued and the dark brown weft is changed to red (represented by dots). The light green at D is changed to purple (cross-hatching), and at E the dark green changes to yellow, so that in this space red, purple, and yellow occupy the three shuttles. At F the red changes to orange, in the pines, where it is heightened by touches of yellow, and in the space G with dark green, which takes the place of the purple shuttle.

Fig. 120 is an example of a small design, quite ordinary in form, which, when woven in the above manner, in lateral stripes of rose-colour, green, and dull gold on a dark blue satin ground, has a most excellent effect. This is woven with only two

FIG. 120.—Modern Broché Tissue.   Designed and
arranged for weaving by the Author.

Small
Broché
Tissue

General
Utility of
the Shaft
Harness

shuttles, one for the ground satin, and the other with changing wefts for the figure.

It is not only for the weaving of fine silk that the shaft monture is useful, but it is equally so for linen, cotton or woollen pattern webs, of either large or small design, such as are used for hangings, furniture, and other purposes. If properly planned, an astonishing variety of weft effect patterns can be designed, which do not require alterations to the loom itself. This is, indeed, the chief advantage of designs in which the weft is most conspicuous. It is obvious that where the warp is only used as a ground or binder to the ornament, alterations are easier to make. Different designs can be woven on the same length of warp, and altogether more freedom is given to the artist in arranging his design. Take, for instance, the simple matter of stripes. If a stripe or stripes of colour are made in the warp, they have to remain in the same position from beginning to end of the web. But, weft stripes, of any size, colour, or distance apart, can be thrown in at will. It is therefore a great advantage to have a loom built particularly with a view to weft effect designs, especially in a studio or small workshop.

Description
of a Most
Useful Shaft
Harness for
Coarser
Materials

As an example of a most useful build of shaft monture for the weaving of these coarser materials, the following may be interesting. The comber-board is the first thing to consider. We will suppose that the width of the web to be woven is twenty-four inches. It might be forty-eight inches,* in

* In the case of the warp being forty-eight inches wide a fly-shuttle would have to be used, and when two

which case the figures of the specification would
simply have to be doubled. The space of the
pierced part of the comber-board must be at least
twenty-four inches, and in view of the material to
be used, fine linen or cotton, it must be pierced
with sixteen hundred holes, arranged in eight rows.
The eight rows of leashes suspended in these holes
will require eight shafts, and the leashes themselves
must have much heavier lingoes than we saw to be
necessary for fine silk. The number of cords in
the pulley-box, or hooks in the Jacquard machine,
should be four hundred, and four leashes should be
raised together by the drawing of each cord for
the figure. One comber repeat will fill the whole
width of twenty-four inches, SO THAT ANY DESIGN
DRAUGHTED ON FOUR HUNDRED SQUARES, IN THE
WIDTH OF RULED PAPER, CAN BE WOVEN ON THE
LOOM.

The binder, in which there must be eight
hundred threads of the same size as those of the
main warp, may either be mounted on eight extra
shafts in front of the figure shafts, or be distributed
in an eight-headle harness. It should be on eight
headles in order that tabby, twill, or satin binders
may be made at will. The entering of the binder
threads, is only in the binder leashes ; they must
pass between each two of the main warp, but not
be entered in its mails. The raising of the binder
harness may be either by means of the treadles and
levers, or by the Jack-in-the-box, unless a Jacquard
or more shuttles were required drop-boxes must be added.
Most of the old draw-loom weaving was done with hand-
shuttles, the fly not being invented till the middle of
the eighteenth century, and the drop-box much later.

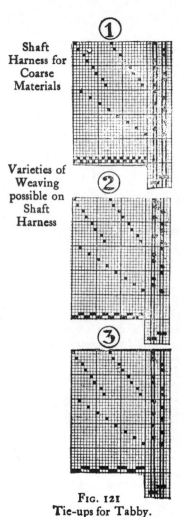

Shaft
Harness for
Coarse
Materials

Varieties of
Weaving
possible on
Shaft
Harness

FIG. 121
Tie-ups for Tabby.

machine is used, in which case all the lifting, both of figure and binder, is done by it.

The reed, for the loom thus fitted up, would require eight hundred dents, and each dent to have two threads from the main warp, and one from the binder entered in it.

Some examples of the kind of weaving to be done with the above loom may now be given. In the first place, tabby cloth, quite plain and even, made by lifting single threads alternately, can be woven, all the threads of both warps being used. This would require all the shafts to be tied up to the treadles as shown at fig. 121, no. 1. No. 2 gives the sketch plan of the entering and tie-up of a tabby of two threads. No. 3 shows the plan and tie-up for three-thread tabby. Tabby of four threads could not be made unless there were sixteen shafts in the figure harness, and above that number of threads would make too coarse a tabby to be of any service.

Double or treble cloth could be made either with single, double, or treble threads, and with or without pattern. Also double cloth,

Varieties of Weaving possible on Shaft Harness

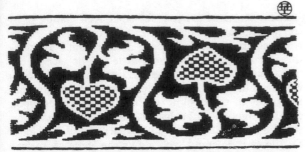

FIG. 122.—Curtain Border.

one portion having double threads and the other portion having single threads, could be woven, and double cloth of two different textures, one tabby and the other satin, could be devised.

Figs. 122 and 122A will show the great utility of being able to weave a perfect plain cloth, with a border introduced at regular intervals. The illustrations are from such a web. It was made for a heavy curtain to fill an archway, and both surfaces were alike. The border being double cloth, it was possible to make the front and back exactly alike, even as to the position of the colours, which in single weaving must always be reversed. The letters of a motto or a monogram might in this way be woven so as to be read rightly on both sides.

Woollen Hangings woven on Shaft Harness

We must now examine three samples of woollen hangings recently made on a loom constructed according to the plan just specified.

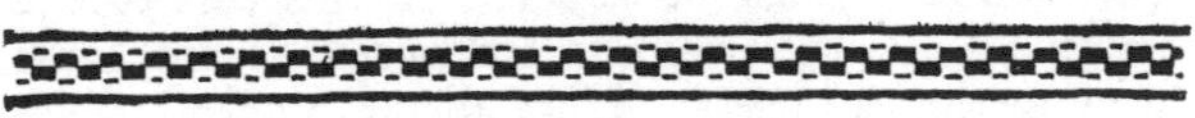

FIG. 122A.—Curtain Edging.

Plate xv was woven for a church hanging in scarlet, blue, and green wool on a ground of fine cream-coloured, mercerised cotton. The ground is a treble-thread tabby, but shows very little on the face of the web—only, in fact, in the bold outlines of the conventional lily and the large leaf forms which compose the trellis of the design. The lily is in scarlet wool, and is only tied down by a satin, which is made on the simple cords of the figure harness. This loose tie allows it to stand well above the general surface of the cloth. The green vase and foliage, and the dark blue background, are tied by a four-headle, single-thread twill, made by the binder harness.

It is often found more convenient to weave this kind of material face upwards as the present example was made.

The order of the weaving was: (1) A tabby shoot of coarse mercerised cotton in a shed made by the tie-up of no. 3, fig. 121. (2) For this shoot all the cords of the figure harness are raised except the background of the design. For the binder the first and fifth binder shafts are raised. Into the shed thus formed the dark blue weft is shot. (3) All cords raised in the figure, except, the foliage and a portion of the trellis leafage. The third shuttle carries a light green weft, and the same binders are raised as for the blue shoot. The spaces between the scarlet lilies (about two-thirds of the design) are woven with three shuttles, but when the lily is reached a fourth shuttle must be added. In this part of the design all the figure cords are raised except those forming the lily itself. Here all the binder headles are left down, as the binding of this part of the

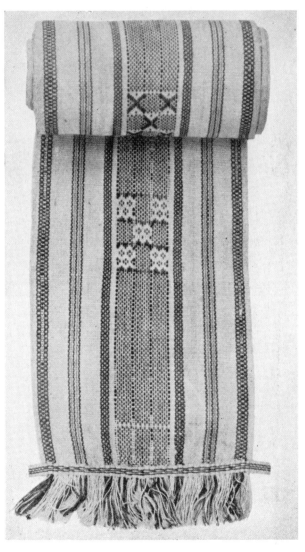

Plate I.—East African Weaving, illustrating
Primitive Work.

British Museum, London.

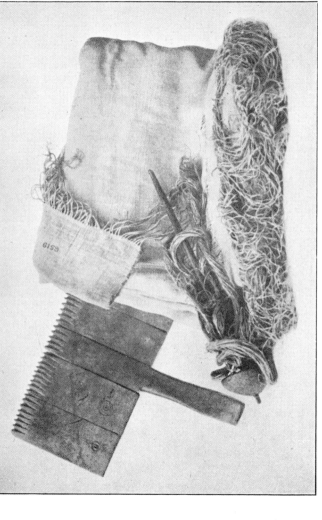

Plate II.—Ancient Egyptian Weaving, 2000 B.C. and later. The heavy comb shown was used for beating the wool together.

British Museum, London

See page 3.

Plate III.—Illustration of Warp and Weft intersected.

See page 5.

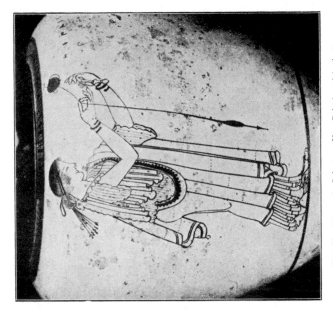

Plate V.—Figure of a Spinster. Vase Painting of Ancient
Greece, 500 B.C.

British Museum, London.

See page 12.

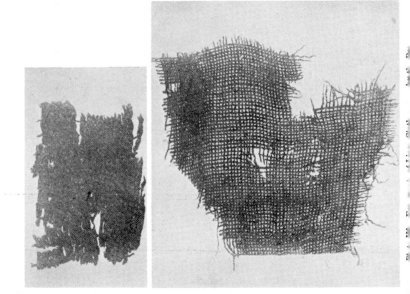

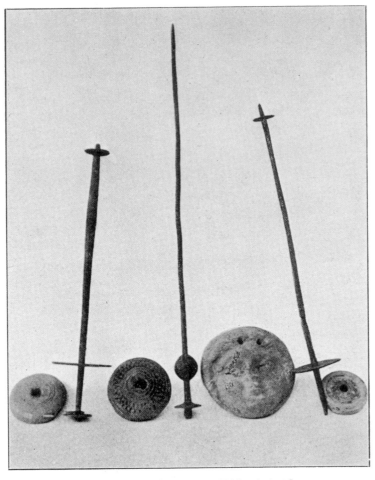

Plate VI.—Spindles, Whorls, and Loom Weights, Ancient Greece.

See page 13.   *British Museum, London.*

Plate VII.—Tapestry Ornaments. Fragment of a Robe of Amenhetep II.,
found in the Tomb of Thothmes IV. Amenhetep, whose Ka name
is woven in the design, reigned in Egypt, B.C. 1500.

See page 133.

Cairo Museum.

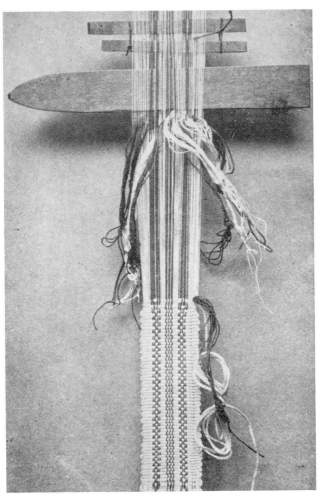

Plate VIII.—Copy (in progress) of a Portion of the East African
Web illustrated by Plate I.

See page 143.   By the Author.

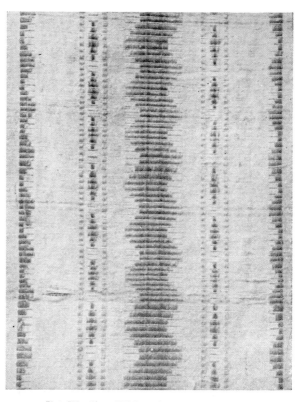

Plate IX.—Piece of Eighteenth-century Silk-weaving,
illustrating *Tobine* Stripes.

See page 228.   *Victoria and Albert Museum, South Kensington.*

Plate X.—Fragment of Seventeenth-century French Brocade,
a most perfect specimen of the Weaver's art.

See page 316.

Plate XI.—Example of French Silk-weaving, time of
Louis XIII.   Size of design, 30″ × 21″.

See page 274.   *Victoria and Albert Museum, South Kensington.*

Plate XII.—Copy, by the Author, of Eighteenth-century Fine French Silk.
A portion of the design only is shown.   The part photographed
is the full size of the original.

See page 333.

Plate XIII.—Copy, by the Author, of Sixteenth-century Italian
Brocatelle. A portion of the design only is shown, about
half the actual size of the original.

See page 285.

Plate XIV.—Spitalfields Tissue in Green and Gold Silk.
Date about 1900.

See page 290.   *Author's Collection.*

This is shown as an example of skilful weaving, not of fine design.

Plate XV.—Wool Hanging, designed, draughted, and arranged for weaving by the Author for St. Christopher's Church, Haslemere. The colours are scarlet, blue, green, and white.

See page 300.

Plate XVI.—Portion of Hanging of woven wool and coarse silk.
Designed, draughted, and arranged for weaving by the Author.
See page 301.

Plate XVII.—Brocade, probably Old English.   The lower portion of
the photograph shows the method of brocading with small
shuttles at the back.

See page 311.   *Author's Collection.*

Plate XVIII.—Figured Velvet.   The ornament is composed of
cut and terry pile.   This specimen is beautifully
designed and perfectly woven.

See page 321   *Victoria and Albert Museum, South Kensington.*

design is by four threads of the figure harness, in the same manner as shown in fig. 116.

The next example, plate XVI, is a portion of a very heavy wool and spun-silk hanging. In this web the binder does not show on the surface, except in the treble-thread tabby ground, as the few ties required on the figure are made by lifting one of the group of four threads raised by the cords of the simple, and are arranged for by the designer on the draught. The binder harness is, however, useful, as it ties in the wool at the back and keeps it flat ; it also helps to force out the figure and make it stand well up from the ground. It will be observed that the two colours of the figure are so interwoven that there are very few long floats of weft which require being tied down. Whenever a float of more than seven squares of the ruled paper is made a binder is raised for the tie. Three wefts, carried by three shuttles, are used in this tissue, and four shoots are necessary to complete one line of the draught.

The warp consists of three thousand two hundred threads of spun silk, warped double. Their being warped double, makes the necessary number of threads (1600) for entering in the figure harness, and the binder must also have double threads like the cane warp. The spun silk for both warps is white.

The weft for the tabby ground is coarse, strong-spun silk, four or five ends being twisted together. This is also white. The weft for the figure is soft wool spun rather finely, several ends (six or eight) being also lightly twisted together. One shoot of the figure is green and the other a very dark indigo blue. One repeat of the bold design

301

fills out the whole width of the twenty-four-inch web.

The order in which the wefts are shot is : (1) The white silk in a tabby shed made by the shafts only, of both harnesses ; (2) the same weft in the alternate tabby shed ; (3) the figure harness alone being used, the green wool is shot into the shed first raised by the simple cords, and is followed (4) by the dark blue in the next figure shed. This completes one line of the design as draughted. This web is also woven face upwards, and the tie-up has to be so made, that, the cords lift first the ground and the blue part of the figure, and secondly the ground and the part of the figure coloured green.

Fig. 123 is particularly interesting, as it shows the great extent to which the changing of the weft in lateral stripes may be carried, with advantage. It is difficult in black and white to indicate the variety of colours used in this pattern, which is arranged to weave with one ground and two figure shuttles only ; but the changing colours are indicated to some extent by dots, lines, and cross-hatchings. Fifteen changes of colour are made in one vertical repeat, and the effect of lateral striping is entirely hidden. The weft changes are shown in the two vertical stripes at the side of the illustration.

The ground in this case is a tabby of double threads only, and is of fine linen. The tabby is made by both harnesses working together, as draughted at no. 2, fig. 121. As in the last example, there is no binder on the figure except in the few places where the length of the floating loops renders it necessary. Where thus required

Fig. 123.

they are made by drawing one cord of the simple.

This pattern is woven face downwards, which makes it very light, both as to the tie-up and the drawing of the simple cords, but it needs the binder harness all raised while the figure is being woven.

The first shoot is one of tabby with white linen weft. The second is fine black or very dark green wool, two or three ends being wound together. This colour runs nearly all through the design, there being only three small spaces where it is changed, once to yellow, at A, and twice to green, at B, B. The third shoot begins with blue at C, and changes at D to green, at E to purple, at F to a different blue, at G to another green, at H to rose-pink, at I to green, at K to brown, at L to blue-purple, at M to green, and finishes the repeat at N with scarlet.

The Split
Harness not
Indispens-
able for
Tissue
weaving It must be understood that all these examples of tissue weaving could be made on the loom as fitted up for damask weaving—that is, with a long-eyed harness in front of the figure harness, if to the latter were added another set of headles to work the separate warp of the binder. In fact, this was the kind of mounting on which the old brocatelles and tissues were made. The split harness is, however, a great improvement, and has many advantages, not the least of which is its occupying so little space in the loom.

There is another kind of harness for silk damask weaving which was also invented by a working weaver of Bethnal Green ; this is called the compound harness. It is most ingenious, and has been extremely useful in connection with the Jacquard machine, for use with which it was invented, but as it is not suitable for use with the draw-loom it is not necessary to describe it here.

The next group of samples for examination require for their weaving a still further development of the monture, which must be explained in the next chapter.

CHAPTER XIX

THE COMPOUND MONTURE

Advantages of dividing the Monture—Description
of the Compound Monture—Examples of Compound Monture Weaving—Old English Brocade—
Eighteenth-century Striped Brocade—French Late
Seventeenth Century Brocade.

Advantages
of the
Divided
Monture

THE scope of tissue-weaving may be immensely
increased by building the monture in two or more
divisions, to be governed by separate sets of simple
cords, and acting on separate warps, all combining to make one web. This compound build of
monture was often used by the tissue weavers of
the sixteenth, seventeenth, and eighteenth centuries,
and enabled them to produce an almost unlimited
variety of webs. It is also even more largely used
in modern pattern-weaving by power, which to a
very great extent consists of warp effects. Warp
effects, in power-looms where very long lengths
of the same patterned material must be woven at
the highest possible speed, are the most economical,
as when once the loom is set up, no matter how
complicated the pattern may be, the actual loom-tending is very simple. In the draw-loom sometimes, montures with as many as four divisions
seem to have been used, but generally two divisions

306

were deemed sufficient. The weavers of the best periods for the most part used weft rather than warp effects in their webs.* The advantages of weft effects have already been dwelt upon in the previous chapter.

For the demonstration of the utility of the compound monture let us make an addition to the split shaft harness for silk-weaving described in Chapter XVII., p. 278. The comber-board is there described as pierced with twenty-four rows of holes, two hundred and thirty-three being in each row. These are lifted in fours by the simple cords, which number four hundred and six, in order to make three comber repeats in twenty-one inches. The leashes, in the twenty-four rows, are also separately suspended on twenty-four shafts. This is the figure harness complete. In Chapter XVIII., p. 287, four extra shafts were added for a separate binder, on which four rows more, of similar leashes were hung, but were not connected as those of the figure harness were with the comber-board. This completed the monture for making brocatelles and broché tissues. On the loom so arranged, brocading in detached spaces could not be done, as the binder warp would be in the way whether it were lifted or not. If left down it would hide or mar the brocaded ornament, while if it were raised it would

* There is a design for silk brocade in the print room of the Victoria and Albert Museum, South Kensington, which has a note at the back to the effect that four simples were required for its production. As it is only a sketch design, not a draught on ruled paper, it is impossible to say how the divisions were made or why they were required.

307

FIG. 124
A Comber-board Slip
308

make the manipulation of the brocading shuttle very tiresome. In fact, a weaver of to-day would despairingly say it was impossible. For making true brocaded tissues, then, some addition to the shaft harness and binder is needed, and this need is met by arranging the figure harness as a compound monture.

Fig. 124 represents a pierced hardwood comber-board slip one inch wide and ten inches long. Twenty-one of such slips would be required to fill the frame of our comber-board. The twenty-four rows of holes in division A are already occupied by the leashes of the figure harness as described. For the compound monture the comber-board would have to be extended above the binder shafts as shown in division B, where six more rows of holes are seen to be pierced; and below these new holes the six shafts of the binder harness are already suspended by their long loops. These leashes must now all be connected with the comber-board in the same manner as directed for those of the figure

harness (see p. 278, fig. 115).   At the top of the
loom the pulley-box must be doubled in capacity, or
a second box having the same number of pulleys
placed in front of it.   Tail and simple cords must
also be added to complete this addition.   Sometimes
the second simple was arranged on the opposite side
of the loom, but more often the simples were
placed side by side, so as to be worked together
when required.   All such details of the construction were, of course, subject to individual require-
ment and convenience.*   All these additions being
made, it only remains to join the leashes of the
front harness, in regular order, to the cords of the
front pulley-box, care being taken to connect them
in the same repeats as the main figure harness.
As the binder warp equals only one-fourth of the
figure harness, it follows that the leashes of the
former must be joined up singly instead of in
fours.†

The additions being complete, the compound
shaft harness will enable the weaver (1) to raise
the binder threads all together or in separate rows
by the shafts as freely as before, and also to use the
main figure harness simple by itself, also as before ;
so that any web that has already been made can be

* It is only possible in such a book as the present to
show the general principles on which these complicated
machines were made.   In practice they were subject to
innumerable modifications.

    † This is not an arbitrary arrangement.   The harnesses
in both divisions may be exactly alike.   In fact, any combination may be planned on the same principle and have
special advantages.

Description
of the
Compound
Monture

repeated. (2) To raise any single thread of the binder or a combination of them, at any place, to make ties for a brocaded figure. (3) To utilise the binder warp in order to make small designs, diapers, checkers, spots, or what not, as a background to the main design.* (4) To lift any portion of the binder out of the way of any other weaving that may be going on. (5) To weave damask-like figures in the background of the brocade, as was so often done with fine effect in the French and Italian webs.

It is difficult to select a few examples of tissues woven on compound montures out of the great number available, any one of which might be chosen on account of some special point of interest in its technique. The space, however, now at our disposal precludes the extended examination which this part of the subject deserves. Three examples must suffice ; these have been chosen as diverse as possible, and will give some idea of the capacity of the drawloom in its highest state of development. Ample opportunity for further study of tissue-weaving is afforded by the fine collection of drawloom woven fabrics in the Victoria and Albert Museum, which is particularly rich in seventeenth- and eighteenth-century examples, French, Italian, and English. There is also in the print room of the same museum a wonderful and most instructive collection of designs for this class of weaving, dating from the beginning of the eighteenth century. The value of these drawings is much enhanced by

* This kind of background effect is particularly characteristic of English eighteenth-century weaving.

310

the designers' and weavers' notes which are written on their margins.

The first example for present examination is a pure brocade, probably old English (plate XVII). The cream-coloured ground is a rich plain tabby, very finely and closely woven, there being eighty shoots of weft to an inch. Two shoots of weft are laid between each line of the brocading, and there are two shoots of brocading to each line of the draught on ruled paper. The quaint floral and landscape design occupies the whole twenty-one inches of the width of the web, and is draughted for six hundred cords. The most convenient ruled paper for this size of design, would be divided into twelve lateral spaces in each of the fifty large squares on to which the design had been first sketched, and as each line is repeated, as we have seen, in the weaving, the proportional number of vertical spaces would be eight. This would therefore be said to be drawn on 12 × 8 ruled paper. The colours are so arranged, that, although there are a great variety of them, as they are brocaded in, there is no necessity for more than four tie-ups for each line of the design on the simple, or for four cards if the lifting were done by a Jacquard machine. For the latter, however, each card would have to be duplicated, as when more than one card is used for each line the second and third, or whatever number are required, must follow in unbroken sequence. The Jacquard machine cannot be turned back to the first card of the line without great trouble ; accordingly a second sequence identical with the first has to be laced in the endless band of cards. This repetition, however, could be done quite easily on

the draw-loom providing the cords were drawn
by a human drawboy.*

The tie-up for this design would be very simple,
as only a few cords here and there would have to
be drawn at each line.

All the colours would have to be painted in on
the draught quite distinctly, in order that the tie-
up might be *read in* correctly by the weaver, and
also that it should be a clear guide to him in the
brocading. Two draughts would have to be made,
one painted in, exactly as the design is to appear
when woven, only without the binders; the other
having all the shapes exactly copied, but without
colour, and the binder ties indicated. In the colour
draught, the colours to rise in each tie-up would
have to be indicated by letters or numerals, 1, 2, 3,
or 4. The colour draught would be for the back or
main division of the monture, and the binder draught,
for the front division. The effect on the loom of this
arrangement, when the tie-up was made, would be
that the back division of the simple would draw up
the figure in large on the main warp without any ties
(see effect of shaft harness, p. 287, fig. 117, no. 1).
Now if the cords of the front harness be drawn
simultaneously with those of the back, all the
threads of the second warp will be lifted from the
figure, except those required for binders. As there

* With regard to two or more colours being tied up
in one line for brocading, it should be pointed out, that,
as each colour is put in with a small shuttle separately,
it follows, that if sufficient space is left between the
parts lifted, any reasonable number of colours can be
brocaded in one line. With a skilful weaver a very
little space between the colours is sufficient.

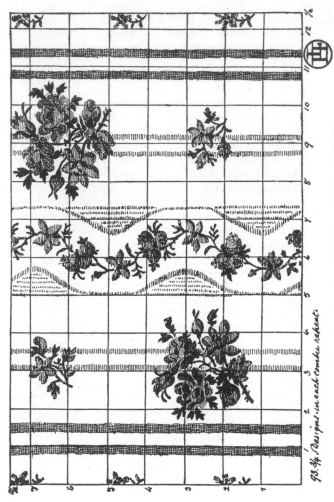

93.¾ Designs in each centre repeats

Fig. 125.—French Brocaded Silk Tissue, Eighteenth Century.

are six shafts for the binder warp, the twill tie may be either a three- or six-shaft twill. The one used in the example (plate XVII) is on six shafts.

The weaving would proceed as follows : Shoots 1 and 2 will be a tabby of the ground and binder together. The brocading shed will next be made by drawing the first tie-up of both the simples together. The brocading wefts in the first shed being laid in the places indicated in the draught, the second tie-ups will open the second brocading shed ; this also being laid, the third tie-ups will open the final shed, for the first line of the design. The third and fourth tabby shoots follow next in order, and the same sheds are to be repeated for the brocading. When the two lines of brocading are thus woven, with two tabby shoots between them, one line of the design, as draughted, will have been woven. The weaving of brocades requires great care and skill, especially when, as in this example, several colours are put in at one drawing of the simple. The weaver has to follow the coloured draught very attentively until he has learned the position and entry of the different colours. Needless to say, brocading must be done face downwards, and the small brocading shuttles are left standing on the back of the web in exact order, like a fleet of little boats, and pass through the shed in regular succession. The lower portion of plate XVII shows the back of the old English brocaded silk, and will greatly assist in the explanation.

The dainty and characteristic eighteenth-century brocaded and striped silk of French weaving (fig. 125) could be woven on two differently

314

mounted looms : (1) On a loom arranged for damask-weaving, with two separate harnesses in front, one to work tabby and the other to weave a satin, with two spaced warps on separate rollers, and with the harnesses also spaced, and *both* entered in the monture. (2) On a divided shaft harness, with one simple and with the warps spaced and arranged on two rollers. If made in the latter way the weaving would be much simpler, and there would be a great deal less strain on the silk, which is always an advantage. The design must first be briefly described, and then the method of preparing the monture for it. The design is shown squared out in preparation for the draughting. The broad stripes on which the large bouquets are placed are of rich satin of a pale blue colour. The narrower stripes, one of which, in the centre, has a wavy ribbon with a garland of small flowers adorning it, and the other, the half of which is seen at each edge of the drawing, are both white tabby-woven silk. The two narrow stripes near each edge are of the same satin as the wide one, and only differ from it in their colour, which is pink, with white edges. These are arranged in the warping. The fine stripes on which the large bouquets are placed are floating white silk weft, as are also the edges of the wavy ribbon and the fine stripes of various lengths which are placed at its side. The bouquets, sprays, and garland are all brocaded in exquisitely delicate tints of pink, creamy yellow, and green. It is not necessary to give a specification of the monture for reproducing this example, but only to indicate broadly the method of its building. The comber-board would be in two divisions, and as there

315

would be an equal number of shafts for both divisions the same number of rows of holes would
require piercing in the board. In the back division
holes would only be pierced in the spaces required
for the satin stripes, and in the front division holes
would be made for the tabby stripe spaces. In this
web there would be no binders for the brocading, as
the smallness of the spaces brocaded renders them
unnecessary. The cords from both divisions of the
shaft harness could be brought into one simple, as
the figures are all raised simultaneously. The
first tie-up of the simple would be of the fine
stripes in the centre of the broad satin one, and
the fine vertical lines and edges of the wavy
ribbon. The second, third, and fourth tie-ups
would be for the three sheds of the brocading.

The order of the sheds, for the shoots of white silk,
in weaving would be as follows : (1) The tabby and
satin groundwork on shafts alone of both warps
together ; (2) the first tie-up on the simple cords
would be drawn and the second shoot of tabby and
satin groundworks lifted. When these shoots had
been made, the first tie-up of the brocading figure
would be lifted by the simple cords and the brocading done ; then the second and third tie-ups and
their brocading, in succession. This would finish
one line of the design. At the fourth pair of ground
shoots with the white weft, the one round of ties
of the eight-shaft satin would be complete, and the
fifth pair would begin with the first tabby and first
satin shafts again together.

The third and last example to be examined is
the fine late seventeenth century French brocade
reproduced on Plate X in the half-tone section

of this Part of the book. It is a superb piece of weaving, and a fine specimen of appropriate and economical design. The fragment from which the photograph is taken is only fifteen inches high and ten and a half inches wide, yet this gives nearly two repeats of a fairly bold design. The figure is turned over in repeating vertically, so that the real design is barely eight inches, and yet on looking at a whole piece of the brocade we should have "no wearisome sense of repetition," which is a quality in design that William Morris commended so highly when describing the early Sicilian webs.* Then again the design is so perfectly adapted to the method of its production that no artist who was unacquainted with the technique of weaving could invent a pattern so suitable for working out in the loom.

The ground of the web is a lilac silk tabby, very rich and warped with double threads. The graceful ornament, consisting of a twisted ribbon and conventional flowers and foliage, is all brocaded in, by means of a multitude of small shuttles. The silks used for the wefts are of exquisitely delicate-coloured dyes, and are varied in a most artistic way in the repeats. The dark green and red wefts are fine chenille threads, which give a velvet-like texture to the portion of the work where they are used. A part of the floral ornament is brocaded with a curiously twisted silk thread, which gives a metallic

* A fine description of the early Sicilian damasks may be found in a lecture on textile fabrics by the late William Morris. The report of the lecture is in the Art Library, South Kensington.

appearance wherever it is used.* The intricate
brocading is not tied down with a binder, but is left
loose or floating, the designer having so arranged the
draught that none of the loops are inconveniently
long.

It was not only on account of its exceeding
beauty that this example was chosen for this
particular illustration, but on account of the
peculiarity of the embellishment of the background
of the figure. This background pattern, is put in
by means of the second or front division of the
monture working on the second warp, which is used
for this purpose instead of as a binder. This ornament is woven in the tobine manner described at
the end of Chapter XIV. As will be gathered
from that description, tobine effects are generally
confined to narrow stripes, vertical or lateral, as small
squares and oblongs, but here we have a kind of key
pattern and spaces between it of plain tabby, and it
does not interfere with the brocading, although it is
in a line with it. All this shows that some means
has been devised for raising and depressing the
tobine warp at any place required by the design
and between any one of the tabby shoots. In order
to effect this, the front division of the monture is
fitted up with ordinary leashes without shafts. The
extra warp, of the same colour as the main one, is
about one-fourth of its richness, and the simple cords
draw from four to six leashes with every cord. The
shapes of the brocading figure have to be tied up on

* The French weavers were very ingenious in twisting
threads of silk and metal, and many beautiful effects in
their webs are due to this special wefting.

the front simple and drawn simultaneously with those of the back. The tobine pattern on the ground is worked in by the tie-up of the front simple while the ground itself is being woven. This tie-up of the front division of the harness would all have to be worked out on a separate draught from that of the brocading.*

* These tobine effects for groundwork patterns became very common and characteristic of English Spitalfields weaving in the eighteenth century. In French work they occur chiefly in stripes.

CHAPTER XX

FIGURED-VELVET WEAVING

Pile and Terry Figured Velvet—The Draught—
The Monture—The Preparation of the Loom—
The Bobbin Frame—Italian and Spanish Velvets.

Figured-
velvet
Weaving

THE weaving of plain velvet has been fully described
in Chapter XIV. It will therefore require but
few words to explain the method of making figured
velvet, which, as far as the actual weaving goes, is
done in precisely the same manner. In one respect
the weaving of figured velvet is not so difficult
as when the pile is plain, as small defects in the
cutting out of the rods are not so apparent.

The design for figured velvet is draughted in
exactly the same way as designs for damask
weaving. Each square of the ruled paper represents a group of from four to eight threads of the
pile. When both cut, and terry, velvet are in one
design they are treated as two colours, and require
two successive tie-ups on the simple.

The leashes of the monture for velvet weaving
are more heavily weighted than for damask or tissue
weaving. They are also mounted on shafts as in the
tissue shaft harness. When both terry and cut pile
are being woven the grooved rod is first placed in
its shed, and the terry one next to it, before the

320

intervening shoots of ground are made. This is the Figured-velvet Weaving only difference in the weaving process. The shafts raise and depress the pile altogether between the shoots, and the cords of the simple raise the pile as required for the design. Plate xviii is taken from a very fine example of cut and terry figured velvet in the collection at the Victoria and Albert Museum.

Although the actual weaving is so similar there is a great difference in the preparation of the loom for figured velvet. Each separate group of threads, lifted for the design by the cords of the simple, has to have a small warp of its own, individually weighted with a tiny piece of lead wire. Eight hundred or The Pile-bobbin Frame a thousand of these, mounted in a frame at the back of the loom, is no uncommon number. It will be remembered that the take-up of the pile warp is so great that the warp has to be at least six times the length of the ground warp. It will therefore be readily seen, that parts of the design, where more or less pile is raised would take up different lengths of warp. Some of the bobbins are found to run out sooner than others, and when they do so they are immediately replaced and the new threads of silk joined to the original ones. In this way the pile warp is kept even, whatever the nature of the design may be.

Figured-velvet weaving seems to have reached its Sixteenth-century Velvet highest perfection in Italy and Spain during the sixteenth century. The webs then produced have never been surpassed, or even equalled, although if good silk, of fine colour were used, in a properly set up hand-loom, there is no reason why velvet, the most sumptuous of all textiles, should not be made as well as ever.

321

CONCLUDING NOTE

It may be surprising, and perhaps somewhat disappointing, to some readers to find that this description of the methods of weaving and weaving appliances, comes to an end at this point. We have traced the history and development of the craft, from its earliest beginning, up to the time when the Jacquard machine was introduced and began to supersede the traditional draw-loom for pattern-weaving. This ending, although perhaps somewhat abrupt, is not unintentional, for it was just at that time that weaving, to a great extent, ceased to be an artistic craft. It was then that the loom ceased to be a tool, more or less complicated, which the weaver himself could keep in order and cunningly adjust, alter, and adapt to any particular work he might have in hand.

With the exception of the fly-shuttle, chiefly useful for weaving wide webs, the Jack-in-the-box, and the split or shaft harness, descriptions of which have been given, no real improvement has been made in weaving or weaving appliances since the middle of the eighteenth century.

As regards the Jacquard machine, the chief advantage (?) it offers is the facility with which designs can be changed in the loom, the endless

322

band of cards taking the place of the weaver's
tie-up. This facility for change only resulted in
the multiplication of patterns ; patterns, for the most
part inferior to the traditional ones already in use.
The Jacquard machine is also responsible, to a great
extent, for the separation of the art of designing
from the craft of weaving.

The speed of weaving has been by means of the
power-loom, of course, vastly increased, but although
this is in some respects a commercial advantage, the
quality of the weaving is far below that of the earlier
times, and the ruthless, rigidly perfect mechanism
of the machine loom has had a disastrous effect on
the weaver as a craftsman.

There can be no question that the best weaving
was done before these innovations of the engineer
and mechanician were made. It would therefore
seem, that the right road to improvement in weaving,
as in all the crafts, can only be found by those who
are willing to return to the traditional methods and
simpler ideals of the earlier masters of craftsmanship.

GLOSSARY *

Batten, the frame of a reed.
Beam, a roller.
Beaming, winding on a warp.
Beaming drum, the essential part of beaming machine.
Beaming posts, supports for a beam.
Binder, the tie for floating weft.
Binder harness, headles for lifting binders.
Bobbin, a reel.
Bobbin-carrier, a reel-holder for warping.
Bobbin frame, part of a warping mill.
Box batten, batten with fly-shuttle boxes.
Breast roll, front beam of a loom.
Brocade, a brocaded web ; originally, silk wefted with
    gold or silver thread.
Brocading, weaving detached ornaments in a web.
Brocatelle, tissue with satin ties in figure.
Broché, web to imitate brocading.

Cane, a new warp.
Cane roll or *roller*, the back roller of a loom.
Cane sticks, sticks for fastening the warp in beam.

* This glossary does not pretend to comprise all the
technical terms used in weaving. These are of infinite
variety, and often have totally different meanings in
districts separated but a very short distance one from
another.

325

Carding, preparing fibre for spinning.

Cards or *cardings*, fibre prepared for spinning.

Cloth beam, the breast roller.

Comber-board, a board perforated to hold the leashes of a monture.

Comber repeat, repetition of a design which does not turn over.

Comber slip, a portion of the comber-board.

Compound harness, two or more harnesses working together.

Compound monture, monture with two or more sets of leashes.

Cords, the simple on which the pattern is tied up in a draw-loom.

Counter-march, a short lower lever in a loom.

Couper, the top levers of a loom.

Cross, the crossing threads of a warp.

Cross, porrey, the cross retained while weaving.

Cross, portee, the cross at the finishing end of a warp.

Cross sticks, smooth rods for preserving the cross.

Damask, a system of weaving introduced from Damascus.

Dent, one space in a reed.

Design, a pattern ; one square of ruled paper.

Diaper, a system of weaving small patterns.

Distaff, appliance used in spinning.

Doubling, winding two or more threads together.

Draught, drawing on ruled paper.

Drawboy, a boy employed to draw the cords of a simple.

Drawboy's fork, implement for drawing the cords in a draw-loom.

Drawboy machine, machine for drawboy's work.

Entering, threading warp in leashes or reed.

Entering hook, thin hook for drawing thread through mails.

Eye, centre loop of a leash.

Fancy web, see *Tissue*.
Figured velvet, velvet with pattern.
Figure harness, the monture or pattern headles.
Float, a loop of weft passing over two or more threads.
Fly-shuttle, a shuttle driven by a picking stick.
Friction brake, appliance for regulating weight.

Gatherer, a part of the heck-block.
Gating, adjusting a loom.
Ground, the plain part of a web.
Ground harness, headles which form the ground of a
    web.
Guiding cords, supports for the pattern loops on the
    simple.

Hand-shuttle, a shuttle for throwing by hand.
Hand-stick, a short stick on which warps are wound.
Harness, a collection of headles.
Headle or *heddle*, a collection of leashes.
Headle frame, a frame for knitting headles upon.
Headle gauge, a tool for making leashes.

Inlaying, see *Brocading*.

Jack-in-the-box, invention which reduces the number of
    treadles required in a loom.
Jacquard machine, a machine perfected by M. Jacquard
    to supersede the drawboy in pattern-weaving.

Lam, see *Headle*.
Leaf, see *Headle*.
Lease, see *Cross*.
Leashes, loops of a headle.
Lingo, the weight of a leash.
Long march, the long levers below a loom.

327

Loom, any arrangement for supporting a warp and keeping it in order for weaving.

Mail, the glass or metal eye of a leash.
Monture, the mounting of a loom for pattern-weaving.

Necking cords, cords joining pulley cords and leashes in a monture.

Pecker, part of the drawboy machine.
Pickers, tweezers.
Picking-stick, the handle of the fly-shuttle motion.
Pile, the cut portion of a velvet.
Plan and tie-up, a sketch showing entry of harness and tie-up of treadles.
Plug, a tube on which weft is wound for the fly-shuttle.
Point repeat, a design repeating in opposite directions.
Pole, the pile warp of velvet.
Porrey, the warp between headles and cross-rods.
Portee, a collection of threads warped together.
Pulley, a grooved wheel.
Pulley-box, the upper part of a draw-loom.
Pulley cords, cords in a pulley-box.

Quill, a tube on which weft is wound for a hand-shuttle.

Race, the beading on the race-block of hand-batten.
Race-block, the lower part of a batten.
Race-board, that on which the shuttle runs.
Raddle, implement for evenly spreading warp.
Ratchet and wheel, a toothed wheel and catch.
Reed, a comb-like implement for keeping warps even and beating weft together.
Reed hook, hook for entering reed.
Retting, steeping flax in water.
Reverse satin, a satin with weft predominating.

Rising shed, a shed in which part of the warp rises, the rest being stationary.
Rocking shaft, part of the drawboy machine.
Ruled paper, paper for draughting.

Satin, a web with infrequent intersections.
Satinette, a short tied satin.
Selvage, the edge of a web.
Selvage bobbin, reel for mounting separate selvages in a loom.
Shaft, a flat lath.
Shed, the opening in the warp for the shuttle.
Shed-stick, a flat stick for opening the warp.
Shedding motion, a contrivance for opening the warp.
Shoot or *shute*, weft ; also throwing the shuttle.
Short march, see *Counter-march*.
Shuttle, a tool for carrying weft.
Shuttle-box, part of a fly-shuttle batten.
Simple, the pattern cords of a draw-loom.
Sinking shed, shed made by drawing threads down.
Skein, a loosely wound length of thread.
Skutching, cleaning retted flax.
Slot, an elongated perforation.
Spacing, arranging threads or leashes in groups.
Spinning, twisting fibre to make thread.
Spinster, a female spinner.

Tabby or *taffeta*, plain weaving.
Tail cords, the upper cords of a draw-loom.
Take-up, the gradual winding of cloth on to breast roller.
Tapestry, tabby weaving, in mosaic, with loose weft.
Tartan, a web striped in warp and weft.
Temple, implement for keeping out the edges of a web.
Terry velvet, see *Velvet*.

329

Thread monture, a monture with single threads in the mails.

Tie, a binder on loose weft.

Tie up, connecting parts of a loom together for forming patterns automatically.

Tissue, a web having one or more binder warps.

Tobine, ornaments formed by one or more headles rising and sinking together.

Trevette, a knife for cutting velvet pile.

Tumbler, a top lever of a loom.

Turning on, beaming.

Twill, a web with a diagonal tie.

Union damask, damask woven of linen and wool.

Vateau, implement for spreading the warp on cane roller.

Velvet, cut, a woven fabric with cut pile.

Velvet, figured, see *Figured velvet.*

Velvet knife, see *Trevette.*

Velvet rod, a grooved rod for the pile.

Velvet, terry, velvet with uncut pile.

Warp, longitudinal threads of a web.

Warping, preparing a warp.

Warping board, for making small warps.

Warping mill, for warping large warps.

Web, a piece of finished weaving.

Weft, the crossing thread of a warp.

Whorl, a spindle weight.

Woof, weft.

Yarn, thread of any kind.

330

INDEX

334

335

336

338

ADDENDA

NOTE TO P.99.—At end of 10th line it should be added that—The batten requires to be very exactly made, and the reed especially must be carefully fitted in such a manner that the swords of the batten and the front of the reed are quite flush.

NOTE TO P.105.—After the word " batten " in the 5th line, the method of fixing the warp to the front roller should have been described thus—The front roller must now be rested on its brackets at exactly the same height as the back roller, and a thin iron rod, having been passed through loops at the ends of two weighted cords and attached by cords or tapes to another rod placed in the groove of the roller, must be fixed in the manner shown in fig. 47A.

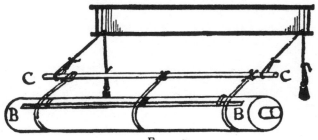

FIG. 47A.

341

The bunches of threads must now be tied to the iron rod as evenly as possible, but in order to do this the back roller must be fixed temporarily so that it cannot turn as the threads are pulled and firmly tied. When the warp is quite evenly tied to the rod the back roller can be released, a little weight put in the weight-box to give some tension to the warp, and the front roller being turned the rod CC can take the place of rod BB, and the warp will be fixed to the cloth roller ready for weaving. An examination of fig. 47B will explain the method of fixing the rod C in the groove of the roller— A being the warp and C and B the respective rods.

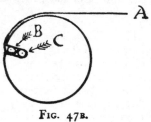

FIG. 47B.